Information Ecology

Also by Thomas H. Davenport

Process Innovation: Reengineering Work Through Information Technology

INFORMATION ECOLOGY

Mastering the
Information and
Knowledge
Environment

THOMAS H. DAVENPORT

WITH LAURENCE PRUSAK

New York   Oxford
Oxford University Press
1997

Oxford University Press

Oxford   New York
Athens   Auckland   Bangkok   Bogotá   Bombay   Buenos Aires
Calcutta   Cape Town   Dar es Salaam
Delhi   Florence   Hong Kong   Istanbul   Karachi
Kuala Lumpur   Madras   Madrid   Melbourne
Mexico City   Nairobi   Paris   Singapore
Taipei   Tokyo   Toronto

and associated companies in
Berlin   Ibadan

Copyright © 1997 by Oxford University Press, Inc.

Published by Oxford University Press, Inc.,
198 Madison Avenue, New York, New York 10016

Oxford is a registered trademark of Oxford University Press

Library of Congress Cataloging–in–Publication Data
Davenport, Thomas H.
Information ecology : mastering the information and knowledge environment
/ by Thomas H. Davenport with Laurence Prusak.
p.   cm.   Includes bibliographical references and index.
ISBN 0–19–511168–0
1. Business—Data processing—Management. 2. Information resources management.
3. Business information services—Management.
4. Management information systems. I. Prusak, Laurence. II. Title
HF5548.2.D3724   1997
658.4'038—dc21   96–45169

9 8 7 6 5 4 3 2 1

Printed in the United States of America
on acid-free paper

To my loving and lovely wife Jodi

for richer, for poorer;
in sickness and in health;
through articles and through books

Contents

Preface and Acknowledgments

Three rather disconnected happenings sparked this book. First, I've had a long-standing desire to improve the lot of information practitioners, myself included. I always felt that the technology-oriented box in which we've packaged ourselves is too small and constraining. This belief eventually led to my work on business-process innovation or reengineering, and when that was finished, I wanted to explore another means of expanding the role of information people.

The second happening occurred in 1986, when I was working as a consultant at what is now CSC Index. A corporate identity consultant charged a considerable sum to recommend that the firm change its name from Index Systems to Index Group. Along with that not-so-profound idea, however, came a tag line of "Management Consultants in Information." I began to speculate then about the possibilities of managing information rather than technology.

But these half-baked notions would have never made a pie without the third event, which was Larry Prusak's arrival at Ernst & Young's Center for Business Innovation shortly after I cofounded it in 1990. Like me, Larry had a strong interest in investigating the management of information in business. Unlike me, he had a background in library and information science, which complemented my technology and organizational-behavior orientation well.

Larry and I decided to start some research on the topic. We assembled a multi-client research program at the center called "Mastering the Information Environment," which eventually comprised more than thirty companies and provided much of the research for this book. I am grateful to those firms, and the pioneering individuals who worked for them, for sponsoring this work and giving us so much access to their successes and struggles.

Originally, Larry and I were going to write this book together, and he did write an early draft of the chapter on information-management processes. He became increasingly interested in knowledge management, however, and I ended up writing the book. Still, because of his support, ideas, and general good humor, his name appears on the title page.

x • Preface and Acknowledgments

Several other Ernst & Young colleagues worked on the Mastering the Information Environment project, and their research appears at various points throughout the book. Jim McGee was particularly helpful in early research about the concept of information ecology. Maylun Buck-Lew and Winnie Rogow worked on the IBM and Hallmark case studies, respectively. Tia DeWeese investigated information mapping. Dave DeLong did work on information behavior and "sensemaking" as a way to understand information requirements. Mike Beers worked on common information, and Randy Russell addressed information sharing. Without all of their efforts, and the support of Bud Mathaisel and Alan Stanford at the Center, and Ernst & Young in general, this book might never have come into being.

Other help along the way came from Rodney Lacey, my research assistant during the summer of 1995, who focused particularly on the topics of information staff and the external environment for information. Neil Burk, Duncan Copeland, Stefano Grazioli, Brook Manville, and Chester Simpson read early drafts and gave me extensive, useful feedback. Martha Nichols, who edited my article on related topics in the *Harvard Business Review*, joined the book as editor late in the game and cleared up my thinking and my prose considerably. If you don't find enough detail in my examples (or enough feminine pronouns), it certainly wasn't because Martha didn't try. Herb Addison at Oxford University Press originally contacted Larry Prusak and me about writing a book for Oxford, and steered it patiently through numerous changes in topic, author, and publication date.

My wife Jodi also pitched in as editor, graphic artist, and negotiator for and protector of my time. I'm sure she'd have written the book and stuck my name on it if I'd asked her. My sons Hayes and Chase had nothing to do with it, but they like to see their names in print, and I like to gratify them.

University of Texas at Austin   T.H.D.

Information Ecology

1

Information and Its Discontents:

An Introduction

The "information explosion," about which so much has been said and written, is to a great extent an explosion of misinformation and badly organized information. . . . The digital revolution has only made the problems more acute.

Murray Gell-Mann,

"Information versus knowledge and understanding"

According to every pundit and computer company sales force, we are in the midst of a new "Information Age," one that will revolutionize how workers work, how companies compete, perhaps even how thinkers think. Few managers will admit to technophobia; with all the money spent on new equipment, no one wants to lag behind. But why is it that most of us, deep down, feel frustrated by information technology? Why do most workers—even CEOs—find it so hard to adjust to new systems and the information skills they require? Why isn't this revolution all it's cracked up to be?

Our fascination with technology has made us forget the key purpose of information: to inform people. All the computers in the world won't help if users aren't interested in the information generated. All the telecommunications bandwidth won't add a dime of value if employees don't share the information they have with others. Expert systems won't provide useful knowledge if the knowledge changes too fast to maintain—or if system designers can't even find experts willing to surrender what they know. Information and knowledge are quintessentially human creations, and we will never be good at managing them unless we give people a primary role.

The status quo approach to information management—invest in new technologies, period—just doesn't work. Instead, managers need a holistic perspective, one that can weather sudden business shifts and adapt to ever-changeable social realities. This new approach, which I call *information ecology*, emphasizes an organization's entire information environment. It addresses all of a firm's values and beliefs about information (culture); how people actually use information and what they do with it (behavior and work processes); the pitfalls that can interfere with information sharing (politics); and what information systems are already in place (yes, finally, technology).

Unfortunately, those who manage information technology in most companies—the programmers, the CIOs (Chief Information Officers—or more appropriately, Chief Information *Technology* Officer), the systems analysts, the IT (Information Technology) professionals—have little patience with the needs of "end users." They throw technology at information problems; and whatever the problems—many of which result from ignoring how people and information relate to each other, not software glitches or idiot end users—this "machine engineering" approach continues to dominate us all. Its adherents firmly believe that

- information is easily stored on computers—as "data";
- modeling computer databases is the only way to master information complexity;
- information must be common throughout an organization;
- technology change will improve the information environment.

Each of these beliefs is based on a grain of truth. However, most managers—whether stubborn systems engineers, or top executives who don't want to get involved with the IT "function"—have relied on the machine-engineering model far beyond its ability to add value. In some cases, implementing a new application system or complicated database has actually set companies back, rather than pushing them ahead.

A satellite manufacturer, for instance, needed more accurate scheduling information from its work cells in order to meet a tough new production schedule. Believing that new technology would solve the problem, its information managers first implemented an expensive mainframe scheduling system, then an easy-to-use PC system. But whatever the technology in place, cell managers furnished inaccurate data about when their tasks would be completed. It turned out human factors were the culprit: managers who revealed their work would be late were punished in performance and compensation reviews; in addition, they believed that if they shared information other managers would use it for their own ends. Production scheduling only improved after a series of senior-management meetings about the problem. Top executives stopped punishing managers who told the truth about scheduling, and agreed (after substantial argument) on which scheduling information to make common across the division.

Executives at a pharmaceutical company wanted to increase information sharing between its research and development departments. They hired a consultant to create a data architecture that included centralized databases and applications. But the effort broke down when researchers and developers couldn't agree on which applications to use for circulating research results. After this setback, information managers took a different tack. They decided the best way to exchange information among different research projects was to create drug development teams, each of which had an information specialist. These specialists passed along information to team members, as well as gathered it from them to share with others in the company or department. Researchers commented that for the first time they understood how the information they created was used later in the development process—the result of a personnel rather than a technological change.

Then there's the consulting firm that had a well-functioning information environment to begin with. Its technology was no better than any other company's, but its people were generally excellent information creators, sharers, and consumers. They were hired in part for their information skills, and they were evaluated and promoted partially on the basis of how they handled information. The firm, which has led the industry in long-term growth and profitability, went to considerable lengths to provide opportunities for face-to-face meetings among consultants who needed to share information. Years before Lotus Notes or the World Wide Web came into being, this firm created printed directories of topic experts and published bulletins summarizing what they had found out from dealings with clients.

These companies have learned, often through painful experience, that better computers and communications networks do not inevitably lead to better information environments. Certainly, no firm I know of practices information ecology in every way. Yet even managers at the satellite manufacturer described above, after rethinking their original assumptions and costly investment, are moving in the right direction.

Rather than a narrow focus on technology, information ecology puts *how* people create, distribute, understand, and use information at its center. Managers who take an ecological approach believe that

- information is *not* easily stored on computers—and is not "data";
- the more complex an information model, the less useful it will be;
- information can take on many meanings in an organization;
- technology is only one component of the information environment and often not the right way to create change.

Breaking down an organization's status quo is never easy. Information ecology calls for new management frameworks, incentives, and attitudes toward organizational hierarchy, complexity, and division of resources—for a start. Yet when managers at all levels fail to take a broader approach to information use, there are real consequences: from millions of dollars wasted on unnecessary technology to salespeople who don't understand how to use a customer database more effectively. Ironically, as information becomes ever more important to us, we must learn to think beyond machines.

Why Technology Is Not Enough

There's no doubt the amount of information technology in organizations has increased, and that it can be a powerful force for changing how we do our work.[1] Technology—including computers, communications networks, and software—has become not only an aid to managing information, but a potent industry in itself. In the United States, more than fifty percent of all capital spending goes to information technology. Spending on IT went from three percent of US GNP in 1990 to five percent in 1995, and has accounted for more than a third of the growth of the entire American economy over the past four years.[2] Over the last decade, IT spending in the United States alone has been estimated at over three trillion dollars.

But information—or at least the effective use of it—has not improved at the same rate as technology spending. Charles Wang, CEO of Computer Associates, one of the world's largest software firms, claims that a third of this spending—a mind-numbing trillion dollars—has been wasted through misuse or nonuse.[3] He argues that this is due to poor communication between business managers and technologists. I would add that assuming technology itself will solve every difficulty is the real problem.

Despite trillions of dollars, pounds, marks, francs and yen spent on IT for business purposes, technology appears unable—at least by itself—to supply us with the information we need to run and manage a business. Despite twenty years of attempts to control information by creating an "architecture" of what is needed by whom and how they might receive it, the centralized engineering approaches employed have often neither informed nor improved our discussions about information needs.

Consider the IBM Corporation. Even given the company's problems over the past few years, it is still the largest information technology firm in the world, and it meets success in many areas. As I'll point out later, it even has some information bright spots. But IBM's information management perfectly illustrates how good technology doesn't necessarily translate into good information. From the mid-1980s to mid-1990s, IBM spent literally billions (reputedly about seven percent of its sixty-five billion dollars in revenues)[4] each year on technology for internal use; managers often claimed that the company was its own best customer. Every IBM manager I ever met had either a PC or a terminal on his or her desk; every function, from research and development to customer service, was supported by major applications.

Yet no IBM manager ever told me their information was better than in companies that spent far less on technology. Indeed, when Jerome York and Frederick Zuckerman came to IBM in 1993 as Chief Financial Officer and Treasurer, respectively, they discovered a very poor information environment, particularly in the realm of essential financial information.[5] It took York two months to get basic information on outstanding warranties on IBM products. Zuckerman was unable to find out how much foreign exchange rates had affected profit margins at IBM Europe or IBM Australia.

I don't mean to single out IBM. Its information problems are no worse than those of many companies. Throughout this book, I'll discuss exemplary firms—including IBM—that are doing something worth emulating. But since the early 1990s, I have consulted with or researched over fifty companies on information management issues, most of them large, sophisticated organizations. For the most part, their information environments are appalling. They don't know what they know or what they need to know. They have little accessible information about their employees, their customers, or even their own products. Even firms that are renowned for specific information systems applications have generally poor internal information environments.

No company can afford such information incompetence, although the cost of having the wrong information—or not using the right information—is difficult to measure. Obviously, a researcher can't read a manager's mind to find out what information she had, when she had it, where she received it from, and how she used it to make a decision. But no one would deny that decisions made based on useless information have cost companies billions of dollars in products that did not sell, acquisitions that did not lead to much-vaunted synergies, redesigned processes that didn't work, and plant or equipment investments that did not produce.

History is also replete with examples of decision-makers who ignored critical information. Some people within the US Army knew that a large group of airplanes was headed toward Pearl Harbor; others knew that six Japanese aircraft carriers weren't where they were supposed to be, yet nobody acted on that information.[6] NASA engineers knew that the seals on the space shuttle Challenger didn't work in cold weather, but the launch still took place on a cold day. On a less tragic note, in the early 1980s, IBM had plenty of information, based on their own research as well as external market trends, to foresee the decline of the mainframe. Yet as late as 1994, when the company's computer division was struggling badly, a member of IBM's board of directors complained that he never knew there was a problem.

Although machine-engineering purists might argue that we just haven't used the technology and tools of information design correctly, forty years of failure is forty years of failure. The tools most frequently employed to design information environments derive from the fields of engineering and architecture; they rely on assumptions that may be valid when designing a building or a power generator, but rarely hold up in an organization. The sheer volume and variety of information, the multiple purposes to which it is put, and the rapid changes that take place overwhelm any rigorous attempt at central planning, design, or control.

As one group of researchers has noted, predominant approaches to information have emphasized the rational, sequential, analytic "left brain" attributes of information and its management. But for these researchers, who are library scientists rather than computer engineers, the "right brain" aspects of information use—that is, intuitive and nonlinear approaches—matter just as much, if not more.[7] Knowledge captured in an emotionally moving story, for instance, or our mood when we peruse a printout, may affect how we handle information much more than its appearance on a computer screen.

A few observers have also emphasized that information has a behavioral, human side that runs counter to the machine-engineering school, but they have largely been ignored.[8] Information architects continue to create models with the naive—and often ludicrous—faith that they will be followed explicitly. Information plans (sometimes) lead to development of computerized information systems, but little attention is given to human factors. The result, as my research shows, is that virtually no one feels their company has a well-managed information environment.

What Is Information, Anyway?

I advocate an ecological approach to information management for any number of reasons. To begin with, the definition of *information* itself is hard to pin down. Take the old distinction between "data," "information," and "knowledge." I resist making this distinction, because it's clearly imprecise. "Information," after all, is both an umbrella term for all three, and also the connection between raw data and the knowledge eventually attained. We also tend to inflate the meanings of these terms. For years, people have referred to data as "information"; now they have to resort to the high-minded "knowledge" to discuss information—hence, the current boom in "knowledge management."

Table 1-1. Data, Information, and Knowledge

Data	Information	Knowledge
Simple observations of states of the world • Easily structured • Easily captured on machines • Often quantified • Easily transferred	Data endowed with relevance and purpose • Requires unit of analysis • Need consensus on meaning • Human mediation necessary	Valuable information from the human mind Includes reflection, synthesis, context • Hard to structure • Difficult to capture on machines • Often tacit • Hard to transfer

Data, information, and knowledge aren't easy to separate in practice; at best you can construct a continuum of the three. Still, coming up with working definitions of these terms is a useful starting place. Defining them can show where a company has focused its IT energy; whether the data it generates has a real use; whether the assumptions for structuring information make sense— and if any of it has paid off.

I define *data* as "observations of states of the world"—for example, "there are 697 units in the warehouse." The observing of such raw facts or quantifiable entities can be done by people or by the appropriate technology. From an information management perspective, data is relatively easy to capture, communicate, and store. Nothing is lost when it's represented as a string of bits, which certainly comforts IT personnel. (See Table 1-1.)

Peter Drucker has eloquently defined *information* as "data endowed with relevance and purpose."[9] Who endows it with these attributes? Humans, of course. Even when a computer automatically transforms a spreadsheet entry into a more informative pie chart, somebody had to choose how to represent such a chart originally. People turn data into information, and that's what makes life difficult for information managers. Unlike data, information requires some unit of analysis. And no matter how simple the informational entity—price, revenue, customer, year—somebody is bound to disagree with your definition of it. Information is also much harder to transfer with absolute fidelity; think of playing "Telephone" as a child, or the outcome of most office rumor mills.

Knowledge is information with the most value and is consequently the hardest form to manage. It is valuable precisely because somebody has given the information context, meaning, a particular interpretation; somebody has reflected on the knowledge, added their own wisdom to it, and considered its larger implications. For my purposes, the term also implies synthesis of multiple sources of information over time. Some knowledge, as Ikujiro Nonaka has long noted, is tacit—it exists symbolically in the human mind and can be made explicit only with difficulty.[10] Knowledge *can* be embedded in machines, but it's tough to categorize and retrieve effectively. Anyone who has ever tried to transfer knowledge from one person or group to another knows how hard that is; not only must receivers use the information, but they must also acknowledge that it actually constitutes "knowledge."

Obviously, the amount of human involvement increases as we move along this continuum of data-information-knowledge. Computers are well-suited for helping us manage data, less so for information, and even less for knowledge. Machine-engineering management approaches also work best—not to say well—on data, worse on information, and worst on knowledge.

Over the past several decades, company executives may have been content with distributing straightforward quantitative information on performance in uniform categories defined by senior managers. Increasingly, however, today's managers are more interested in capturing ideas—explanations or context for financial results, best practices, market and competitive intelligence, solutions to customer problems, learning from a conference, even attitudes and values. Ideas can be distributed in the form of text, photos, and graphics, or as audio and video recordings. An idea may constitute one page or an entire book. It may be on paper, film, or computer. Ideas are not a new form of information, but effective use of them can now give companies a competitive edge.

More important, the information and knowledge of senior managers is not the only valuable source in an organization. While the decline of hierarchy has probably been exaggerated, an increasing number of managers are attempting to capture the insights, observations, and experience of their employees at all levels.[11] New technologies, including groupware, electronic networks, and multimedia applications, do facilitate the management of more complex information forms.

There's just one problem: this kind of information is unruly. An information architect's predefined categories can't capture its fuzzy, frustrating diversity. And if machine-engineering approaches haven't worked well for structured information, they're hopelessly unsuited for structuring ideas.

The Research Points to Information Ecology

When I've used the term "information ecology" in my consulting practice, I've gotten mixed reactions at first. Some managers find the concept a refreshing break from IT techno-babble. Others distrust anything that reeks of "green" approaches to business. I consider ecology, the science of understanding and managing whole environments, only a metaphor. Still, metaphors can be quite powerful; they often drive behavior and help to build a new organizational vision.[12] Rather than modeling an information environment on machines and buildings, I argue for an approach better suited to living things.

When we begin to think of the many crisscrossing relations among people, processes, support structures, and the other elements of a company's information environment, we have a better model for managing the complexity and variety of current information use. You could also describe information ecology as "holistic management of information" or "human-centered information management."[13] The essential point is that this approach puts humans back at the center of the information world, banishing technology to its rightful place on the periphery.

It places the primary emphasis not on generation and distribution of reams of information, but rather on the effective use of a relatively smaller amount. An information ecologist, like an architect or engineer, would still plan a company's information environment; but that planning would allow for evolution and interpretation. It would relax some of the central controls that never really worked anyway, and make the people who need and use specific information responsible for it. In short, ecological approaches to information management are more modest, behavioral, and practical than the grand designs of information architecture and machine engineering.

While this ecological approach may be new to information management, it's quite familiar to business strategists and economists. The use of ecology as a metaphor goes back at least as far as the late 1950s, when the economist Charles Lindblom described how public managers "muddle through" most decisions.[14] The most consistent advocate of an ecological approach has been Henry Mintzberg; in many articles and books he has pointed out that business strategy and management are not predictable, well-oiled processes but are "emergent," based on the vagaries of politics, conflicting motivations, and imperfect perceptions.[15] The Mintzberg organizational vision—one that very much appeals to me—allows for both deliberate and emergent strategy. He describes this managerial combination as something akin to craftsmanship, in which the outcome is shaped both by the design of the craftsperson and by day-to-day exigencies.[16]

There's no clear body of research to tell us how firms should manage in Mintzberg's emergent environment, whether it comes to strategy, policy, or information use. But in my own work, I've encountered many companies that have started to grapple constructively with their information problems. The list below highlights the forty-eight firms that served as sources for my work on information ecology. In each, I conducted research—through both structured and semi-structured interviews and surveys, as well as more free-form

List of Firms Studied

AT&T	American Airlines	American Express
Andersen Consulting	Asea Brown Boveri	Barclay's Bank
British Petroleum	Chase Manhattan Bank	Chemical Bank (now Chase)
Chrysler Corporation	Coopers & Lybrand	Dai-Ichi Pharmaceuticals
Dell Computer	Dow Chemical	Dun & Bradstreet
DuPont	EDS	Ernst & Young
Ford	Genentech	General Electric
General Motors	Hallmark	Hewlett-Packard
Hoffman La Roche	Hughes Space &	IBM
Internal Revenue Service	Communications	Johnson & Johnson
Lithonia Lighting	Lotus Development	McKinsey & Company
Merck Medco	(now IBM)	Millipore
Mitsubishi Electric	Monsanto	NationsBank
NYNEX	Pacific Bell	Polaroid
Sematech	Sequent Computer	Steelcase
Standard Life	Teltech	Toshiba
Union Pacific Railroad	Xerox	

consulting interviews—with information and IT providers, information users, and senior executives.

I mention most of these firms later in the book in specific examples; some are described anonymously. In addition, I surveyed 35 information managers from 25 of these companies on cultural and behavioral aspects of ecologically oriented information management.[17] Based on these many sources, I will present a set of ecological practices—a wide variety of approaches that have been tested by different companies—as well as a general description of information ecology.

How This Book Is Organized

The first section includes this introductory chapter and the two that follow. Chapter 2, "The Illusion of Control: Our Information Past," addresses problems with previous approaches to information management, including an analysis of IBM's original Business System Planning model. If you prefer to skip the historical details, I suggest you cut straight to Chapter 3, "The Best of All Worlds: Information Ecology." There I outline the components of an ecological organization and end with a look at the UK's Standard Life Assurance—one of the most ecologically oriented companies around.

The next section, Chapters 4 through 9, focuses on the information environment of organizations. This is the core of the book; the components discussed here are probably the most amenable to managerial change. Each of these chapters concludes with an assessment survey for that particular area of information management.

Chapter 4, "Information Strategy," emphasizes the importance of developing an overall strategy for information use. Here I discuss Chemical Bank, Dow Chemical, Genentech, General Motors, Johnson & Johnson, Merck Medco, Millipore, NationsBank, and other companies.

Chapter 5, "Information Politics," delves into the infighting, jealousy over division of resources, and political battles information ecologists should expect. I describe the political aspects of information use at ABB, Hewlett-Packard, Hughes Space and Communications, and a small oil company.

Chapter 6, "Information Behavior and Culture," looks at how people really use information, what they want, and why it's so hard for them to change. Among the companies that have wrestled with this topic are American Airlines, Buckman Laboratories, Polaroid, Springfield Remanufacturing, and Wal-Mart.

Chapter 7, "Information Staff," considers the information responsibilities of various information providers—not only IT people, but also librarians, guides, and content editors. I present the critical information staff issues of Coopers & Lybrand, Hallmark Cards, and McKinsey here.

Chapter 8, "Information Management Processes," analyzes why companies need to address how information work is done on a day-to-day level. I describe several key steps of an information management process that all organizations have in common and discuss specifics at AT&T Universal Card, Chase Manhattan Bank, Dean Witter, IBM, NYNEX, and Toshiba.

Chapter 9, "Information Architecture," presents several alternatives to the machine-engineering approach for structuring and modeling information. Exemplary companies detailed in this chapter include American Airlines, American Express, IBM, Teltech, and Xerox.

The final section of the book covers the last three chapters. Chapter 10, "Connecting to the Company: Information and the Organization," takes on the overall organizational environment for information management: this includes its business situation, technology investment, and physical arrangement. Here I look at Chrysler, Lithonia Lighting, NEC, National Semiconductor, 3M, Steelcase, and Verifone.

Chapter 11, "Information and the Outside World," focuses on a company's external environment, including the business, technology, and information markets that affect it. I also discuss the various relationships between a company's information environment and this external environment. Firms described in this context include Digital Equipment, Monsanto, Shell Oil, and Southwest Airlines. Chapters 10 and 11 conclude with assessment surveys for managers as well.

Chapter 12, "Implementing Information Ecology," closes the book with some practical suggestions for managers, and tells the story of fictional Good-Drug, a company that does everything right.

Where Do We Go from Here?

Part of the appeal of the rational, machine-engineering approach to information is that it gives managers and professionals something clear to do. After all, if we're not supposed to design information environments in great detail, how *do* we spend our time constructively? Surely there's more to information life than "fighting fires"? Of course there is. But when managers begin to take an ecological approach, their roles may no longer be so well defined, or their control over information so assured.

I would never argue that technology and formal engineering of information environments have no value. Certainly, IT has made it much easier to access many types of information; new technologies for high-bandwidth communications, object management, multimedia computing, to name but a few, are enhancing everyone's information environment. Formal information planning has its uses, especially when managers are dealing with a specific information domain, and when they intend to build a computer system to support that domain. It's even more useful when they expect little change in that domain over the next several years. Unfortunately, there are few companies in contemporary industrial societies in which these conditions prevail across an entire organization.

The alternative to architectural control—information ecology—has never been articulated before this. While many firms have adopted aspects of a human-centered approach to information, until now there has not been an overarching framework for ecological information management. Yet many managers understand the human aspects of information use intuitively. Like the student who discovered he had been writing prose all his life, they may already be practicing information ecology without knowing it.

My task is to make managers aware of what they know in their gut. More important, I want them to make this intuitive knowledge explicit in order to build a more competitive, creative, and practical information environment for everyone involved. Only then will the "Information Age" and the "Information Revolution" become more than frustrating hype.

2

The Illusion of Control:

Our Information Past

We tried information architecture for 25
years, but we got nowhere.
We always thought we were
doing it incorrectly.

A director of information management,

Xerox Corporation

Since the 1950s, computers have enabled us to capture and store much larger volumes of information. Consequently, managers have gone from a cautious interest in planning and monitoring organizational performance to the current frenzied clamor to know *everything*. Of course, it's impossible to know everything about how a business operates; that was true in 1900, and it will still be true after the year 2000. Yet the desire for control is never far from most managers' hearts. It has often seduced them into attempting to quantify the inherently unquantifiable, or ignoring certain types of information that aren't easily represented on a computer.

What we think of as modern information management began roughly a century ago; it emerged through what has been called the "control revolution" in business operations.[1] The dawn of the corporation, with its multidivisional, multifunctional organization, created a greater need for coordination and control. Information systems historian Joanne Yates[2] has cogently described the mundane beginnings of information management in the form of business correspondence (generated by the typewriter) and document filing systems (stored in the cabinets still common in any office). Advances in transportation and production technology also called for a much faster and more efficient means of handling an organization's information.

Early on, information management involved four different approaches. They correspond roughly to four modes—or "streams"—of information in a modern organization: (1) unstructured information; (2) intellectual capital or knowledge; (3) structured information on paper; and (4) structured information on computers. Though the four streams have different intellectual origins, at times they have overlapped when put to practical use. In addition, the popularity or influence of a given information stream has varied widely over the years. Structured information on computers came out of nowhere in the 1970s to dominate information management; in the 1990s, knowledge management is now all the rage.

Nevertheless, the four approaches have several problems in common. The information they use overlaps with other types, the management styles they've adopted have not been adequate, and they have largely ignored behavioral and social factors in information use. Below I will discuss each of these "control" approaches separately, showing how all could benefit from a more ecological perspective. Then I'll focus on the one that still dominates—management of structured information on computers.

Control Approach 1: Unstructured Information

Attempting to handle the stream of unstructured information generated by an organization—or an entire society—is the oldest approach around. Librarians, market researchers, executive assistants, and policy analysts have gathered information like customer reactions to new products or the trade "secrets" of competitors as far back as the twenty-first century BCE, when clay tablets were gathered together in the first library in Sumeria. Needless to say, this approach has a bit of a head start over the others.

But it hasn't varied much for centuries, because the approach itself is unstructured and labor intensive, requiring highly skilled workers and offering few economies of scale. Historically, gatherers of unstructured information relied most heavily on printed sources, including books, journals, and reports. Over just the past ten years, of course, there's been tremendous growth in the availability and use of on-line information; in 1993, for example, there were over 4,000 commercial databases in the United States alone.[3] Yet if anything, widening this particular information stream has only made it harder to manage, not to mention control.

In the past, unstructured information management was largely an ad hoc activity. Workers gathered information for a specific purpose and delivered it to decision-makers for their use. Librarians were the only group of workers extensively trained in this area of information management. Over the past two decades, librarians have been managing printed information, as well as participating in its acquisition, distribution, and storage in computerized forms.

Even so, their role is still largely a passive one: they handle information requested by others.[4]

Unstructured information providers like librarians do have unique skills. They often have a better understanding of information's content, and they're closer than any other type of provider (though usually not close enough) to the user. They sometimes add value to the information they collect—synthesizing, interpreting, and packaging it to suit the purposes of whoever requests it. But the ad hoc nature of their work, the passivity with which information is provided, and their inability to leverage their activities beyond personalized service to individual users has limited the effectiveness of this group's work. While librarians and their use of on-line services have a definite place in an ecologically oriented organization, they're not enough.

For example, managers at the New York Capital Markets division of an international bank decided that widely distributing information about its clients and potential deals was crucial to its success, and that traditional library-type intermediaries created a bottleneck. The firm acquired the groupware program Lotus Notes and gave its investment bankers direct access to a system called "Market Talk"; one component of the system automatically captured external news in categories predefined by users. Other components allowed bankers to share information (where ethically appropriate) on pending deals and changes in clients' organizations. While the system did increase overall external information costs in the division, it also increased information use dramatically. Many of the bankers now wax enthusiastic about how the information has led to more and better deals.

This example illustrates the direction unstructured information management may take in the future. It will rely less on a central function—for example, a library or competitive intelligence group—and more on people from around the organization who have knowledge worth sharing. And it will not try to control the flow of that information, especially for short-sighted financial reasons, since such control might actually undercut the main goal of any business: to compete successfully in the marketplace.

Some unstructured information—rumors, gossip, stories—will always remain that way. That's life in increasingly decentralized organizations. For providers and managers of unstructured information, the greatest challenge will be determining when and how to exert control—and how much computerization is appropriate for a given class of information.

Control Approach 2: Intellectual Capital or Knowledge

While many managers say the knowledge of their employees is a company's most valuable asset, few firms have actively begun to manage this information stream on a broad scale. Knowledge management has thus far been addressed either philosophically or technologically, with little pragmatic discussion of how knowledge can be managed and used more effectively on a daily basis.[5]

Certainly, companies have long focused on hiring knowledgeable people, and on increasing their employees' knowledge through training and education. There have been efforts, both systematic and ad hoc, to improve the transfer of knowledge from laboratory to production in the new-product development process at such firms as IBM, AT&T, and Xerox. And anyone who works in an organization knows how many company pamphlets, instruction manuals, and other paper documents exist to help—supposedly—capture and distribute knowledge.

Only recently have computers become an effective tool in managing knowledge or intellectual capital. That's largely because new software can capture structured text, discussions, and graphics or video. Firms have begun to encourage employees to contribute to knowledge bases and discussion databases. Hewlett-Packard, for example, maintains a database called Electronic Sales Partner that allows various professionals to view any proposals, white papers, presentations, or product literature that might aid the sales process. The same company also has a discussion database called Trainer's Trading Post in which education-oriented HP employees give their opinions of courses offered by HP and course materials on-line.

But only limited progress has been made in capturing knowledge for expert systems and neural networks, because of the technical difficulty of keeping such knowledge up to date. The celebrated XCON (Xpert CONfigurer) for configuring computer-system orders at Digital Equipment, for instance, is no longer used. A widely publicized neural network once employed for picking stocks in Fidelity Investments' Disciplined Equity Fund has also been dropped.

Knowledge is often sprawling and messy, and the ways in which knowledge workers use it are manifold and unpredictable. More to the point, early attempts to "engineer" knowledge have often failed. An ecological approach to knowledge is critical, then, simply because humans are essential to shaping, interpreting, and muddying this most complex kind of information.

Control Approach 3: Structured Information on Paper

Paper-based records and documents have ruled the information roost until very recently. For the vast majority of its history, this stream has been dominated by what is now called records management—defined by one British records-management practitioner as "the management of any information captured in reproducible form that is required for conducting business."[6] That would include computer (or at least magnetic tape) based information, but paper, of course, has been the medium of choice for the first several thousand years of records management.

Governments were the first to manage records in libraries or national archives; the earliest Sumerian repositories date to 5000 BCE. France established a national records office in the eighteenth century, England in the nineteenth, and the United States in the twentieth. The document registry, in which workers number and track incoming or outgoing documents, was a key focus of these organizations.[7] Corporations really only began to manage the full life cycle of documents in the mid-1940s, but most large firms still have records management units in operation today.

Records management dominated this information stream until the early 1970s, when managers began to incorporate the broader notion of "Information Resource Management" (IRM). In some respects, IRM is an early form of information ecology, though its subsequent problems in practice illustrate certain pitfalls to avoid. This movement reached its fullest expression in the US federal government; the Commission on Federal Paperwork developed and articulated many of its principles, which were later embodied in the Paperwork Reduction Act of 1980.[8]

In addition to the somewhat simplistic objective of reducing bureaucratic paperwork, these principles included measuring and managing the cost of information, setting up efficient modes of information storage and retrieval, emphasizing increased organizational awareness of the value and use of information, and, most profoundly, recognizing that excessive paper results from an organizational lack of policy and accountability, rather than a simple paper-handling problem. In businesses and to some degree in government, IRM quickly encompassed not only records and forms but also computerized information and databases. Like information ecology, it advocated integrated management of multiple information types.

Apart from government paperwork reduction, however, IRM did not have a long-term, major impact on how information was managed in either the public or private sectors. Its managerial advocates seldom realized their high and worthwhile ambitions. Like approaches to managing unstructured information and knowledge, IRM has made some important contributions to information management, including its promotion of a combined approach to computerized information and stored records; its recognition that information has significant economic value; and its overall treatment of information as a valuable resource. But IRM as a movement, sadly, is now dormant.[9]

All budding information ecologists need to heed this cautionary tale. For one thing, IRM was much more admirable in theory than in practice.[10] Its advocates made overly rational and systematized assumptions about how organizations worked, and about how easily information could flow around those organizations. IRM advocates assumed that organizations worked as systems, rather than as individuals and communities with diverse interests, and consequently found it hard to motivate anybody. IRM's ambitious goals collided with the *realpolitik* of government agencies and departments, many of which didn't always want information to flow freely to rival managers or even their own workers. And while most managers understand that information has value, assigning a specific value to a specific, idiosyncratic chunk of information has always been difficult.

Many executives perceived, perhaps accurately, that IRM was a self-serving ploy of information managers, who would have had to become "czars" of all types of information in order for IRM to work. The mismatch between IRM objectives and real-world information environments meant that it eventually degenerated into technology management. In the words of John Leslie King and Kenneth Kraemer, two academics who have studied IRM in government extensively,

> IRM is enacted to treat information as a resource, but in practice its focus is mainly on the management of information technology. The great breadth of IRM objectives is so far out of the reach of most managers that, in practice, their IRM "strategy" immediately devolves to management of technology. The goal of managing information seldom is resurrected.[11]

One could argue that even a "compromised" verson of IRM has value. But I believe the baby has already been thrown out with the bathwater. There are still a few so-called IRM managers, particularly in US government agencies, but they are now virtually indistinguishable from traditional information systems managers in other organizations.

And yet, even the old-fashioned realm of records management requires a more ecological approach these days. The volume and complexity of information is simply overwhelming traditional methods. As one advocate of records management points out:

> We have mountains of paper files and computer printouts. Rolls of microfilm and stacks of microfiche are filling boxes and cabinets. Audio and video tapes are hidden away in corners and desk drawers. Diskettes are scattered throughout offices, computer tapes are consuming warehouse space, and optical disks are filling cabinets. Today, we also face new information systems in the form of voice and video.[12]

A centralized, highly engineered approach to this vast amount of information is clearly untenable. Even the most carefully maintained records are of no value unless they are used. Information management strategies that make every employee a records manager seem to be the only viable alternative. And general tactics that focus on how people in organizations create, store, and use records will be more valuable than those involving only technology or records architectures.

Control Approach 4: Structured Information on Computers

Using computers to handle structured information has become the most popular approach to information management, partly because of the problems associated with the other three streams. Its advocates believe computerization can deal with the exploding reams of paper in any organization, direct information use rationally, quantify and easily distribute an organization's knowledge, maybe even cut down on personnel costs by getting rid of librarians and other information providers. Yet almost anyone who works in an organization knows these assumptions are not only utopian; they're often dead wrong.

From the early, post–World-War-II days of computer information management, IT gurus championed technology to solve information problems, and IT has improved rapidly since the first mainframe applications. With each advance in processing speed, memory, storage capacity, and software came an expectation of better information environments. Supposedly, managers and professionals would get the information they needed because they'd have more powerful tools at their disposal—timesharing or fourth-generation languages or relational databases or personal computers or neural networks—or whatever shiny new discovery comes next. Technology proponents are perpetually optimistic, even though the most "revolutionary" advances in technology—the first mainframes, PCs, e-mail—have seldom led to evolutionary improvements in information use.

Given this technological focus, IT professionals have mainly concerned themselves with managing computer-based data, rather than information more broadly defined. This has its uses; yet the heavy emphasis on what can be represented on a computer has often ended up denying that unstructured information or knowledge has any value. Sometimes it's as if these "fuzzy" kinds of information don't exist for the people in charge of the machines, although such information—a boss's explanation of how to interpret a competitor's numbers, a conversation with a colleague, ideas generated in a development meeting—is what most of us rely on.

Still, in the 1960s, as computers became more reliable and were used for more than financial transactions, information managers focused on structuring data efficiently. Some, quite sensibly, did not want the decisions made around an organization based on differing versions of the same data. This wasn't a large problem for most companies, since almost all computer-based information was maintained centrally. The desire to avoid redundancy was fueled more by a need to reduce costs and optimize system performance.

As computers become more powerful and data storage cheaper, you'd think avoiding redundancy would be less of a concern. Yet technologists still worried about it. In the 1970s, they began to advocate separating data from computer applications, again for initially sensible reasons. One database of customers, for example, could serve more than one application, which meant that people in order processing, sales promotions, and billing would all be using the same numbers.

These technologists concluded that the only way to avoid redundant data storage across applications was to develop plans or "architectures" of key data elements and classes and their relationship to applications. IT experts came up with various ways of building such plans, but IBM advanced the most popular one. Called "Business Systems Planning" (BSP), this approach was the information-planning tool of choice for a generation of computer and data managers. While BSP was relatively concerned with data, its primary focus was on the development of information systems applications.[13]

BSP advocates also emphasized the need for an independent analysis of data requirements, and the relationships between data and business procedures or processes. For example, what data were used in a company's shipping process? And did the shipping function have the ability to create, read, update, or delete that data? IBM researchers (notably E.J. Codd) pushed these concepts, and by the late 1970s they had become part of "information engineering," a methodology promoted by IT consultants James Martin and Clive Finkelstein.[14] Information engineering is based on the following principles:

- "top down" identification of business information requirements through interviews with senior executives (this also served a marketing purpose, of course, for IBM and its imitators);
- "bottom up" identification and detail of all computerized information items or elements used in the organization;
- alignment of key data entities and classes with the processes using them within the organization;
- grouping of data class and process relationships into specific computer applications and databases.

BSP, information engineering, and its successors brought a new level of planning and rationality to information management. Throughout the late 1970s into the 1980s, many IT organizations hopped on the bandwagon. Even in the 1990s, BSP and information-engineering approaches are still applied under the general name of "information architecture."

So what's wrong with this eminently rational picture? First, while their primary objective is to facilitate interactions between information providers and users, these approaches usually end up creating barriers to communication. The abstraction, technical orientation, and complexity of information modeling tend to drive away users. Even the less technical representations of the approach are hardly appealing to the average marketing or manufacturing manager. For example, Clive Finkelstein earnestly writes:

> The purpose of normalization can be stated in a non-technical way as: *The application of a formal set of rules which determine those key attributes which uniquely identify each data attribute, and which place each attribute in an entity where it is fully identified by the whole primary key of that entity.* [15]

If this definition is nontechnical, God forbid that managers should be exposed to the technical one. I've frequently observed how negatively managers respond to this kind of techno-babble. Here's a typical comment from a manager at a pharmaceutical firm who was involved in an information-engineering project:

> I deal with pieces of paper, regulatory submissions. It's grunt work, and these meetings were way too abstract for me. They drove me flipping crazy. I'd tell them what I did and the computer people would tell me that their charts said that. We talked a lot about the way things *should* be. It was torturous, and it went on for months. I left out of frustration. It was a stupid waste of my professional time.[16]

The complexity and detail of BSP and information engineering approaches also mean that they're frequently never completed;[17] and when they *are* finished, managers often decide not to implement them.[18] When allocators of corporate resources must decide between investing in information architecture and a more tangible, obviously useful system for order processing or customer-service problem tracking, they tend to choose the latter. At American Airlines, for example, more than 200 data modelers were redeployed in 1994 to help develop a new frequent-flyer system. In most cases, however, top executives aren't given a choice. That means more company resources are often thrown after information architectures and plans, and more years wasted.

When these technical methods are applied broadly to model information needs, not only do they fail to add value, they also distract from business change. This is particularly true when the methods of information architecture are also expected to redesign business processes, as some "enterprise engineers" would have it.[19] While machine-engineering designs and architectures may work for individual systems, they often bog down when applied to the information needs of an entire enterprise. An enterprise model of information can easily take more than a year to complete; by that time, the business has changed and the model is usually out of date.

Rank Xerox UK, for example, embarked upon a broad program of information and process modeling in the late 1980s.[20] The goal was to use information-architecture techniques and computer-based modeling tools to design new business processes, then to use those models to generate code automatically for a new set of supporting information systems and databases. When a new Managing Director arrived after several years of this work, he asked for a simple model describing the old and redesigned processes. Not one could be found; all that existed were very detailed data models largely reflecting the status quo processes. The technicians had lost the objective of business change in the details of modeling. Now Rank Xerox UK, using simpler approaches (flow charts and process cost build-up charts), has achieved some successful changes in its work processes, and it uses information architecture only to design specific systems.

Obviously, machine-engineering techniques apply only to those types of information that fit easily on a computer. They primarily address highly structured data involving past financial or operational management within the organization. Other forms of information that appeal to managers—including external market numbers, structured communications inside and outside the firm, text or graphics-based records—generally can't be handled by any of the methods I've observed. Therefore, many executives have decided to cancel enterprise-modeling projects, with little fuss or argument, even after costly initial investments.

Machines Still Rule—But Why?

These four approaches to information management—particularly structuring computerized information—all have their strengths in the right context. But overall, we continue to ignore the real problems, reassuring ourselves that technological progress means information progress. We spend a great deal on system solutions that don't provide the right information, or don't get used. We assume that an information management solution is finished when the technology has been implemented—*if* it ever gets implemented. The overemphasis on technology eventually even reflects poorly on technology itself, because non-technologists assume that their inability to get the information they want is due to inadequate equipment.

Of course, it's not fair to lay all the blame for our love affair with the machine on enterprise modelers and other IT specialists. If techno-babble and abstract systems jargon were the only problem with implementing machine-engineering systems, a company could eventually make a successful translation for other employees. But the struggles over information use in companies go far beyond that kind of language problem. The machine engineering model of information management is rooted deeply in our culture. We all participate, to a greater or lesser degree, in a culture that values technology and "scientific" control over the real, unpredictable human world.

To begin with, the organizational structures that provide information support to businesses don't often help much with information. Despite titles like "Information Services," "Chief Information Officer," and "Information Center," most such functions are preoccupied with technology—if not hardware, then software, applications development, and communications. Few of these groups could provide, for example, a listing of key information types around an organization (including information not on computers) and their locations. If you approached the Information Systems help desk of the typical company and asked, "Where can I find information on our competitors in South America?" I doubt you'd get more than a blank stare.

Even corporate librarians, perhaps the last bastion of those interested in information content, have increasingly become enchanted with technology while neglecting other sources of information. Many library and information science programs in universities have put computer-oriented training at the center of their curricula. Librarians perform more and more computer database searches; indeed, I have encountered many librarians and researchers who seem to have forgotten that some information can't be found—or trusted—in on-line databases.

Then there's the IT press. Despite names like *InformationWeek* and *InfoWorld*, these magazines focus almost exclusively on technology, probably in part because their main advertisers produce high-tech equipment. Although, broadly speaking, the information industry is large, it's much more diffuse than the IT industry. No information providers match the clout of IBM, Digital Equipment, AT&T, and Microsoft. One of the largest providers, Dun & Bradstreet, has recently broken itself into three companies, all of which have fewer promotional resources separately. The Information Industry Association represents information providers, but this is a vaguely defined body with many different subgroups and diverse interests.[21]

In the past several years a few sources have begun to focus on information itself. These include *CIO* magazine and books like *Managing Information Strategically* by Jim McGee and Larry Prusak, *Information Proficiency* by Tom Buckholtz, and *Infotrends* by Jessica Keyes.[22] Other books now address effective creation and management of knowledge in business, for example, Ikujiro Nonaka and Hirotaka Takeuchi's *The Knowledge-Creating*

Company and Dorothy Leonard-Barton's *Wellsprings of Knowledge*.[23] Still, the number of pages devoted to managing information is nowhere near the pages about technology that roll off the presses.

Not all industrialized societies are as technology-obsessed as we are. Japan, for example, has a management culture that emphasizes human information in much greater proportions than in Western business. A 1995 survey found that Japanese senior managers were less likely than their US counterparts to feel they must use computers (eight percent vs. sixty-four percent), get involved in corporate IT construction (thirty-six percent vs. sixty-eight percent), or rely on their corporate information systems departments as a source of management information (two percent vs. twenty-eight percent). Characteristically, the study's authors, Fuld & Company and Fujitsu Research, subtitled it, "How Different Management Styles Have Resulted in a Competitive Disadvantage for Japan, Inc."; they cite the difference as a factor in the current Japanese economic downturn.[24] Yet in my experience, Japanese managers are much more interested in information and knowledge than those in the US, and are more diligent about applying it in their decisions and actions. We should be very careful about explaining this difference as a competitive disadvantage for Japan; it might be just the opposite.

The Trouble with Computers

Our information past has not only overemphasized technology; it has also devoted too much energy to information on computers. Information providers—specifically those in an information systems organization, which normally has far more employees than any other provider—focus on that narrow band of what can be contained in bits and by algorithms. That's because computerized information is easy to manipulate, distribute, and store. But it's not particularly flexible or informative. The same attributes that make computer-based information easy to load into the computer, and easy to manage once there, make it less valuable to humans.

People prefer information that is timely and rich in contextual cues. We like information that involves sequence and causality (that is, a story),[25] which is presented with humor or given a unique interpretation—information that's visually rich in color, texture, and style, and clearly has relevance for our work and lives. Perhaps this seems obvious. But what we get from computers is usually dated information with little or no context or clues to meaning, devoid of sequence or causality, presented in impoverished formats, in much greater volumes than we care to sift through.

While it is technically possible to represent quite complex aspects of reality in ones and zeros, usually much of the value is lost in the translation. Even if we could put on a computer the late-breaking news from the CFO's (Chief Financial Officer's) office that quarterly results will be down, we would also like to know whether the board has been told of the problem, if it's due to the recession in Europe, or if our major competitor is doing any better. The computer rarely shows us the pained facial expression of the CFO as she relates the news, or explains the obfuscational wording of the memo that tells us something is really wrong.

Plenty of empirical research indicates that senior managers prefer information that doesn't reside on a computer. Various studies have demonstrated that computerized information doesn't provide the variety, currency, and relevance to their problems that managers require. As a result, most executives rely on verbal information as their most important source. One summary of these studies suggests that this preference hasn't changed substantially since research on the topic began in the 1960s.[26]

Managers tend to get two-thirds of the information they use from human sources; most of that is through face-to face-conversations, the rest from telephone conversations. The other third is structured information, most of which comes from documents about the external environment, from market research reports to industry magazines and the *Wall Street Journal*. Whenever I ask my consulting clients or research site managers how many of them get the information they need from a computer, almost none say they do. A recent Conference Board survey of strategy and planning managers also found that "Substantial skepticism was expressed by respondents about whether corporate information problems can be solved by better computer systems."[27]

Information managers would probably be better off if they declared a five- or ten-year moratorium on new technology and focused on information use itself. But the world of information technology continues to advance, and some resources will have to be devoted to implementing new capabilities. Some of those capabilities will be useful in mastering the contemporary information environment—the ability, for example, to capture, store, and distribute unstructured text, audio, and video. At the very least, IT managers should spend their time implementing this particular set of tools, since they have the most potential to provide the kind of information we want.

Many types of information can be put on contemporary computers, from entries in the general ledger to videoconferences and expert logic. What I want to emphasize here is the distinction between focusing on simple "state data" and information that adds value for its human users. Information ecology, which prescribes a looser approach to structuring information, is much more appropriate for managing information of all kinds—not just the data that can scroll down a computer screen.

3

The Best of All Worlds:
Information Ecology

We will have to learn, before understanding any task, to first
ask the question, "What information do I need, and in what
form, and when?. . . The next question people have to learn
to ask is, "To whom do I owe which information and when
and where."

Peter Drucker, "What Executives Need to Learn"

The well-known ecologist Garrett Hardin has pointed out that if you want to
manage an entire ecosystem, "you can never do just one thing."[1] Up to now,
most companies have done a little better than that in managing information:
they have undertaken two things. They've applied technology to information
problems, and attempted to use machine-engineering methods to turn data into
something of use on computers. Unfortunately, neither "thing" constitutes a
holistic approach to information.

Information ecology includes a much richer set of tools than that employed
to date by information engineers and architects. Information ecologists can mobi-
lize not only architectural designs and IT but also information strategy, politics,
behavior, support staff, and work processes to produce better information environments. When managers manage ecologically, they consider many avenues for
achieving information objectives. They rely on the disciplines of biology, sociol-
ogy, psychology, economics, political science, and business strategy—not just
engineering and architecture—to frame their approach to information use. And
they look beyond a company's immediate information environment to the overall
organizational environment—how many buildings, offices, and physical locations are involved? What kind of technology is already in place? What's the current business situation?—as well as the external market environment.

Besides thinking holistically about an organization, there are four key attributes of information ecology: (1) integration of diverse types of information; (2) recognition of evolutionary change; (3) emphasis on observation and description; and (4) focus on people and information behavior. All four are analogous to aspects of ecology in the physical world. While the fully ecological approach to information would adopt all of these attributes, each is valuable in its own right. Adopting any of them will help organizations move in a more ecological direction—an important fact to keep in mind when information ecology seems like a daunting project.

Holistic approaches do have their downside. Working on many dimensions at once requires broad managerial skills and patience. It's also difficult to decide where to start, and what sequence of activities to pursue, when there are many tools available. And when change *does* occur, managers sometimes can't pinpoint a specific intervention or cause, making it hard to figure out information ecology's bottom line.

As I've already emphasized, wholesale change never comes easily, particularly when managers don't have as much control over the process as they'd like. Even so, we can't let that scare us off. The techno-utopian and machine-engineering approaches to information have already wasted far too many resources in far too many companies; they're simply not up to current information demands. In this chapter, I'll discuss why the four ecological attributes matter, why we need a working model for information ecology, and how a real company, the UK's Standard Life Assurance, has successfully implemented ecological techniques.

Ecological Attribute 1: Integration of Diverse Types of Information

As biological ecologies thrive on species diversity, information ecologies thrive on information diversity. Indeed, many organizations have already begun integrating management of diverse types of information: computerized and noncomputerized; structured and unstructured; text, audio, and video. Such integration has been driven not only by new technologies but also by the need to better leverage nontraditional forms of information.

Unlike the other ecological attributes, information integration will happen to some degree without conscious action. At this point, computers increasingly capture, access, and manipulate all types of information in some form (even if the form remains inadequate or has yet to add value). The organizational structures and processes used to manage computers are becoming de facto integrators.

Still, true information integration won't happen without major changes in management approaches and organizational structure. Existing information planning approaches, for example, deal with only one type of information. Just consider logistical processes in most warehouse facilities, where information planners address the quantities and volumes of items shipped, but not equally vital information like customer complaints about late shipments. Even departments for the provision and management of information usually only work with one or two kinds. In most organizations, there's scarcely any contact between the information systems, library, and competitive intelligence functions. Even fewer firms have information liaisons who can help find a useful nugget among multiple online sources, pie charts, and databases. In fact, information providers who wish to meet their customers' needs shouldn't be directing people to any particular type of information; they should combine all the information media available.

More important, if non-computer providers of information—be they middle managers, market analysts, or executive assistants—want to direct the inevitable integration of information in their company, they need to begin explicitly addressing how to do so. They must meet with each other, perhaps for the first time; identify the key topics on which they should focus their energies; and understand how diverse information sources, formats, and perspectives can be brought to bear on an issue for the good of the organization. They must resist the headlong rush to grind all information into a format that is palatable to a computer. Given the diversity in any information ecology, it's up to non–IT-oriented providers to package information in forms that engage and spark the information consumer.

Ecological Attribute 2: Recognition of Evolutionary Change

Just as we expect physical ecologies to evolve over time, we should assume that information ecologies constantly change. That means the information systems in place also need to be flexible. Since it's impossible to understand or predict fully how a company's information environment will evolve over time, information management must allow for change—even if it's not clear exactly what that change may be.

While I've sought a stable, predictable information environment for years, I have yet to find one. Once I thought I had in a privately held Northwest timber company. Timber is timber, and thus it shall ever be, or so I assumed. The need for wood being fairly constant, this privately held timber company would appear to be insulated from the usual market pressures. When this firm undertook an information engineering project, I thought, at last! Here's a company that will benefit from an entirely rational, machine-oriented approach. But as any information ecologist could have told me, nothing ever stays the same.

In the middle of the project, the US government ruled that spotted owls in Western timberlands were an endangered species. If the firm didn't know where spotted owls lived in its forests, it couldn't cut timber. The information engineering effort was halted—after incurring great expense—and the firm began to wrestle with how to capture and use information on spotted owls. Much of the relevant information, of course, was in documents, maps, and photographs. While computers can now contain such information, the company saw no immediate benefit in computerizing it all; out of necessity, they moved beyond machine-engineering approaches.

In fact, most IT managers do recognize that information environments are always changing. By now they know that traditional approaches to systems modeling and development can easily become obsolete before they're finished. In developing new computer-based systems, information technologists are realizing that they can neither anticipate the future for three to five years, nor freeze changes during the development cycle. To address this evolution, some firms employ systems-development approaches like iterative prototyping and so-called Rapid Application Development.

But managers understand much less about how to deal with evolving information needs in general. Are there analogs to systems-development approaches in non-computer areas? What's the right compromise between building information structures that last and structures that can easily be modified? What approaches to managing continuous change from physical ecology can be borrowed and applied to the information world? While nobody knows the full answers to these questions—and they'll differ from business to business in any case—recognizing that evolution is an organizational fact of life is a necessary first step for all managers.

Ecological Attribute 3: Emphasis on Observation and Description

Perhaps the earliest ecologists were the biologists and naturalists like Darwin, who began by simply describing the world—from the Galapagos to the British countryside—in all its complexity. Only then could he and others understand why a species fit into its environment, or the dynamics of environmental change. Similarly, we must become more descriptive in our approaches to information management. It's the height of ignorance and hubris to believe we understand the information requirements of an organization after only days or weeks of interviews with a few people; yet this all-too-common assumption drives many information engineering projects.

While information engineers emphasize modeling the future, information ecologists take a more humble approach. As Henry Mintzberg might say about strategic planning,[2] if we can't anticipate the future, we shouldn't plan it in detail. Describing and understanding the existing information environment is a major undertaking in itself.

Indeed, the information environment in any large organization is highly complex. Describing who has what information, the various sources of information support, how information and knowledge are used in work processes, and the organization's intentions and objectives for information is an essential, if sometimes overwhelming, task. Given the multiplicity of information sources and uses, and the close relationship between the information environment and the broader business environment of any organization, predicting the future is virtually impossible. For example, a company can't know who its competitors will be in the future or what information about them it will need; it makes much more sense to focus on describing the competitive information a company has *today*, along with the support staff for gathering new information when it becomes necessary.

Emphasizing description over future planning will take many different forms. In the area of information architecture, for instance, a new emphasis on description means developing maps of current information rather than models of the future information state. In the realm of information processes, it means creating a thorough understanding of existing processes before designing new ones. We need to start asking, How is information gathered, shared, and used *today*? Who are some particularly effective information users *today*, and what can we learn from them? We know so little about information use in organizations that the first step is to observe the relevant "species"—information users—in their natural settings.

Ecological Attribute 4: Focus on People and Information Behavior

Any attempt to manage ecology in the physical world requires the participation of a broad range of inhabitants. Efforts to prevent water pollution, for example, rely just as much on persuading the residents of a city not to dump crankcase oil in the sewer as on building new filtration plants. When it comes to ecological information management, focusing on the people involved means not simply providing information—or even usefully observing what workers do—but also facilitating its effective use.

In the past, providers of information have focused almost exclusively on the production and distribution of information. What the recipients have done with it upon receiving it has been nobody's business. Therefore, we have little idea of how to help individual workers seek, share, structure, and make sense of information. And we also know little about shaping or developing positive information cultures—those broad patterns of information attitudes and behaviors that recur throughout an organization.

But at gut level, most managers can see why the different approaches taken by the following companies matter. Xerox, like many initially successful companies, had an information culture that valued (at least implicitly) guesses and intuition. Then David Kearns became CEO in 1984. He slowly and painfully changed the culture to one that now emphasizes fact-based management, attempting to base decision-making on hard evidence whenever possible. Of course, facts shouldn't elbow out informed intuition entirely; but Xerox did need to establish a healthier balance.

At General Motors, the information culture until recently emphasized financial information and the authority of the information presenter over the quality of the actual information. If a powerful product manager wanted to introduce a new car model, market research was often conveniently ignored by the product manager and the executives who approved product decisions. But CEO Jack Smith succeeded in making the information culture more oriented toward operational and quality information. For instance, new information was presented at board meetings, and senior management meetings addressed new topics and measures.

In short, information behavior is a vast untapped dimension of information management. I devote all of Chapter 6 to information behavior and culture, but the importance of paying attention to people and what they do pervades this book. From where I stand, if a managerial action or initiative doesn't change information behavior, there's no point in bothering with it.

A Model for Information Ecology

A physical ecology—say, the Amazon rain forest—is not a single entity, with only a few, unvariable components. Even a specific geographical area usually includes a number of micro-environments. In the overall ecology of a rain forest, for example, the environment of the treetops—which is exposed to the open sky and includes monkeys, butterflies, birds—differs from the shadowy world under the leaves—the snakes and sloths, other monkey species, butterflies, birds—and differs again from the soil underground, with its complement of worms, mold, and other parasites. These environments overlap and affect one another, even if they seem very different. If somebody contaminated the rain forest's groundwater with selenium, for instance, all three environments would change—probably for the worse, although no one can fully predict such outcomes. It's possible that killing off a number of trees in one area might allow more space for tree-top dwellers in another.

In any information ecology there are also three environments. The *information environment* of a company is the main focus of this book. But this environment is still rooted in the broader *organizational environment* surrounding it; both of these, in turn, are affected by the *external environment* of the marketplace. In actual practice, these environments overlap and have

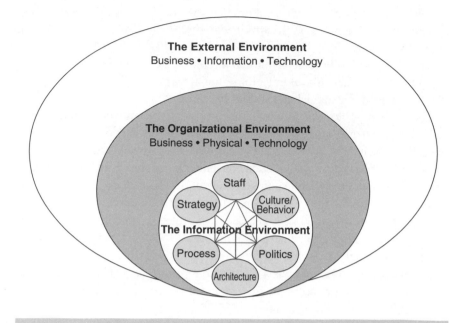

Figure 3-1. An Ecological Model for Information Management

fuzzy boundaries at best. That's why information initiatives can involve all three, whether managers are aware of the connections or not.

To date, there are no practically oriented approaches that encompass all components of an information ecology—that is, how an aggregate of individuals, in a particular organization, in a particular industry affected by broader market trends, works with, thinks about, focuses on, and generally manages information.[3] But description is a fundamental attribute of information ecology. And to manage ecologically, we must first understand the overall landscape in which information is used. To this end, I propose the following model for information ecology (Figure 3-1), one that indicates the many interconnected components of this approach.

The Information Environment

The inside circle of this model is the core of an ecological management approach. It encompasses the six most critical components of information ecology—strategy, politics, behavior/culture, staff, processes, and architecture—each of which is detailed in a chapter of its own.

Information Strategy. Companies frequently have strategies for managing financial or human resources, and you could argue that organizations don't need yet another strategy. But I would argue back that making explicit the high-level "information intent" of a firm actually makes a lot of sense in an information-pervasive world.[4] Information strategies revolve around the question, "What do we want to do with information in this organization?" More important, they must involve top management. As I discuss at length in Chapter 4, information strategies—like any kind of business strategy—are likely to change and will require revision based on any number of internal and external factors. Rather than casting specific intentions in stone, developing a set of basic goals or "principles" is a better vehicle for expressing a company's information strategy.[5]

Information Politics. This critical component involves the power information provides and the governance responsibilities for its management and use. I and other writers have treated this vexing topic elsewhere in some detail,[6] and I devote Chapter 5 of this book to it as well. Occasionally firms I've observed identify their existing political structure and the type of transition they would like to make—say, from an information monarchy (in which a single powerful executive makes every decision) to federalism (in which a broader group of managers arrives at consensus on information policy). More frequently, however, companies attempt to implement information strategies or initiatives that are inconsistent with their political structures—and they fail. For example, several firms I know of are trying to create an information environment of greater sharing, without realizing or acknowledging that they have a feudal information environment in which business unit executives hoard information as a matter of principle.

Information Behavior and Culture. These two related factors may matter most in creating a successful information environment—and they may be the toughest to change.[7] Such positive behaviors as sharing and gaining lasting knowledge from information are too important to be left to chance or individual initiative; instead such behavior must become a basic management objective—and not just the province of IT managers or one czar. As with other resources, managers can use various incentives, outright rewards and punishments, education, even exhortation to influence information behavior. Obviously, some approaches work better than others. Given that so many people are frustrated by or scared of IT to begin with, exhorting employees to use the latest machine or system probably won't have much more effect than asking everyone to trust each other.

All of a company's information behaviors, good or bad, make up its information culture. Particular information cultures determine how much those involved value information, share it across organizational boundaries, disclose it internally and externally, and capitalize on it in their businesses.

Information Staff. People are still the best identifiers, categorizers, filterers, interpreters, and integrators of information. By this I don't mean the

IT people who run the computers and networks, but those who provide and interpret information. The all-important information staff of a company handles the more valuable forms of information, such as organizational knowledge and best practices. If the information in these categories is to be of value, it must be continually pruned, restructured, interpreted, and synthesized—all tasks that computers do poorly.

Just as researchers on manufacturing technologies in the automobile industry discovered that the most productive plants use hybrid human and technological solutions,[8] the best information environments don't automate away the human role. A good information staff therefore includes many kinds of people, such as content specialists (librarians and market researchers); designers and facilitators of information bases; and information liaisons (guides who help users identify their needs). In Chapter 7, I discuss these various roles at length.

Information Processes. This component describes how information work gets done. Some researchers have attempted to understand how knowledge work processes can be improved.[9] Larry Prusak, my former colleague who now consults for IBM, has also described how firms can take a process view of information management, providing examples of particular steps in a process.[10] However, his research focused on just the work of information providers. In the ideal situation, a company takes a broader view, defining information processes as all those activities performed by information workers. To be sure, facilitating the many ways in which a firm's managers, scientists, administrative personnel, and accountants identify, acquire, understand, and act on information should satisfy the most ambitious information ecologist.

As I describe in Chapter 8, the two "traditional" options for changing how work gets done are usually called process improvement, which emphasizes incremental change, and process innovation or reengineering, which sometimes (though not always) leads to radical innovations. Whatever option managers go with, information ecology first calls for a thorough description of how any piece of information work is done.

Information Architecture. The last of these six critical components will be most familiar to information managers. When used parsimoniously for specific purposes, such a machine-engineering approach can indeed improve a company's information environment. However, "information architecture" is also a confusing concept that can embody several alternative meanings.[11] What I mean by it in ecological terms is simply a guide to the structure and location of information within an organization. The architecture can be descriptive, involving a map of the current information environment, or prescriptive, offering a model of the information environment at some future date.

This distinction between current maps and future models is a critical one. As an insurance company information manager once told me, "Since we never fully implement our models, we never have a useful map of the structure and location of our current information." Perhaps information systems professionals instinctively resist mapping the present because it is messy and "wrong"; yet their abstract information visions are rarely realized, and so their work has little practical value.

In the information environment, ease of understanding and communication should always outweigh detail and precision. Information ecologists view architectural blueprints as a means for changing the behavior of information users, not as a technical exercise.[12] Even a map of the entire current information environment may be impractically large and time-consuming; information managers will do much more for users if they map specific topic areas. In Chapter 9, I present a mapping-oriented approach to information architecture, along with several extended examples based on what real companies have done.

The Organizational Environment

While a company's information environment will be the site of most management initiatives, it's always rooted in the broader organizational environment—including the overall business situation, existing technology investment, and physical arrangement. Each of these three components of the organizational environment are described in Chapter 10.

Business Situation. How the specific aspects of an organization's business situation affect information initiatives will vary across firms and industries. But whatever the specifics, information ecologists need to pay attention to a firm's business strategy, business processes, organizational structure/culture, and human resources orientation. Clearly, these aspects mirror components of the information environment. As such, business strategy, for example, will influence information strategy—and vice versa.

Technology Investment. A company's overall investment in IT will certainly influence its information environment, but the most critical factor here is simple access to information. The increased prevalence, ease of use, and power of desktop workstations and local area networks have provided a good infrastructure in virtually all firms. And some new technologies are more information-oriented than those of the past, allowing the management of text, graphics, video, and audio in all their richness.

However, the effects of the personal computer revolution aren't always so salutary for the broader information ecology. Components of the information environment like strategy and culture do influence technology investment, though not as much as they should. In the equivalent of Gresham's Law, in which "bad money drives out good," a heavy focus on technology can actually drive out information. IT applications may also limit creative thinking about how information can be displayed and structured. I've heard scattered complaints, for example, about the damage spreadsheets have done to creative thinking about financial information. Too often managers invest in expensive technologies without seriously considering what information initiatives they will facilitate. As a result, the initiatives don't fare well, and the technology is not used to maximum advantage.[13]

Physical Arrangement. It may seem intuitively obvious that this component affects information management and use. At the most basic level, we share more information with colleagues in the same physical space. Systematic studies of organizational communication have shown that physical proximity increases the frequency of communications within groups.[14] And some firms have attempted to manage information by creating spaces that facilitate interaction.

In the information ecology model, physical arrangement includes the physical aspects of information media as well. At the most micro level, documents are media that structure and present information. Xerox, after becoming "The Document Company," has done substantial work on how attributes of documents—such as amount of text on the page or use of color—help or hinder information transmission. Some firms even make effective use of posters, white boards, and post-it notes—all physical media that don't require complex technologies. Increasingly, of course, firms can choose between physical and technological means to facilitate communication.

The External Environment

Any company's information ecology is bound to be affected by external factors, many of which the company can't directly control. Governments create new regulations, customers' requirements evolve, and competitors take unpredictable steps. A country's politics or cultural trends usually act on a given company rather than the other way around. Few firms have the clout to shape the entire external environment by their own actions, especially if the Dow Jones takes a dive or war breaks out in Saudi Arabia.

Still, companies want and need information about the external world. In any information ecology, the external environment consists of information about three basics: general business markets, technology markets, and—perhaps the most important type for our purposes—information markets. I discuss each of these in detail in Chapter 11.

Business Markets. These create general business conditions for firms, which affect both their ability to acquire and manage information, and the types of information they need. Ideally, changes in customers, suppliers, business partners, regulators, and competitors would be reflected in the information that exists inside the company.

Technology Markets. Here is where available technologies that may affect our information world are bought and sold. At any given moment, a company must know what is available for purchase in the market, and then decide whether and how a given technology might be of value.

Information Markets. This third component of the external environment—in which everything from industry trends to mailing lists are bought and sold—can provide critical resources for effective information ecologies. While individual companies primarily focus on what information to buy from information markets, many firms are now considering whether to sell information themselves. American Airlines, for example, makes more money selling information to travel agents in many years than it does flying airplanes. Monsanto has recently begun a new service business that sells information about "what works" in agriculture to farmers. Stan Davis, the consultant who came up with the term "mass customization," has described this trend as "informationalization" and argues that all firms should evaluate their potential for generating income this way.[15]

New information sources are becoming available as I write, of course, and it doesn't always make sense to generate your own. Still, when managers scan information markets for potential services to buy, they need to evaluate their business relevance, information quality, and authority—the degree to which the information is accepted as an industry standard. In the automobile industry, for example, firms like R.L. Polk and J.D. Power are clearly authoritative sources of information; companies happily purchase sales and customer-satisfaction data from them.

Some external information markets resemble the Moroccan bazaar more than the New York Stock Exchange—but that's not necessarily a bad thing. Companies should identify all possible ethical means by which information can be gathered, including job interviews, trade shows, even newspaper employment ads, and put the information into a form in which it can be understood and used. The problem here comes not in gathering the information, but in systematically capturing, leveraging, and verifying it. Information gained at a trade show, for example, is often remembered and used only by the person who had the conversation.

The Information Ecology "Web"

Creating change in an information ecology is clearly a complex, multifaceted undertaking. As in a natural ecosystem, a change in one environment will affect the others. Information ecologists ask questions like, How does our information strategy affect our business strategy, and vice-versa? How do information politics reflect or help to shape broader organizational politics? How do all of these factors relate to overall business success?

We know that information systems often don't meet the business objective for which they were intended,[16] although firms have long tried to make information systems (if not information initiatives) align with business strategy.[17] However, information ecology argues for a higher level of integration than that—an explicit acknowledgment that the many different elements form an interconnected web. Based on everything I've observed in companies, I believe true information changes are connected not only to strategy, but also to organizational structure, culture, a firm's physical arrangement, and all the other components of this model.

Here, we no longer overemphasize technology but place it in a balanced perspective. Certainly, the technology available in the broader marketplace, as well as the specific technologies that an organization chooses to implement, can affect what information is available and how easy it is to access. In fact, I include technology in this human-centered model to show that technology and people are inextricably related. Certainly, some technologies are more human-oriented than others; but rather than simply assuming more technology yields a better information environment, thinking ecologically means accounting for how politics, strategy, behavior, and other human factors all intervene in this relationship.

In a consumer products company, for example, an information strategy might focus on getting better information about customers—both retailers and consumers. Information process plans might address how consumer behavior is better understood through scanner data or frequent-buyer programs. Approaches to information behavior could focus on development of better analytical skills in order to draw conclusions from vast amounts of consumer transaction data. Information staff might include a "category manager" who analyzes sales of particular brands. Managers might also emphasize information about the external environment—competitors, consumer trends, the economy.

When it comes to planning, of course, ecological thinking calls for a certain humility. No manager will ever be able to anticipate all of the events that drive the nature and success of an information ecology. On a more day-to-day level, highly detailed plans tend to inhibit communications about information changes and directions. I have no doubt this model can help planners, but I suggest employing it modestly, with a grain of salt.

Indeed, no company that I've worked with fully employs an ecological approach. Information ecology remains a vision, a new way of seeing the world of information use—but I'm convinced it's an absolutely essential perspective. Even if information ecology has yet to be realized, some companies have begun grappling with their own information environments out of competitive necessity. From the way they balance, shift, and revise the many complex connections we can learn what works—and what doesn't.

Real-World Ecology: A Look at Standard Life

Take the UK's Standard Life Assurance, which has successfully changed major elements of its information ecology. Based in Edinburgh, Standard Life is one of the world's largest and most profitable mutual life insurance companies.[18] It was founded in 1825; by 1992, it had revenues of £5.4 billion. But after decades of stable business conditions, Standard Life's *business markets* underwent rapid change. Growth had exploded, products were proliferating, competitors were merging, and regulation was shifting with lightning speed. Furthermore, the company faced new competition from financial service companies such as banks and building societies.

The firm's *business situation* consequently had to change as well. Top managers articulated a new business strategy and related mission, new objectives, and new values: in particular, they emphasized fast response, expense reduction, and customer satisfaction. They gave the go-ahead for major reengineering efforts of business processes like insurance underwriting and policy administration. Given the changes in regulation and competition, the senior management team, called the "Senior Executive," also started paying closer attention to the external environment. These managers could see that demand for business information was clearly increasing; but they were concerned that Standard Life employees were relying too much on external *information markets,* with too little coordination to be cost-effective.

In order to better manage and coordinate these changes, the Senior Executive focused its collective gaze for the first time on Standard Life's information environment. In practical terms, however, top management wasn't really involved and allocated few resources to the effort initially. For roughly a year after declaring that Standard Life needed improved information management, nothing happened.

But in 1993, a new *information staff* organization was created. Called "Information Management and Architecture," this small group began to plan and initiate ways to improve the overall state of Standard Life's information environment. The group recognized a number of information problems at the firm, including how hard it was to get people to perceive and understand an information issue in a common way; how hard it was to define and focus information projects so they might lead to tangible outcomes; and a widespread tendency to treat information as data.

To address these and other issues, the new group set itself four main goals, which constituted its *information strategy:*

- to focus on business areas or information topics with the greatest potential payoff for the firm;
- to develop the conceptual models and tools—even the right language—to enable Standard Life employees to better recognize, understand, and discuss information issues;
- to help everyone, including senior managers, see the "big picture" that is, information's importance to the firm;
- to establish the place of information within Standard Life's strategic business planning framework.

Several of these goals inspired specific initiatives to create new systems or support groups. In 1994 Chester Simpson, who headed the Information Management and Architecture Group, took another ecological step. He developed a generic model for *information management processes:*

- formulate the problem;
- identify information needs;
- locate/capture appropriate information;
- analyze/interpret it;
- manipulate/package it;
- distribute it;
- store and dispose of it;
- use it.

Simpson thought Standard Life did a relatively good job of distributing and storing information, perhaps because these steps involved information technology. However, he believed that the analysis of information, and feedback about it when used—all human issues in information management—were often neglected. Simpson's group used his information-process model to underpin virtually all projects it undertook. And another "value-added model"—one developed to help people see why they transformed information and what gave it value—influenced the group's work as well. This model highlighted key information attributes, including:

- *truth*—a user's confidence in the information;
- *guidance*—when information points the way toward actions that need to be taken;
- *scarcity*—when information is new or not freely available to competitors;

- *accessibility*—how available information is to users in a form they can use and understand;
- *weight*—the features that give information "weight," making it compelling and more likely to be used (an attribute that I call "engagement").

A number of new projects were based on these models. For example, one addressed the still relatively new Competitor Analysis (CA) function within Standard Life. The CA team provided senior executives with a series of strategic profiles of leading or potential rivals within the UK marketplace; but evidence had mounted that executives weren't using this material to make decisions or for corporate planning. A series of interviews with the Senior Executive and a second tier of managers revealed major differences between the way CA team members expected their information to be used, and the way executives actually did use it.

The CA people assumed their "product" would matter most for decision-making and planning. However, managers at both levels wanted to gain inspiration from the material as well, hoping that it would spark them to ask big questions like, "What new things in our business should we be thinking about?" By looking at what their peers in rival companies were doing, Standard Life managers also wanted confirmation for their own actions. In addition, neither Simpson's group nor the CA team had expected to find that anybody but senior executives was reading the competitor reports. Yet several managers had been handing them out to their own staffs as a way to stimulate thought in their divisions about how things might change.

To put these unexpected findings into practice, Standard Life's information staff was realigned significantly. Because the Senior Executive already received a great deal of high-level competitor information from contacts with their peers in the insurance industry, the division responsible for the CA team diverted its resources into charting best practices across the business spectrum—something the division had only tentatively approached up to that point. The CA team then became part of Marketing to take advantage of this division's experience with gathering competitor information in relation to products and markets.

Other projects undertaken by the Information Management and Architecture group put more emphasis on *information behavior*. Information managers talked to executives and observed meetings to figure out what information people needed. And a "communication" project in one Standard Life division looked at not only how the behavior and attitudes of information providers facilitated users' access, but also how the level of trust between managers and staff affected sharing.

Simpson's group recommended that the company improve its *technology investment* by bringing in Lotus Notes for several information distribution applications—for instance, to help disseminate marketing research. Finally, these information managers used *information architecture* to clarify the locations of Standard Life's information resources. They conducted an "information audit" on a limited scale; this involved interviews with approximately forty groups within the company that provided or created information, such as Competitor Analysis or Market Research. The audit, which focused on how to understand and improve the information processes of these groups, then led to a larger effort to document the information resources within the entire UK organization. The result: "InfoGuide," Standard Life's first electronic guide to information. Implemented in 1996, InfoGuide can be accessed through both mainframe and Lotus Notes software applications.

Note that Standard Life didn't address all components of the information ecology model. Even with such forward-thinking approaches to strategy and processes, the company's *information politics* changed much more slowly. Standard Life had a hierarchical structure, which emphasized communication of "complete information"—that is, conclusions rather than questions or hypotheses. Consequently, individual employees were seldom rewarded for open-ended thinking or questioning management decisions. Politically, it operated somewhat feudally—with various business executives maintaining a tight hold on the information keys to their castles—combined with a strong current of technological utopianism. Standard Life's *physical arrangement* was also not ideal; employees were spread throughout more than twenty buildings in Edinburgh alone.

What's most encouraging, however, is that Standard Life's *information culture* has begun to shift. Some information initiatives have fallen by the wayside; but there's been a tangible improvement in the organization's ability to think about and employ information. For starters, the firm's information feudalism is beginning to crumble, because managers in different divisions now realize they need to share information across organizational boundaries. In addition, employees all over Standard Life are using "truth," "guidance," and other terms generated by Chester Simpson's group—and Simpson assumes that if the terms are being used, providers are genuinely trying to add value to their information.

Initiatives to improve customer information and knowledge are now cropping up around the organization. For instance, the Sales division is employing various means to identify new sales leads through multiple distribution channels. Then there's the new drive to understand customers not only in terms of their financial need but also according to what motivates their financial decisions; the information gathered for this effort has been used to identify seven customer categories, all based on their behaviors. Another project, now in its third year, attempts to tie indicators of customer service to specific actions by

Standard Life; those involved here have moved past how to collect and analyze this information to how to distribute it through the organization so that people will use it.

Leaders of these initiatives act in complex, ecological ways. Like the members of Simpson's group, they expect their information environments to change, yet take on focused, short-term projects rather than losing themselves in grand designs. The upshot is that customers are now much more aware of the value of Standard Life's information products. And the Senior Executive is discussing information strategy for the first time in its existence.

Standard Life Assurance has at least moved beyond the easy rhetoric that information is important to business success, developing plans and taking actions in areas not normally addressed. This happened, in part, because Standard Life's managers adopted an ecological perspective. While the information ecology model (like all other management tools) offers no miracles, it can direct attention to new areas. Those areas may involve behavior, culture, and politics simply because they've been so grossly neglected by information and general managers in the past.

Standard Life's efforts certainly argue for formulating a good *information strategy*. When top managers put together a plan for what information they need, and how it should be used—the subject of the next chapter—they have started down the right ecological road.

4

Information Strategy

The point is that the economic value from generating, using,
and selling information is growing significantly faster than the
value added by producing traditional goods and services.

Stan Davis, *20/20 Vision*

Because creating an information strategy can potentially encompass all aspects of an information ecology, it's a good place for managers to begin. Yet at the risk of sounding like an amateur Zen philosopher, I believe the final strategic destination means much less than the journey there. Any good strategy promotes communication, debate, consensus; more than anything, it gets managers to talk to each other. Strategy is about choices and emphasis—which types of business to pursue, products to create, markets to address.

Information strategy also means making choices, not carving out a master plan in stone. Ecologically minded managers will strategize about which information to focus on, what information activities to emphasize, and how information will help their organization meet its objectives. Of course, such issues change over time and can never be fully resolved. As I've noted earlier, my rather atypical attitude resembles that of Henry Mintzberg, who is both a specialist on strategy and a sometime researcher of managerial information needs.[1] Mintzberg's rigorous observations show how planning really happens in organizations—for better or worse. Like him, I argue that

- strategy is a continual, incremental process of setting and resetting organizational direction;

- strategy should not be elaborate or detailed, because we cannot anticipate the future in detail;
- strategy is a dialogue rather than a document;
- strategy and planning should be done by business managers, not "strategic planners."

I also find the concept of "strategic intent" helpful.[2] This term indicates that a strategy can specify only an approximate destination for an organization, one we'll probably never reach. If managers insist that the only success-ful strategy is one that has been fully implemented, they're headed for a fall, especially in the ever-shifting world of information use. But if they think like information ecologists, simply viewing strategy as a guide to action, these managers may find that "success" means more than implementing a local area network or creating a Web site.

In this chapter, I'll describe four possible ways to focus an information strategy: (1) on specific information content; (2) on a firm's common infor-mation; (3) on information processes; (4) on new information markets. Then, based on the experiences of a number of companies, I'll discuss how infor-mation strategies can play out—and succeed—in practice.

Why Do We Need an Information Strategy?

It's true that many organizations don't have information strategies. What's more, most of them survive despite this managerial lack, so why clutter the strategy shelf with another binder? While I hate proliferating memos and meetings as much as the next person, there are at least five good reasons to think strategically about information:

- information environments in most firms are a disaster;
- information resources can always be better allocated;
- information strategies help organizations adapt to change;
- information strategies make information more meaningful;
- the kind of information strategy I propose is not that burdensome.

In the past, we could count on people in a variety of jobs to make the information environment better. But many of the positions that used to involve information management—planners, executive assistants, researchers, and middle managers in general—are now gone in many firms. Contemporary computers and communications networks provide greater information access, but access is not the problem. Insufficient resources exist to understand, interpret, and add value to information. Most important, when the organizational and external business environments change, a company's information environment usually needs to change as well.

For example, a major automobile manufacturer has gone through significant downsizing over the past several years. The company has eliminated management layers, creating cross-functional teams instead. These changes can be beneficial in themselves; but at this firm they've had unintended consequences. For one thing, the managers who remain receive more information than ever before. A manager is expected not only to respond to communications from his or her own business function, but also to coordinate actions across cross-functional processes. In addition, these processes are being coordinated worldwide, which means managers must exchange information with their peers all over the globe.

Information overload is the result, with no information strategy to address the problem. Individual managers complain that they get more than 100 e-mail messages a day in addition to voice mail, faxes, regular telephone calls, and a heavier-than-before load of paper mail. As one manager told me, "If I am to keep up with my job I have to spend all of my time, both on and supposedly off the job, communicating. I don't have a life anymore."

Perhaps the most important rationale for creating a coherent information strategy is to increase the appreciation for information. This may seem counterintuitive; why create a strategy for something if people don't already think it's important? Unfortunately, managers don't always understand the difference between information and its associated technologies. They assume, even when using information every day, that its management is the province of technologists. They may even engage in discussions of *technology* strategy— whether to employ mainframes or client-server computers, for instance, or how many telecommunications carriers with which to deal—without realizing an *information* strategy would be much more relevant to their broader business strategies.

There will always be individuals in key management positions who believe that the speed of the latest Intel chip is more significant than improving customer information. These individuals were formerly confined to Information Systems departments in firms; thanks to the personal computer revolution, they can now be found almost anywhere.

Indeed, that's still the main problem for Standard Life Assurance. Despite the fact that top executives say things like, "We are not an insurance company, we're an information company," many other managers feel these executives don't really grasp the importance of information management. The Senior Executive has devoted few resources or little attention to the topic in the past, even though the need for better information keeps "popping up." Therefore,

Standard Life's information strategy doesn't cover as much ground as it could; the company's information movers and shakers have promoted the concept with some visible successes, some direct lobbying, and circulation of key documents and management frameworks—but wouldn't it be better if they could also state clearly what information directions the company intends to pursue, and how doing so will contribute to success in the insurance business?

Given the technocentric attitudes of so many IT managers, information consciousness-raising isn't the best place to start when developing an information strategy. For a number of pragmatic and political reasons, it makes more sense to begin with content—what information is most important to a company's bottom line. Then managers can figure out how to create a dialogue about strategy, making it "real" for all involved.

Because few firms have consciously developed information strategies, we can't rely heavily on the experience of others. But if you've read this far, I'm willing to bet you already appreciate effective information use. Perhaps you even have faith in the need for explicit information strategy, so bear with me while I detail how some companies have taken their first steps. While many of them haven't formalized their information content emphases, they all exemplify the necessary conversational give-and-take.

Focus 1: Information Content

Part of the journey toward an information strategy involves deciding what to discuss. Again, strategy is about choices, and no organization can devote the same amount of attention to all information. What's chosen should be driven by larger business concerns. One research study found that while managers typically have access to a wide range of information, most of them really only pay attention to one major information type—financial, operational, or market-oriented information—the type that best addresses an organization's strategic uncertainties.[3] In such cases, there's little point in managing diverse varieties of information that no one will use.

Many firms decide they should focus on their customers, though defining who that customer is can be difficult. In the health care industry, for example, a firm's customer might be a patient, a hospital, an insurance company, or an employer. At Medco, a provider of prescription drugs recently acquired by Merck, information managers began to emphasize employers as customers. Since employers pay most medical bills, and are normally the party that contracts with Medco to manage drug costs within a health plan, Medco managers decided that they need to learn more about employer information requirements. They want to be able to answer quickly—sometimes even to anticipate—employer requests for information on patterns of prescription drug usage and costs.

To accomplish these explicitly defined strategic-goals, Medco information managers set up an employer database, visited employee health plan administrators, and analyzed transaction databases to spot patterns and trends. The necessary employer information began to take shape, although Medco managers felt for a time their efforts would be in vain if Bill Clinton's government health-care plan was actually implemented (it wasn't). Now Medco remains the leader in its industry despite much tougher competition.

Meanwhile, the biotechnology firm Genentech views physicians—all those who prescribe the drugs created by Genentech—as their primary customers. The firm's information strategy, which is well understood by top managers but has never been formally documented, involves providing information on Genentech drugs to physicians, and receiving information from the same source, through multiple channels. Genentech's sales representatives aren't the typical pharmaceutical "detailers" who enter doctors' offices armed with gifts and free pills but little information. Instead, they are well-trained on the chemical and medicinal properties of Genentech drugs, and carry laptop computers full of additional information, such as clinical-trial results. Physicians have responded positively to Genentech's approach, often prescribing its drugs instead of less expensive (and, Genentech maintains, less effective) alternatives. This same information strategy has recently been adopted by Astra/Merck, a joint-venture startup in the more traditional pharmaceutical arena.

Other firms focus on competitive rather than customer information in their information strategies. At Monsanto's agricultural chemicals organization, for instance, researchers didn't know much about the offerings and strategies of competitors, largely because two of Monsanto's products, Roundup and Lasso, were so successful the company initially had little competition. But when patent protection on Roundup and Lasso neared expiration, managers decided each researcher had to learn more about competitors. The company implemented a Lotus Notes system with an information-gathering tool called Hoover. Whenever a competitor was in the news, researchers would find out about it through this system. Researchers thought the system was especially valuable when the agricultural chemicals division began to introduce genetically altered seed hybrids, a market with a completely new set of competitors for Monsanto.

Johnson & Johnson's Pharmaceutical Research Institute also chose to address competitive information. Top management had allowed drug development teams to remain oblivious to the activities of competitors—until one of those teams wanted to introduce a drug for a clinical problem that had already been released by a competitor, potentially leading to millions of dollars wasted in development costs. As a result, information specialists joined each drug development team in order to increase the attention paid to competitive efforts. It can take as long as ten years to develop a new drug, so it's hard to know yet if such changes have paid off. Still, J&J scientists on these teams undoubtedly have a greater awareness of the market for their drugs.

NationsBank, the third largest US bank in assets, now focuses on nontraditional competitors. Senior managers have started viewing non-bank financial institutions as rivals just as threatening, and sometimes more so, than other banks. Rather than creating an explicit strategy that emphasized such competitors, however, NationsBank management went about it more informally. Most executives could readily cite the major non-bank players: Fidelity for investments, GE Capital for equipment financing, Countrywide Funding for mortgages. And Hugh McColl, NationsBank's CEO, frequently addressed the topic and the specific competitors in management meetings.

Of course, if top managers are planning to undertake critical business initiatives, odds are good that better information is necessary in that business domain to support the initiative. NationsBank's interest in non-banking competitor information, for example, coincided with a business strategy emphasizing entry into new geographical and financial services markets. In this case, McColl explicitly instructed market researchers and strategic planners to focus on nontraditional competitor information.

Sometimes even relatively prosaic information can become the focus of an information strategy. Over the past decade, Digital Equipment managers have had difficulty in accurately predicting quarterly earnings. The firm's complex organizational structure, multiple order-processing systems, and varying business processes twice led to earnings predictions by analysts that were much higher than the real outcome. Each time this caused a major drop in Digital's stock price. Gathering more accurate order and financial information has thus become Digital's strongest focus, though given the repeated problems, perhaps not strong enough.

Obviously, a firm may emphasize different information content at different points in its business cycle—or as it evolves (and, one hopes, grows) over the years. Depending on the business, a company's information strategy can also address any of these content areas:

- obtaining more consistent product information within a company;
- using information from suppliers and channel partners;
- improving logistical information for better coordination and customer service;
- getting better information on current and potential employees to facilitate growth, retention, or new hires.

An information strategy that focuses on particular types of content allows an organization to coordinate how its gathers, analyzes, and acts on the most important information. Managers can always spend money to buy information and the computers to manipulate it; but the truly scarce resource in any organization is the time people have to make use of it.

Focus 2: Common Information

Rather than emphasizing specific types of information, some firms focus on sharing common information. It's not the easiest course for an information strategy, but there can be sound business reasons for it. Companies typically seek to share common information in order to ease communications across divisions, functions and/or business processes. More often than not, this focus on commonality remains implicit; but because creating and maintaining common information is so difficult, ecological managers should address it explicitly as an element of strategy.

Firms that have done so, with some success, include General Motors, Millipore, Dow Chemical, and Hewlett-Packard's Worldwide Customer Service Division. Before 1990 General Motors, for example, was notorious for not sharing components in building its vehicles; at one time, it had sixty-five different turn-signal levers in its cars! Yet the company got the number of turn signals down to twenty-six by the end of 1993 through sharing common information—part numbers, product descriptions, even market segments—across business functions. Maintaining this common information required cooperation across Design, Engineering, Manufacturing, and Marketing. GM's information managers commissioned a set of high-level models that described business processes and the information required by them.

By focusing strategically on information sharing, these managers combined a traditional (if less detailed) approach to information architecture with behaviorally oriented initiatives—such as policing common definitions of key terms. Vince Barabba, GM's head of information management, also directs market research. Whenever he sees or hears about a presentation with non-standard market-segment categories (such as an atypical definition of the luxury market), he immediately tries to get the potential offender to use GM's standard categories. Barabba told me that drift in the firm's definitions for various market segments was at least partly responsible for the many similar car models produced by GM divisions in the 1980s.

Millipore managers also want to create common processes and systems, and their information strategy explicitly focuses on creating common information.[4] However, as a medium-sized company focused on the high-performance filtration business, Millipore's overall objective differs from that of larger companies like GM or Dow Chemical, which generally adopt common information strategies to facilitate global coordination across multiple types of businesses. Millipore's managers believe that its organizational flexibility will be greatly enhanced if the entire company shares common processes and systems. Indeed, they were able to split the organization into nine product-oriented business units with much greater ease because of a shared information environment.

But even if decentralizing in this manner happened more smoothly than if the business units had each struggled with their own information, that doesn't mean sharing common information went off without a hitch. Millipore's top managers formed teams in each major business area to identify key information terms and meanings. Team members, including sales, finance, manufacturing, and logistics workers when order information was discussed, argued vociferously for weeks about what certain business entities should be called and how they should be defined. Should a "sale" be recorded when the order was taken, for example, or when the product was shipped? As one manager noted, "They cared as much about changing the names of these entities as if we were changing their own names." Millipore ended up using the common information strategy to develop an entirely new (and common) information systems architecture. Managers do feel that greater flexibility has been achieved, although they wrestle with converting this benefit into hard savings or earnings.

In fact, common information is frequently a high-cost strategy, both to implement initially and even more to maintain. At Dow Chemical in the late 1980s, top managers focused on common information through implementation of SAP (Systems, Applications, and Products), a broad, cross-functional information system package developed by the German company of the same name. These executives wanted Dow units around the world to use SAP; in fact, they believed this system would force managers to adopt common processes and information—something that had become increasingly necessary for the company given global customers and manufacturing strategies. Technologists first attempted to implement SAP for a specific worldwide business (styrofoam). Even within the styrofoam business, however, each function and geographical location had to be persuaded of the virtues of implementing a common system and processes. Senior managers put their full weight behind achieving this, but the effort was treated as a technology initiative rather than an information strategy.

Here again, an approach that overemphasized technology—even with management's explicitly stated strategic goal of sharing common information—led to an expensive and time-consuming change process. When Dow tried to expand SAP into other product areas, those managers cried out that not only were their businesses unique, but they also had unique information needs. SAP is a very complex package that offers multiple options; yet some business units still wanted more customization of the system. This project has gone on for over six years; some Dow managers, as well as a few of their competitors, estimate that the system has cost more than $500 million to date. While a number of other companies are now implementing SAP, Dow's less than resounding success so far indicates that any company's information strategy has to rely on more than a computer-based information system.

Focus 3: Information Processes

Information strategy can also focus on particular phases in an information-management process. In Chapter 8, I'll detail how ecological managers can approach and redefine information processes. Still, a good information strategy will probably address process improvement at some level, because getting a handle on an information process can be just as important—if not more so—than specific information content. Once again, the need for enhanced information sharing in an organization often raises its thorny head. Even when a firm has successfully identified the content to emphasize—or even the general need for sharing common information—particular processes for carrying out these strategic goals, from collection to use to disposal of relevant information, may be quite flawed.

Many pharmaceutical firms, for example, now attempt to speed new product development by sharing information more consistently throughout the development cycle. At one firm, information about a drug's poor absorption with food in a patient's stomach was not communicated to the researchers who designed the clinical trial. As a result, they began an expensive and time-consuming clinical trial that yielded less than optimal results. By the time these researchers uncovered the miscommunication, the trial had to be redesigned and restarted; needless to say, precious months were lost during which the drug might have been earning revenues.

Several professional services firms, including Andersen Consulting, Booz Allen & Hamilton, Coopers & Lybrand, Ernst & Young, and McKinsey, have also begun major efforts to capture and share knowledge around the organization. Individual professionals learn new things everyday about their clients, so the firm that is able to capture and leverage such unstructured knowledge will be able to compete more effectively in this idea-driven business. To realize this strategic goal, such firms have improved information processes by developing idea-sharing networks, creating CD-ROMs of firm expertise, and appointing professionals to structure and maintain the knowledge. Information and knowledge can flow more readily from one client engagement or office to another, and the same knowledge can be resold multiple times.

Processes that emphasize sharing information may extend outside an individual organization. Many companies now electronically share logistical, pricing, and marketing information with channel partners as a key element of their information strategies. Some managers are also beginning to discuss sharing more value-added information and knowledge with outsiders. DuPont's legal strategy, for instance, emphasizes reducing the number of law firms with which it works; in addition, the company links the firms it does use electronically, requiring them to share knowledge of DuPont's legal situation, along with approaches and precedents used in litigation.[5] Clearly, this is an ambitious information strategy, one that requires law firms, individual lawyers, and DuPont managers to change their behavior substantially. Yet it has already enabled DuPont to cut its legal costs substantially in 1995.

At General Motors, Vince Barabba and other senior executives have concerned themselves with the process designed to improve use of market information. Specifically, they found that market information about the kinds of cars that appeal to customers had not been used effectively within the company, especially during new car development and product launches. Barabba points out that GM's research about the likely success or failure of its new cars in the marketplace was usually correct, yet this information was often ignored by developers and marketers, sometimes merely because it arrived in their mailboxes or on their computer screens too late.

As a result, General Motors didn't begin developing new vehicles such as the minivan until after Chrysler and other competitors launched their best-selling models—even though GM's preliminary research indicated that minivans would succeed in the marketplace. (Note that GM is probably not the only automobile manufacturer with this problem. Ford may have had early market research suggesting that a second driver-side door on its Windstar minivan would appeal to customers, but managers didn't act on it right away. However, with the success of Chrysler's new minivan, which has such a second door, Ford is belatedly back at the drawing board.)

In order to address these problems at General Motors, Barabba and other managers are now implementing a new product-development process in which market information analysis is explicitly considered. For each major step in the process, the type and sources of necessary information are specified. A car designer, for example, should consult focus-group results early in the design process. GM has also created an "Inquiry Center"—a centralized source of market information and support in applying it.[6] In general, many researchers and managers of marketing information are focusing on the processes that enhance its use.[7]

Focus 4: New Information Markets

Some companies emphasize new information markets—not just information use internally—to build another source of revenue. I devote much of Chapter 10 to the potential value of new information markets; but again, in order to leverage such markets effectively, managers need to address them explicitly in their general information strategy. Indeed, because of the businesses they're in, many firms now generate large amounts of valuable information about aspects of their own or their customers' businesses. Assuming such information is available, top managers must decide whether selling that information in the marketplace fits their overall strategy.

There are legendary examples of success, of course. American and United Airlines have made billions of dollars from selling information about their and other airlines' flight schedules to travel agents. Grocery stores sell information about what moves in their stores to market research companies, who in turn sell it to consumer products firms.

Ross Operating Valve Company, headquartered in Michigan with plants in the US, Europe, and Japan, is considering new markets as a key element of its information strategy. Ross has traditionally prospered by making pneumatic valves. However, in an effort to become a more agile competitor, the company developed some proprietary CAD (computer aided design) software and a library of valve designs. It's been giving customers access to this information, free of charge, as part of its general marketing approach. But now Ross's top managers want to sell the information as a product in its own right. Henry Duignan, the firm's Chief Operating Officer, anticipates that information and knowledge will eventually yield higher profits for Ross than valves.[8]

Still, despite such seductive possibilities, several factors should influence whether a firm goes into the information business. Selling information is bound to affect a company's market positioning, competitive relationships, and ability to use its own information internally. As with Ross, customers of a company's core products and services will undoubtedly complain about having to pay for what they once received free. And information furnished to paying customers must be of higher quality, more up-to-date, and easier to understand and access than that distributed internally. Managers formulating an information strategy need to determine whether revenue or profit potential outweigh these valid concerns.

Firms may also need to make less dramatic decisions about information markets. For one thing, there's the classic "build vs. buy" issue. One firm may choose to buy key information from outside the organization, while another may conclude that its interests are best served by compiling the information itself. Whether it's information about product sales, customer satisfaction, credit, or competitors, companies now have plenty of choices for where and how to get it—and such choices are the stuff of strategy.

Putting Strategy to Work: Information Principles

Deciding on your information strategy's focus is at best half of what matters on this journey. Creating a real dialogue about strategy among the decision-makers involved—not to mention realizing information management goals in practical terms—forms the all-important second half of a sometimes uncomfortable ride. Because putting strategy to work can vary so much from company to company, I'll stress not a "method" for information strategy, but some tools and techniques that managers can use along the way.

If strategy creates dialogue, those involved first have to decide who should participate in this dialogue. Typically, senior managers believe they should be the key (or only) players in developing strategy—and if a company is in the midst of deciding whether to create an information-selling business, for example, senior managers will have to make such a call. Even in these cases, however, more players should participate in the discussion. Most likely, middle managers or professionals will be the ones who come up with the idea to sell information in the first place; and they'll be the ones who do the market and competitive analysis that makes the decision possible, not to mention the planning and implementation that make it real.

Broad participation is one side of the information-strategy coin; the other is that senior managers *must* join the debate at some point, not delegate it to their functionaries or technologists. This is especially true if a company is about to devote significant organizational resources to information content or processes. Ironically, as Standard Life Assurance's experience suggests, senior managers are often reluctant to participate in the first crucial stages of developing an information strategy, often because few of them understand information concepts or the related technology well enough to discuss it.

Yet most managers do have an intuitive understanding of information and its importance to the organization. Senior executives don't normally rise to their positions in organizations without making effective use of information in some form. That's why managers must break down barriers to understanding and participation as soon as discussion of a firm's information strategy begins. At the very least, they need to acknowledge that communication gaps are a natural part of such a discussion, and should not be considered hopeless obstacles.

One simple, straightforward approach to building strategy of any kind involves the use of principles, or statements of direction and position on key issues. Other researchers have discussed principles in terms of leadership of organizations more broadly, and also in terms of creating information technology strategies in which senior managers can participate.[9] Even some of the principles for technology-oriented strategies that I've observed in action contain information management as a component. Consider the following information principles from different industries:

- *A US bank:* We define corporate management information as: that information needed to support legal and regulatory requirements; and/or that information required by corporate staff functions to perform the duties assigned by executive management; and/or cross-group information under the custodian of a business unit but also beneficial to multiple business areas for effective business analysis and development.
- *A US railroad firm:* Every manager is accountable for the timeliness, accuracy, integrity, security, and recoverability of all data created, maintained, or used by his organization.
- *A US telecommunications firm:* Data redundancy is allowed to provide ease of access but must not violate any data integrity issues.
- *A US insurance firm:* Database designs should be driven by local unique needs rather than common or shared needs.
- *A US pharmaceutical firm:* Every employee has a responsibility to identify, communicate, and utilize opportunities for sharing information.
- *A European chemical firm:* Information is presumed to be available to all authorized employees unless specifically restricted by the data owner.
- *A US county government office:* Data will be managed in such a way that direct access to data by citizens will be provided to enhance the convenience of County services and information to County citizens.

These principles cover a variety of issues despite the fact that they deal primarily with computer-based data. Some are more effective than others; advocating the statement of principles should be easy to understand, signify a clear position, and avoids a generic value like "motherhood"—such as "Information is a critical business resource." In the principles above, for example, the bank's are the only ones to clearly define what constitutes corporate information.

Organizations may also find it useful to articulate not only the principle but its implications, as this computer company did:

Principle: Data are owned by the company, not any specific individual or department, and are assigned to designated Data Trustees for developing standard definitions. Owners of business processes that create or update data are responsible for implementing the data standards.

Implications:
- An enterprise-wide classification of data by subject area will be developed;
- A Data Trustee will be designated at the corporate level for each subject area;
- The Data Trustee will be responsible for determining the standard definitions for "Enterprise Data" for each subject area;
- Business experts will establish the standard names, definitions, formats, structures, domains, and business rules for Enterprise Data under the supervision of the Data Trustee;
- Local Data Trustees for each applicable subject area will be established within each business unit to assist in implementing the standard definitions for Enterprise Data and for establishing the standard definitions for business unit-specific data;
- Business-process owners will be responsible for the accuracy of the data values when they create or update data.

At this company, both IT and general managers feel the principles have helped them carry on a dialogue about information management. They've made some progress in sharing common information and in improving the quality of information by specifying ownership responsibilities and privileges. Perhaps most important, the company's general managers are now much more aware of the importance of information strategy and direction after participating in creation of the principles. They even emphasize the various purposes a strategy can serve, distributing their principles widely to customers in order to demonstrate the company's prowess in managing information and technology.

On the other hand, it's far easier to draft principles than to implement them in any real way. As the overly technical jargon here indicates, the computer company's IT organization initially came up with these principles and implications. In addition to the Data Trustee role mentioned, these IT managers emphasized the need for Enterprise Information, as well as the ways in which such corporate-wide information could be managed and shared. Yet their method for developing the information strategy ultimately undercut its effectiveness.

In this case, corporate senior managers did review the first draft of principles, but geographical division heads weren't consulted. Subsequently, after the principles had been widely circulated, several divisions decided that they were "enterprises" and defined their own enterprise information—including definitions of customers and products—accordingly. When a new CEO asked for a list of the firm's 100 largest customers so that he could send a "get acquainted" letter to them, he was told that creating such a list would require several weeks of effort. And since each country maintained the information in a different format, with many overlaps across country boundaries, the list would have to be created manually!

Also note that the data trustee role was assigned to middle managers who headed functions in related areas. The head of market research became the data trustee for customer information, and so on. However, the Trustees weren't given any additional resources with which to maintain the standardization and quality of enterprise information, and their previous responsibilities weren't reduced. Not surprisingly, they basically found it impossible to perform the trustee role under these conditions. Perhaps in part because of its information woes, this company was acquired shortly thereafter.

Of course, the type of principles selected, their implications, and the specific wording depends on a company's business situation and overall information environment. In the case of mergers and acquisitions, creating a consistent set of principles is more important than ever; companies in this position may find themselves forced into the exercise, whether they like it or not. Consider the following positive example, in which some managers may have been initially reluctant to share information or focus on its use.

At Chemical Bank, top managers realized they needed information-management principles shortly after the bank merged with Manufacturers Hanover (but before it merged again with Chase Manhattan). The two banks had different information cultures—Chemical, for example, shared its information widely, while that of Manufacturers Hanover was largely kept within departmental boundaries—which created a barrier to integrated bank management. But because top managers of the new Chemical Bank decided early on to create a set of information principles, each functional or product group within the bank was allowed to raise concerns about information issues and suggest principles for the final master set. The IT group, for example, drafted a principle that addressed access to information:

Principle: Working within corporate guidelines, each group will have unlimited access to management information required to manage its own business. Each group will have liberal access to other groups' management information where a legitimate business need exists. Overall rules for allowing access to management information will be set by major types of information (e.g., customer information, exposure information, profitability information).

Implications
- A process for requesting and granting access to Corporate Management Information will need to be established.
- Cross-group management information is prioritized, scheduled, and delivered according to negotiations between interested groups.

Because Chemical's information strategists allowed for broad (and sometimes heated) debate on the issues, the principles largely "stuck" after implementation—unlike at the computer company discussed above. The process was initiated again when Chemical merged with Chase Manhattan.

The virtue of principles is their simplicity and common sense; when they are drafted sensibly, no complex methodological detail should stand between managers and an understanding of key information issues. However, a small group of information managers can draft a set of principles in a few hours. Unless executives feel they truly understand the topics under discussion and their implications, they won't abide by such a group's conclusions. The more vehement the debate, the more likely managers are to stand by the consensus they eventually reach. In short, the process of developing principles is much more important than achieving a quick result.

Other Information Strategy Techniques

Even if consistency and common sense are the essential elements of information strategy, some traditional strategic techniques may help managers develop specific initiatives or processes. These include analysis of the business or an appropriate industry; a functional or "value-chain" approach to strategy; and benchmarking.

Business/Industry Analysis

A fundamental strategic analysis can identify which information to focus on. Managers might analyze any or all of the following factors:

- their company's basic position in the marketplace;
- traditional and alternative competitors;
- external forces driving market demand;
- the structure and function of the organization;
- how much the organization needs to change to succeed in its current business environment.

As with so many elements of information ecology, developing a strategy is part of a complex web of crisscrossing threads. Using a traditional business analysis, for example, an ecologically minded manager might see that her firm is highly integrated horizontally and that business functions like sales, manufacturing, and logistics are tightly connected. In information strategy terms, she might then advocate focusing on a high degree of common information, particularly about customers and products, which functions can share.

Some research does assess information requirements in situations where there is a high level of organizational change. For example, in firms undergoing "strategic turnarounds," new top managers in one study collected and issued information involved in overcoming organizational inertia and unlearning old behaviors; structuring and communicating new performance expectations; and gaining allegiance to the new agenda for the organization.[10] In each category, these managers included specific types of information—for example, a new mission statement for overcoming inertia. If your organization is undergoing such a turnaround, perhaps you should also be gathering this type of information.

Managers might also try applying traditional industry analysis techniques to assessing their internal information environments. A manufacturing company, for instance, established a new internal information function to provide better information for managerial decision-making. But the head of this unit soon realized there were already competing providers on the scene: the market research, competitive intelligence, and information systems departments within the company; and consulting firms, market research firms, and universities outside it.

So he met with his employees to do a "five forces" industry structure analysis of the buyers, suppliers, existing rivals, substitutes, and potential new entrants for the internal information provision business at this company.[11] According to this manager, the analysis helped the company focus on a competitive niche involving customer information that had been poorly served in the past.

Looking at the Value Chain

If a firm emphasizes certain functions within the value chain—that is, how the various functions of the business add value for customers to its products and services—as part of its business strategy, there are corresponding implications for information strategy. If a value-chain strategy emphasizes distribution and partnership relations with retailers, for instance, then its information strategy should focus on product and shipping information, and it must coordinate its information strategy with that of major retailers who sell its products.

Procter & Gamble and GE Lighting have coordinated their information strategies with Wal-Mart's in an effort to improve logistical processes—and because Wal-Mart, the powerhouse of this particular retail channel, imposed such coordination for its own competitive advantage. The links between these firms involve continuous replenishment of product (CRP) on Wal-Mart's shelves by the vendors. Wal-Mart furnishes the vendors with daily sales information at each store; the vendors supply Wal-Mart with electronic shipment and billing information.

Both parties in such a relationship can benefit: the vendor can lower inventory costs and plan on a predictable flow of product; the retailer needs fewer personnel and, in passing on some of the savings to customers, gets higher sales volumes. Note, however, that the information exchanged in such a partnership isn't only electronic data. The initial relationship between Wal-Mart and Procter & Gamble was forged in a fishing-boat conversation between P&G's Lou Prichett and Wal-Mart's Sam Walton. And in an effort to better transfer less structured information, a dozen Procter & Gamble employees relocated to Wal-Mart's headquarters in Bentonville, Arkansas. It must have been the potential for new information that motivated the move; there isn't much scenery in Bentonville.

Just as the study mentioned above described the information needs of companies during strategic turnarounds, other research indicates what information different functional managers really use. In interviews with executives at twelve North American manufacturing companies, the management accountants Sharon McKinnon and Bill Bruns have created the first enumeration of information requirements by function.[12] These researchers found out what information managers wanted in sales, manufacturing, and production environments. Anyone who's interested in providing useful information to a marketing, financial, or operations manager need only turn to McKinnon and Bruns's book, *The Information Mosaic,* to get a good introduction to information content strategy. (See Table 4-1.) In the past, those in charge of information management have believed that the proper strategy is to ask managers what information they need. With solid research like this behind us, however, we can get a running start on telling managers what their information requirements should be.

Table 4-1. Summary of Managerial Information Requirements

Production	Purchasing/Logistics
Labor counts	Inventory availability
Output units	Price of inputs and outputs
Order quantity	Carrier rates and locations
Product specifications	
	Planning
Sales/Marketing	Financial performance
Orders	Program effectiveness
Customer information	
Market prices	

Source: from McKinnon and Bruns, *The Information Mosaic*

Benchmarking

Perhaps the most obvious traditional approach to identifying aspects of information strategy is benchmarking. We can turn to other firms that do a good job of information management to identify aspects of our own information strategy. Although information management often contains little of the quantifiable measures that benchmarking requires, there are some exceptions. In addition to providing information access, many firms are beginning to offer information that has been interpreted and analyzed in useful ways. Bloomberg, a provider of business and financial information, for example, started off by providing not just information about bond prices, but textual explanations of why they moved—which eventually led to the company's successful establishment of a financial news service.

Indeed, many of the firms I describe in this book would be obvious candidates for benchmarking partnerships. Executives who wish to understand the effect of mergers on information management, for example, should consider contacting Chase Bank. The most valuable partners would be those with a well-conceived information strategy and a similar business situation to one's own. As in many areas of life, there's no point in inventing an information management approach from scratch if it can be borrowed from somewhere else.

What Information Strategy Can Do for You

Consider the following combined approach to information strategy taken by the Exploration and Production (E&P) business unit within a major UK oil company. Unit managers set out to define how they wanted to manage information in the year 2001, and hence called their strategy exercise "Information Management 2001." Even though this is an oil company unit, just creating the document helped to confirm that, as the head of E&P said, "information is the most important resource we have." These managers defined the current information management situation as the "barricades scenario," because there were so many obstacles between people and the information they require. Then they came up with an improvement strategy that covered business processes, IT, people, and information itself.

The E&P managers had recently identified its key processes, and as a part of the strategy exercise they further specified the key information in each process. They identified which information needed to be managed in common across the unit, and which could vary freely. They also created some principles for information management, such as "Information should be stored flexibly so that it can be used in multiple ways," and "Information about the information (meta-information) is required to manage it." In addition, these managers developed a culture in which information providers viewed their users, for the first time, as customers. And in order to establish common information, managers made sure a broad cross-section of customers would be consulted. Other key roles and responsibilities for information—such as who (or what group) owned, supplied, or maintained given kinds of information—were specified at the E&P unit. Unusually, technology received relatively little attention; information managers largely specified common technology standards so that information could be easily exchanged across the unit.

Without using the term "information ecology" (not the most comfortable phrase for an oil company), this firm clearly adopted an ecological approach. Their strategy document concluded, "Our recommendations require a set of related activities to be undertaken together; no single one will achieve the goals." Although the creators of this information strategy did come up with an actual document, in their view the most important aspect of developing the strategy was to start a dialogue about information. To that end, they encouraged everyone in the company to "trash" the draft document in order to stimulate thinking. And their goals were modest: "To identify some first steps to demonstrate the viability of the approach." Two years later, the E&P unit is still debating certain aspects of the strategy, particularly the need for more common information with acquisition of the SAP program. Nevertheless, these managers feel discussion of information issues has become institutionalized within the unit.

In any event, information ecology calls for such a broad approach. From where I sit, since there are few information strategies in place, any efforts should lead to improvement. Even so, the rankest ecological beginner will soon recognize that single initiatives may not yield real change. The sample "Assessment Survey" that follows indicates how managers might begin taking a longer and broader look at how information is used.

Information strategists need to avoid excessive detail in one area; they should always consider process as important as content. But more important, the journey toward good information strategy is bound to cross a number of roads and bang into barriers, including the subject of my next chapter. In the frustrating realm of information politics, managers, professionals, and other employees often bang heads—or, at the very least, raise their voices.

Assessment Survey for Information Strategy

The greater the level of agreement with the statements below, the better an organization manages information strategy.[13]

✳ A comprehensive information strategy has been developed for this organization.

*   A wide variety of senior and middle managers as well as professionals—
    from both information and non-information functions—actively partici-
    pate in strategy-development sessions.

*   In designing our information strategy, those in charge clearly articulated
    the difference between technology and information.

*   One or more senior managers is responsibile for implementing the infor-
    mation strategy.

*   Our information strategy is easy to understand and takes a position on key
    information issues in the organization.

5 $\vdots$

Information Politics

Information is not innocent.

James March,

Decisions and Organizations

Information is affected daily, even hourly, in virtually all organizations by power, politics, and economics. This is no secret.[1] Yet few managers want to deal consciously and systematically with information politics, perhaps because to do so would somehow undercut an organization's existing hierarchy. Therefore, power plays or political wrangling over information—when they do muscle themselves into managerial awareness—have been treated as an aberration rather than as a natural and inevitable component of information management. And the all-important economic ramifications of information politics are often dismissed, since it's hard to quantify information value.

Indeed, information politics remains "undiscussable" in many organizations, all of which have implicit models of information governance. Yet the negative consequences of information politicking have led awry many projects intended to improve information use. Researchers have zeroed in on politics, for example, as a major factor in the failure of systems-development projects.[2] Other studies suggest that resolving conflicts over information and technology is strongly associated with the success of development projects.[3] Once again, Standard Life Assurance's failure to address information politics straight on means this company undercut its other laudable efforts to take a more ecological perspective. This is a typical problem when middle managers attempt to take the lead in substantially improving a firm's information ecology.

Curiously, many observers acknowledge the importance of information technology governance but still ignore information politics. Endless speculation is devoted to the role of the CIO, the significance of outsourcing IT management, and the relative merits of centralized vs. decentralized IT structures.

Yet I believe focusing on the governance of information is equally important, if not more so. Which matters more—who operates the data center, or who decides what information will be gathered and used within a firm? Are personal computer standards more important than information standards? Is the architecture of information less significant than the architecture of technology? The effective use of information, much more than any new technology, can change how an organization runs.

Clearly, attitudes toward information and technology predispose organizations, nations, and societies to particular political arrangements. Yet the reverse can also be true, especially in a business organization. In fact, information management can be used either to distribute power or to concentrate it.[4] Some firms effectively control information centrally; others employ similar techniques to promote information openness and broader decision-making. It's a matter of choice, one that's based on any number of idiosyncratic factors like a company's size, major business or businesses, and organizational structure. But whose choice and how those choices play out is the essence of information politics.

There are several viable models for governing information.[5] My main point is that managers—especially corporate executives—need to talk honestly and directly about the political nature of information, regardless of how they decide to govern it. Addressing information politics explicitly is what matters for information ecology. Any of the four models I'll describe below—federalism, feudalism, monarchy, even anarchy—may be desirable for some type of organization. They form a continuum of local vs. centralized control of the information environment (See Figure 5-1).

The trick, of course, is matching your organization to the political structure that best suits it. These models are primarily concerned with information politics, but I'll also briefly discuss a market-based model of information governance, since politics and economics are often inextricably related. I'll also discuss a variant of information politics based on a utopian faith in technology.

Information Federalism

My favorite form of governance—for information and in general—is federalism, though it's not appropriate for all organizations. Federalism involves rep-

Figure 5-1. The Continuum of Information Control

resentative democracy, a weak central government, and a high level of local autonomy. In information terms, this model emphasizes that only a few information elements need to be defined and managed centrally, while the rest can be left up to local units. Federalism requires rational negotiation between central and dispersed groups, and it is the model that most explicitly recognizes the importance of politics. Federalism treats politics, including the politics of information, as a necessary and legitimate activity by which people with different interests work out among themselves a collective definition of purpose and the means for achieving it.

Information federalists recognize the value of both *information universalism*—where a term means the same thing across an organization—and *information particularlism*—where a small business unit can define "customer" in the way that best suits it. This political model offers a range of options, with pure information democracy at one extreme and a stronger central government at the other. Like the US government, the players involved shift within this range, or at least argue about it. Therefore, the best federal organizations manage a healthy tension between central and dispersed information control, which continues to shift over time.

At Hewlett-Packard, for example, "the HP way" specifies that decentralized units should largely manage their own destinies. Yet at a minimum, the company has to centralize reporting of financial results. At times HP has let business units proliferate their own financial measures; then, when reconciling localized and centralized performance become too burdensome, ledger items are pruned back. Of course, the process sounds much easier than it really is; but the constant negotiation at HP creates a financial information environment that evolves with the business.

As with the other political models, federalism can have a relatively benign face, such as HP's, or a somewhat despotic one. Asea Brown Boveri's reliance on ABACUS, its internally-developed financial information system, for instance, represents the more control-oriented form of federalism. In tune with the model, ABB's over 4,000 profit centers are expected to report only financial results and their number of employees to headquarters. But woe to the profit center manager who does not deliver the expected numbers. One manager wrote the following to a profit-center manager in France:

> The current level of performance is unacceptable. I will not accept excuses. When I arrive next week, be prepared to discuss in detail your steps to improve profit to agreed levels and to reduce inventory by 16 percent within 3 months.[6]

Indeed, a former country manager within ABB described ABACUS to me as "a tool for beating up on managers."

Yet ABB's senior executives argue that they had to emphasize results during the first years after the 1990 merger of Asea and Brown Boveri, when there was a recession in many of the company's major markets. Now ABB is beginning to focus not just on sharing financial results across profit centers, but also on best practices, process performance, and customer information. Managers claim their approach to sharing this type of information has become more "democratic."

For example, major account managers are now required to describe their customers' core business processes, critical success factors, and other key business issues to improve information sharing. At the same time, each account manager is allowed to capture and record the information in formats that make sense to him or her. According to one corporate staff executive, "If Percy Barnevik [ABB's CEO] were to require everyone at ABB to record customer information in a particular way, there would be many chuckles but little compliance."

Federal models can also be adjusted for different types of information. Paul Strassmann, who has both written about information politics and managed them himself as head of information management at the US Department of Defense, rightly argues that "To deal with the inherent conflicts between autonomous business units and headquarters, which happen in most large organizations nowadays, the management of information should operate as a multi-layered federation." Strassmann breaks down an organization's information into seven categories or "layers": "personal," "local," "application," "business," "process," "enterprise," and "global."[7] He sensibly points out that individual layers of governance should be defined and managed separately.

You could also "segment" federal governance according to type of information. In most information federations, financial information is defined and managed centrally. Even the most diverse conglomerate must pull together some common financial information each reporting period. But sharing customer information across business units is much less common and certainly more problematic. Some units may not trust others with information about their customers. Even when various unit managers sufficiently trust each other, they're right to be concerned about who puts information into the form needed by another group within the organization.

Take Chemical (now Chase) Bank, where the creation of a set of information management principles after a merger raised the sticky issue of whether customer data should be shared throughout the bank. Should the private bank furnish information on wealthy individual customers for use by the capital markets division in promoting a bond offering? If so, which of the two groups would be responsible for identifying likely prospects, notifying relationship managers, and outputting the customer information in a form that capital markets could use? Eventually, Chemical Bank's senior executives agreed to define "corporate management information" shared throughout the company as:

- that information needed to support legal and regulatory requirement;
- and/or that information required by corporate staff functions to perform the duties assigned by Executive Management;
- and/or Cross-Group information under the management of a business unit but also beneficial to multiple business areas for effective business analysis and development.[8]

Sharing "Cross-Group information" may strain the bounds of federalism; but these managers added another principle that stated all such information be "prioritized, scheduled, and delivered according to negotiations between interest groups." In fact, for large, diverse businesses like Chemical Bank, federalism is ideal. There can be no synergy across business units without shared information, and information might be said to be the "glue" of corporate federalism. More to the point, the level of information sharing fully determines operational integration.

This kind of political massaging may seem both messy and time-consuming. Yet any large company contains competing information interests, and the sooner managers recognize this as a political fact of life, the better. When considering whether information federalism is the model for your organization, keep the following points in mind:

- Federalism can't be established through any means other than extensive negotiation, even heated arguments. And both business unit and corporate managers need to understand how valuable information is to participate actively in the debate—and to make federalism work.
- Some locally defined information is a healthy sign; it means information-based innovation is taking place. Just as pundits often call the states of the US "laboratories of democracy," individual business units can be laboratories of how to use information effectively.
- Federalist administrations govern through the consent of the governed.

If key information users don't feel their interests have been adequately represented in deliberations over information, they'll develop their own sources of information and subvert the federal structure.
- Successful information federalism requires trustworthy information managers, "honest brokers" between corporate and local interests. They should facilitate negotiation among the true stakeholders for information rather than building their own information empires.

Of course, federalism won't work for some companies. The primary criteria for corporate federalism in general are also relevant for information federalism: size and diversity.[9] In small, single-industry businesses (Ben & Jerry's, the ice cream company, is one tasty example), there's little need for small business units to define their own information. While such firms could have "functional federalism," in which business functions define much of their own information, that would make an integrated business system impossible. Then there are companies with many business units and little synergy, where another political model may make pragmatic sense.

Information Feudalism

Let's turn from my favorite political model to one I believe usually causes far too many problems. Information feudalism—when business unit managers control their information environments like lords in so many separate castles—is one of the most common approaches to information management, and one of the most unexamined by those in charge. I and two co-researchers previously found that half the firms we studied had strong elements of information feudalism. More important, senior executives at these firms had never explicitly planned for this model and had little understanding of its consequences.[10]

So, yes, information feudalism isn't generally as healthy for a large company as federalism; but sometimes it's appropriate. In fact, under the right circumstances, you could call it a very extreme version of federalism. If business units have different products, different customers, different performance measures, and different forms of almost all relevant information, why should corporate managers force units to share (other than for regulatory purposes)? Feudalism in such organizations allows manager "lords" to adapt their information closely to business needs.

For example, NBC managers have argued that their nonfinancial performance measures are wholly different from those of GE Aircraft Engines, GE Plastics, and most other General Electric business units. And they are right.

NBC managers have pointed out, for instance, that the corporate desire to improve "inventory turns" doesn't apply to TV shows; as a result, their parent company now allows them to develop business-unit–appropriate information. Partly because of its hard-fought independence in information and other areas, NBC is presently the most successful US television network.

Unfortunately, NBC's success is not the norm. Information feudalism is often poorly adapted to an organization's needs and can do a lot of damage. It results from a narrow-minded focus on a business unit's information objectives, without consideration of larger business issues. As a result, firms that should be operating across integrated business processes are unable to do so. Those that should be cross-selling to customers can't. And companies that should be sharing components in different products don't.

Hughes Space and Communications (HSC), a very successful builder of satellites, exemplifies the pitfalls of information feudalism—and how managers might go about addressing them.[11] While this firm never failed to deliver satellites on time in the past, by 1993 increasing demand for its products created a greater need for coordinated, rapid production. Therefore, effective scheduling information became critical for HSC. Consistent, accurate schedules allowed movement of satellites from one work cell to another, as well as efficient use of scarce research resources (such as the vibration chamber). But while HSC had relied on a computerized scheduling system for years, individual work cells either didn't use it or furnished inaccurate schedules. One program manager, whose job it was to move satellites through work cells on time, put it this way:

> "You are after reliable component delivery dates. People lie and hide their margin; you may have to calibrate each person and adjust what he/she is telling you. The real issue is the truth in scheduling. We reward the biggest liars and punish the aggressive schedulers."[12]

Fortunately for Hughes, information providers there, while working on a project to create a new, client-server scheduling system, finally realized that information politics were "an underlying cause of the weekly scheduling problems." They found that each work cell would create its own local schedule, update schedules at its own preferred intervals, and have local definitions of crucial terms like "completion." Some units called a component that had been integrated onto a satellite "completed"; others wouldn't define it that way until the component had been thoroughly tested in an integrated system or subsystem. In the satellite integration and test area alone, providers uncovered eleven different yet redundant schedules; needless to say, the connections between them were hard to establish.

In a session with general managers, HSC information providers concluded that the firm's information politics were clearly feudal. While some managers felt that the analysis of information politics was very revealing, "It was clear that senior management was uncomfortable having these issues raised openly." But the scheduling project's team leader kept these political issues in mind, and began brokering individual information agreements among work cell leaders. In other words, he is now trying to create a more federalist model from the middle up. While it remains to be seen if this one manager's efforts are enough, he is making progress on improving the management of scheduling information, and thus far Hughes has continued to meet deadlines with the enhanced rate of production.

Information Monarchy

When one individual or function controls most of a company's information, the political result is a monarchy. The monarch—who should be a very senior manager but may not be—specifies what information is important, establishes meanings for key information elements, even attempts to control how information will be interpreted. This political model can benefit a relatively small, single-business firm. Most monarchs at least understand information's value to business. And the kings and queens who rule a particular business unit or type of information may operate within a broader organizational context of federalism or feudalism.

But the approach is not without its own problems, especially when the monarch is a low-level functionary rather than a senior executive. If the "queen" in charge of information is just an IT functionary—even CIO herself—that means everyone else above her in the organizational hierarchy doesn't care enough about information to give her any power. To be blunt, the monarch for enterprise information should be the CEO; the head of a function can assume the crown for functional information, and so on. Rarely do Chief Information Officers even attempt to play a monarch, for good reason. Whether or not they should be in charge of information, they seldom have the political clout or resources to carry off broad initiatives.

On the other hand, sometimes an information monarchy arises simply because top managers are frustrated by less efficient political models. At an oil exploration firm, for example, there was widespread confusion about the use of the term "oil location."[13] Information architects had defined the term on multiple occasions, but their recommended usage never stuck. Some users thought oil location meant the oil's original geographic coordinates in the ground; others defined it as the well from which it sprang; still others used the term to refer to current location in a tank farm of pipeline.

Each definition found its way into computer databases. As a result, reporting wasn't standard, and it was difficult to share even the most basic information on the production of different sites. The firm could not get consistent estimates of the oil produced by a specific location. Among other problems, this meant managers couldn't accurately monitor the performance of specific wells, coordinate the allocation of crude to the closest refinery, or figure the taxes owed to states and counties where the oil was pumped.

The CEO of the firm finally seized the information crown. He decreed in one meeting that henceforth oil location would mean only one thing—the source location determined by company geologists—and that anyone who publicly used another meaning would be fired. Whatever you say about this extreme approach, or however you feel about heavy-handed CEOs, it worked.

Information Anarchy

The fourth model for information governance isn't really a "model." Information anarchy, in which every individual fends for himself or herself, is only rarely something an organization would consciously choose. Anarchy usually emerges when more centralized approaches to information management break down, or when no top executive realizes the importance of common information to the effective functioning of the firm.

In addition, information anarchy has been made possible—and much more dangerous—by the introduction and spread of the personal computer. Suddenly individuals and small departments find that they can manage their own databases, tailoring information to their own needs at any time they desire and at minimal cost. Almost all anarchistic firms have a high proportion of autonomous knowledge workers: scientists, consultants, computer programmers, systems developers, and so on. It's not that their managers *want* information anarchy; but they feel powerless to prevent each professional worker from creating her own information environment.

The good thing about anarchy is that it indicates a thirst for effective information, defined on a user's own terms. These information users aren't generally scared off by new IT systems, and they value information because it directly affects the work they do. With individual knowledge workers, there's every reason to tolerate information particularism, at least on a small scale; needlessly trying to define or structure the creative use of information generated by such professionals makes little sense. However, when it comes to business organizations, this laudable desire for information should quickly be harnessed into a more effective political model, not some poor—and counterproductive—reflection of the cyber-anarchy of the Internet.

Indeed, the shortcomings of information anarchy are obvious. When everyone has his or her own database, the numbers for revenues, costs, and customer order levels in one database will quickly diverge from those in another area. I know of several firms in which this kind of information anarchy—almost always unintentional but surprisingly common—was the source of late or inaccurate quarterly earnings reports.

A firm can't survive for long with such discrepancies. Intel, for example, had a relatively anarchistic information environment, largely because technology so pervaded the company, and managers and professionals were rewarded for autonomous, creative actions. Around 1994, however, top management realized such anarchy was too expensive, since the company couldn't sufficiently coordinate necessary information. Intel is currently moving toward a federalist information environment, in which the software package SAP will supply common information in defined areas.

There's only one firm where I've encountered managers who chose anarchy with their eyes wide open. This software firm had previously tried to develop an overall structure for information management by asking key managers what information they needed to run the business. When no consensus on information needs could be achieved, the managers determined that a bottom-up structured exchange of documents across its network—using a new software technology developed for this purpose—would yield all of the required information.

Each manager and worker was then free to create, share, and use the information that was most useful to him or her. The only information that carried more weight than any other was the financial information used for official reporting purposes—and the pronouncements the CEO made at breakfast meetings. Information anarchy seemed to work for this company, though it didn't grow as fast as some of its competitors and was eventually acquired. Now it is a barony within a large feudal organization.

Market-Based Models

The distribution of power is not the only criterion for information governance, and sometimes none of the four political models discussed above quite fit a company's situation. In some organizations, the demand for information controls how it is governed—or at least it should control it. Market-driven organizations, for example, might put a variety of different types of information into a database, but only maintain that which is heavily accessed by users. A market orientation often implies decentralized management of information resources: owners can name, format, update, and dispose of information as they desire. Information providers and facilitators are self-supporting, but they can charge for any information or services that their customers are willing to pay for, at market prices.

McKinsey and Company, for example, lets the market rule its information management. Its information and knowledge managers don't attempt to specify what content will be most useful in consulting engagements. Rather, they let the market work; virtually anyone at McKinsey can offer up new frameworks, methods, or techniques, and their value (and worthiness for investment in further development) is determined by how much they're used by others at the firm. Of course, the invisible hand of the market is sometimes supplemented; consultants who have done a good job in the past are more likely to receive seed resources to develop new content.

One precondition of market-based information politics is the ability to determine demand. At McKinsey, this is assessed by placing practice documents into a firmwide repository, and then monitoring the withdrawals or usage of particular contributions. Another means of assessing demand might be to simply ask information consumers within a firm what information they find valuable, an obvious tactic that's only rarely used.

The strength of market management, however, can also be a weakness: a lack of clarity about information ownership. Most companies have difficulty assigning full ownership to information that might be considered a corporate resource. Information is also difficult to price because of its intangibility, its reproducibility, and the differing extent to which it informs potential buyers. Still, even if few organizations have adopted a pure market governance model, most will employ aspects of it. They may, for example, assess the popularity of different information entities, then focus their resources on the most popular information.

Technocratic Utopias

Finally, there's one other model to which many organizations subscribe. I've already alluded to techno-utopia in other contexts, and, sure enough, these utopians also assume that technology will solve all problems of information governance. If an organization needs to improve access to information, they're convinced that once Lotus Notes is installed, the problem will be solved. For sharing common information, utopians place all faith in the SAP applications mega-package. Indeed, after I discussed this issue at a conference, one earnest attendee said to me, "You're right about this technocratic utopia business. But object orientation really is going to address most of the issues of information management."

While the other models—even feudalism—all have something to recommend them, there's little positive I can say about technocratic utopianism. Its biggest crime is distracting managers from addressing the real issues of information governance. Whether we like it or not, information politics involves competing interests, dissension, petty squabbles over scarce resources—even violent arguments that can rock a whole company and "make heads roll." I wish that a reverence for technology *could* resolve the tensions in any social organization; then again, tension isn't the worst thing in a business world that requires ever more creativity at lightning speed.

If you hear a comment resembling, "As soon as we get the (fill in an information technology), we will be able to (fill in an information behavior)," you should recognize the unrealistic claims of utopianism. Begin to counter it with down-to-earth questions of your own: Who controls the IT purse strings? Could those resources be used for a more effective information initiative? How do information managers build a power base and create momentum for change? How do we get R&D and Marketing to stop fighting?

Political and Economic Tactics

The above political and economic models are the strategic—and, I hope, explicit—choices firms make about information governance. But there are also tactical approaches that managers and workers employ every day. These may weaken or strengthen the firm's particular political model(s). Individual information politicians may thrive, even when an overall organization doesn't manage information politics well. Sometimes political tactics are open and visible; more frequently they operate behind the scenes, taking place in closed-door discussions between two people or individual musings. Managers should try to become familiar with the day-to-day alternative approaches to information politicking, and work either to supplment or subvert the firm's dominant political model.

Political tactics are well-known to any astute observer of office politics. They include such behaviors as information exchange, leaking, brokering, and selective dissemination or use of information. *Information exchange*—or "dealing"—is simply when two parties agree to share information with each other: "I'll give you product complaint information, if you give me earlier notice of recalls." Information exchange can also occur more formally between organizations—when companies share benchmark information within an industry, say, or when competing firms decide to cooperate on a particular project or with a large customer.

But information exchange becomes a pragmatic political maneuver when it's used in secretive information environments. For example, lower-level managers in a highly feudal system can cut private deals with their colleagues in other departments without any formal change in the information hierarchy. These may sound like cloak-and-dagger moves, but they come into play all too often when top managers fail to address the real political issues behind information use. All good information politicians seem to know the following rules of thumb for such exchanges:

- Don't tell the corporate lawyers what you are doing.
- Don't actually give up your information until you get the other party's.
- Ask to see a sample before doing the deal.
- Make sure the other party's information would be as incriminating as yours—or ideally more so!—if revealed.

When exchanges are mediated by a third party, this is known as *information brokering*. At its best, successful brokering can facilitate information management in an organization; and undoubtedly, some managers will have to play this role in order to carry out a company's information strategy. The aspiring broker should identify a particular information domain (such as customer information), identify a party that needs information, and find another party that has it. The task then is to find common ground between the potential information exchangers. Of course, brokering only succeeds if the broker is honest and is not solely arranging the deal for his own benefit. When the broker works between two different organizations, that person is likely to be what's known as a boundary-spanner.[14] Boundary-spanning can be very useful for organizations, which benefit from the exchange of information across functional or business-unit boundaries. It is, however, a questionable career strategy for individuals.

Leaking information is another way to open up an overly restrictive information environment. Leaks, of course, can be used for individual or corporate benefit, but regardless, they're almost always accomplished surreptitiously. Leaks often make the information seem more important than it really is; as a result, much unimportant information is leaked so that its apparent value will be magnified. Any aspiring information politician who wishes to master the art of the leak should spend a few years working in Washington, London, or some other capital.

Selective dissemination of information is another long-term tactic of the politically astute. It involves releasing some information—but not all—in order to accomplish some objective. Middle managers are notorious for filtering out negative information from their superiors, but this is a very primitive (and often harmful) form of selective dissemination.

New CEOs and political leaders often practice a form of selective dissemination by portraying their organizations in overly negative terms when they assume office, then later (though as quickly as possible) in overly positive terms.[15] Selective use of information is a variant of this tactic, as studies on information signals have shown.[16] Asking for a great deal of information before making a decision may lead others to assume the choice is based on rational analysis, even if the decision-maker doesn't use all the information. Sometimes an information politician may want others to believe that information provides the rationale for a course of action, when in fact it's otherwise motivated.

A variety of economic tactics can also reinforce desired information behaviors and attitudes. For example, patterns of information pricing and subsidy can greatly influence how often and how well people communicate. If electronic mail is free and voice mail is charged to my budget, I'll bend my messaging needs to suit the electronic medium as often as possible.

Most organizations don't now charge for internal communications, but one way to reduce information overload fast would be to charge people by the amount of information they send and number of people to whom they send it. Managers could not only ask employees to stop sending most broadcast and multiple-copy electronic messages—no more "Come to the Saturday 10K Run!" or "Help! I lost my earring in the third-floor Women's Room" or even "Who knows the sales numbers in Singapore?"—but also give users an e-mail budget, in which they're only debited for broadcast messages.

Indeed, if each employee had a "communication budget," it's likely that communications would then become much more targeted and restricted to important messages. (Perhaps it should cost more to send messages to senior managers; they, at least, believe their time is worth more.) And if charging mechanisms were in place, companies could establish subsidies for the types of information or communication they want to encourage.

Exchange of knowledge, for example, should be free; it's difficult enough to transfer knowledge without economic barriers. Yet in practice, many companies charge those with valuable information (generally through computer fees) to provide it to others. As a result, the information is often not supplied, since the owner is essentially punished for doing so. A manufacturing company's sales department, for instance, charged salespeople who weren't in the office when they dialed into a sales-reporting system. These call reports gained the salespeople little, yet they were asked to use a scarce resource to provide them. Even though the reports were mandated by top management, many salespeople simply did not comply.

Measurement can also become either a short-sighted effort with little reason to be, or a useful economic tactic. Information is notoriously difficult to measure in any way other than cost. Some firms practice selective measurement of costs, assessing only the costs of externally supplied information. Obviously, it also costs a company to generate and distribute information internally; but if these costs aren't measured or assessed, companies often gravitate toward producing everything themselves—unless the information is of very poor quality.

Perhaps the only reliable way to measure information's value is to have the user rate it. After all, the degree to which a piece of information really informs is in the eye of the informed. An information recipient could ask herself, "How valuable was this information to me?" and pay the provider accordingly. To institute such a measurement system would probably be very helpful in encouraging providers to add value to information. If nothing else, it would open the field to market forces.

Of course, it would be difficult to extract payment based on perceptions of information value, but there are other means of rewarding suppliers of valued information. One increasingly common approach is to evaluate job performance in terms of the information supplied by an employee. This might be done by supervisors or evaluation committees (as at McKinsey, where consultants aren't promoted unless they have contributed to the stock of useful knowledge), or by peers, who are often the best judges of how well a coworker adds value to or shares information. It's not difficult to add information sharing, for example, to the list of evaluation criteria employed in peer evaluations, and I know of several firms that have done so recently.

As you can see from this discussion of tactics, managers use them—whether information ecologists or technologists, federalists or monarchs—to influence behavior. Indeed, the political realm of any organization is all about influence, for good or ill: getting other managers behind an initiative, compromising to build coalitions, rewarding individual employees for what you want them to do. Incentives for "good" behavior can span everything from money to power to new technological toys to increasing a creative person's access to more information.

Regardless, as the next chapter underscores, paying attention to the human side of information use is mandatory for any good politician. For the information ecologist, it's the equivalent of kissing babies.

Assessment Survey for Information Politics

The greater the level of agreement with the statements below, the better an organization manages information politics.)

* Senior managers take an active interest in defining information categories and entities.

* Senior managers meet as a group to debate corporate information needs.

* The information entities to be managed centrally in my organization are clearly defined, with other information needs left up to individuals, business units, or functions.

* Information managers consciously assume political roles (such as dealer, broker, leaker) in order to further strategic objectives.

* Information politics can be discussed openly in our organization.

6
.
.
.
.
.

Information Behavior and Culture

We have spent a great deal of time and money bringing
water to the horse, but we don't even know if he's thirsty,
and we have no idea how to get him to drink.

A Pacific Bell manager

Changing how people use information—and ultimately building a support-
ive information culture—is the crux of information ecology. Yet in many areas
of business, managers at every level have discovered, to their chagrin, that
the behavioral and cultural dimension of change is often the most difficult to
accomplish. Whether firms are trying to improve quality, redesign processes,
or increase customer satisfaction, they find that "the soft stuff is the hard
stuff." And designing new work processes, organizational structures, or business strategies can seem like child's play compared with changing day-to-day
attitudes and behaviors.

Companies continue to plan complex and expensive information systems
that won't work unless people change what they're doing. Yet firms rarely
identify the ways in which behavior and culture must change if their information initiatives are to succeed. Even the terms "information behavior" and
"information culture" are scarcely recognized by managers. Of all the elements of information ecology, information behavior and culture are perhaps
the least explored.

Simply put, *information behavior* refers to how individuals approach and
handle information. This includes searching for it, using it, modifying it, sharing it, hoarding it, even ignoring it. Consequently, when we manage informa-

tion behavior, we're attempting to improve the overall effectiveness of an organization's information environment through concerted action.

While behavior involves acts by individuals, the notion of culture involves groups or organizations—particularly the values and beliefs of the group. By *information culture*, I mean the pattern of behaviors and attitudes that express an organization's orientation toward information. Information cultures can be open or closed, factually oriented or rumor- and intuition-based, internally or externally focused, controlling or empowering. A company's information culture can also include organizational preferences for certain types of information channels or media—for example, face-to-face communication vs. telephone or teleconferencing.

Some organizations have definite beliefs about how information should be presented, such as IBM's historical predilection for overhead projection "foils." Other cultural attitudes include antipathy to particular technologies, such as First Union's distaste for voice mail (which might more accurately be expressed as its CEO's distaste imposed on the broader organization). As with any sort of culture, managers must often come to grips with their information culture subjectively, impressionistically, learning how to describe it rather than trying to analyze it formally.

Nevertheless, a few researchers have conducted empirical studies of information cultures in limited domains. One unpublished study of information behavior in pharmaceutical firms, for example, found that firms with more open information environments had higher levels of research productivity.[1] Another study of twenty-five electronics firms found a positive relationship between encouraging the use of scientific and technical information, and corporate performance.[2] Other such studies have focused on how information culture can influence environments of technical innovation. In general, this research suggests that acquiring and sharing information—in textual or verbal form—is correlated with higher innovation and scientific and engineering productivity.[3]

Unfortunately, the results of such studies haven't reached the mainstream of management practice. In my own research with fifteen large firms, I found most had taken few steps to change workers' attitudes toward information; in fact, none emphasized the human aspects of information use. Of the thirty-five information managers I talked to at those firms, only a third felt that any particular internal group had assumed a responsibility for information behavior or culture.[4] When I pushed them, the majority of these managers agreed that information behavior and culture were important, but few could describe specific ways in which either had been explicitly managed. Those who could referred to conventional approaches to information management, such as data-modeling exercises, that hadn't really changed the status quo.

My primary purpose here is to argue for the importance of behavioral and cultural management, to detail the critical types of information behavior—sharing, handling information overload, cutting down on multiple meanings—and to describe how managers can start making changes. In fact, some companies actively (though unconsciously) manage information behavior, even if few executives can explain what they're doing. In this chapter, I'll provide ecological language and models to help managers orient themselves toward the messy—but extremely worthwhile—human world.

Why Manage Information Behavior?

No organization stands out for its management of information behavior. But I believe this realm of information ecology is absolutely essential for a number of obvious, and perhaps not so obvious, reasons. First of all, at least forty percent of American workers are information workers—not just dealing with information in their jobs, but manipulating information as a frequent, primary activity. Regardless of their specific positions, such workers spend a good proportion of their time acquiring, using, and sharing structured information. If managers don't pay attention to what these people are doing, then they aren't managing a significant component of work life.

Furthermore, in almost every firm, executives would agree that some portion of the firm's value lies in its knowledge. But to take better advantage of an organization's knowledge, changes in information behavior must be instituted. Some widely publicized technologies (for example, expert systems, "groupware" applications like Lotus Notes, decision-support systems) can help capture and disseminate organizational knowledge, but they're of little help if the people involved aren't already predisposed to use information effectively. From where I sit, successful knowledge management always occurs through a combination of technological and behavioral change.

Better management of information behavior can also lead to control of information costs. In almost every organization I've studied, information acquisition from external sources is neither efficient nor cost-effective. Part of the problem is that the individuals or groups that acquire information don't share it well—which argues for reinforcing the right kind of sharing behavior to control a major source of overhead costs.

There's also what I call a "why not?" rationale for managing information behavior. A number of observers have noted that information and its associated technologies have become a critical organizational resource, on the level of such other business necessities as financial and human resources. Indeed, the metaphor that likens intellectual capital to financial capital is relatively well established.[5] We have elaborate structures and processes—policies, procedures, approval limits—for managing financial and human resources behavior. Most of us even understand that firms have financial cultural traits—tight-fisted versus free-spending, for example—and human resources traits—secretive versus open. So if we consider information an equally important organizational resource—and many senior managers at least say they do—then it stands to reason that information behavior and culture should be managed accordingly.

Presumably the primary objectives of managing financial behavior are cost control and the maximization of shareholder value; for human resources behavior, management objectives generally include maintaining productivity, equity, and quality work lives. In these terms, the objective of managing information behavior is not only internal effectiveness, but also the achievement of competitive advantage. It's the *use* of information—not its mere existence—that allows managers to make better decisions about products and processes, to learn from customers and competitors, and to monitor the results of their actions. Such advantage should not be left to chance, and can't be achieved without managing the human aspects of information.

Of course, information behavior is as least as difficult to manage as financial and human resources behavior. Information is often less tangible than finance, with no common currency or language; in fact, its value is always more difficult to calculate than currency. No one has yet established a common and easily measured unit of information; there's no equivalent of the dollar, the therm, the pound, or the joule. But though there are technical difficulties to information management, the toughest aspects involve its strong human flavor. As in managing human resources, an organization must achieve consensus on information meanings and uses.

Perhaps one reason why information behavior hasn't often been explicitly addressed by firms is because it's tough to manage. What behavioral management that does exist usually has a negative, controlling feel. A few organizations have policies about confidentiality of electronic or paper-based communications. Several educationally minded companies offer remedial training in such communications skills as reading, writing, and listening. A few firms discourage "loose lips" in elevators or public transportation. Under the banner of quality improvement, some have addressed the issue of how employees use factual information to make and justify decisions. Quality programs sometimes also attempt to improve the performance of front-line communications people, such as receptionists and telephone operators. On occasion, a company implementing a major new information system will train users not only on the use of the system itself, but also on the way in which they should use the information it produces.

To a greater or lesser extent, these are promising approaches. But such behavioral initiatives generally happen in isolation, not backed by larger management goals for building a positive information culture. At best, specific initiatives are only first steps down the ecological road.

Sadly, while many people use, generate, or distribute information, the only real managers of information behavior in most firms are lawyers. They often try to control information property rights and flow, particularly when intellectual property, sensitive financial information, or external ventures are involved. But their usual advice is to hoard information rather than to share it; such a course of action may always be safe, but it won't create competitive advantage. Just the notion of "intellectual property" implies clear boundaries of ownership and strict control over information, and ignores the difficulties of managing information as if it were property. Clearly, lawyers won't often be the information users we want to emulate—which means other managers need to define the information behaviors they *do* want.

What Kind of Information Behavior Should We Encourage?

I've found there are three critical types of information behavior that improve a company's information environment: sharing, handling overload, and dealing with multiple meanings. If organizations intend to create healthy information cultures, their employees need to do all three.

Information Sharing

Perhaps the simplest of behaviors to understand is sharing. We're supposed to learn how to share tangible goods like candy and toys in childhood; nevertheless, throughout our adult lives we still wrestle with how much we should share our money, property, and time, probably because sharing always sounds easier to do than it is. While most managers have a good idea of what it means to share information, they usually don't find it any easier than sharing money—for good reason. In any organization, those who control the right information also have the most power.

I define information sharing as the *voluntary* act of making information available to others. Sharing should be distinguished from reporting, which is involuntary exchange of information on a routine or structured basis. The term "sharing" implies volition; the sharer could pass information on but doesn't have to. Reporting is usually up and down the structural hierarchy—up to superiors and down to subordinates—within functional boundaries. Such vertical flow is probably the most common type of information exchange in US firms, although even reporting doesn't necessarily go well. Advocates of Total Quality Management emphasize distributing information about a firm's strategy and objectives at all levels so that employees can formulate their own work plans accordingly. This is sometimes called "policy deployment" or "*hoshen kanri*" in Japanese.[6]

More relaxed vertical information flow, or TQM's less hierarchical distribution, is a good idea. But information sharing between peers—or horizontal information flow—is likely to make the biggest difference to a firm's information environment. There's nothing new about the idea of sharing information, but more and more business leaders realize it's a desirable behavior. For example:

- managers of a pharmaceutical firm hope that its scientists will share information about new drug compounds throughout the entire new drug-development process;
- sales managers want field sales personnel to share information with each other about competitive initiatives they see in the field, and to share feedback about products with engineering and design departments;
- consulting firm leaders want their professionals to share best practices they observe among clients in an internationally available database;
- customer-support managers at a computer firm want their workers to add typically-encountered problems to a knowledge database, and to answer ad hoc requests from other personnel when received via electronic mail.

Managers become particularly interested in information sharing when they want to make business processes cross-functional. In new product development processes, for instance, design engineers must talk regularly with manufacturing engineers, who each must exchange information with the production line. In order-management processes, sales, accounting, logistics, and manufacturing organizations all need to share information.

Yet in most Western firms, neither formal nor informal information travels well cross-functionally.[7] There are all sorts of barriers that prevent horizontal information flow, including functionally based information systems, incompatible information architectures, and political and cultural differences that can be reinforced as early as the university training of future scientists, engineers, marketers, and accountants. Some researchers have argued that one of the keys to the success of Japanese management approaches is effective horizontal information flow.[8]

But creating more horizontal information flow doesn't happen by simply mandating it—or implementing a new e-mail system. Here's where an ecological perspective can really help, because influencing behavior usually involves a number of related initiatives. Establishing cross-functional process-es is an important step. That means performance needs to be measured and rewarded differently, since most managers are judged by how well they opti-mize functional performance and receive few incentives for operating cross-functionally. In addition, they must become familiar with the competing subcultures that exist: the differences between marketing and R&D, for instance. Top management might encourage career paths that take executives through a variety of functions; just as some companies have their rising stars work in different international offices, they could have a promising engineer, say, try out project management or even marketing. Another strategy might be to have managers treat other departments as customers whose needs must be understood.

In Japanese firms, the most common approach to creating horizontal information flow is rotating managers between various functions throughout their careers. The Japanese business culture emphasizes experience as a pri-mary basis for learning; if, say, I've been a marketing manager in the past, when I become a finance manager I'll bring a much greater appreciation of marketing problems and perspectives to my new job. Cross-functional infor-mation flow is also facilitated through frequent face-to-face meetings with other managers both on and off the job, and a decision style that emphasizes consensus.

The Western firms that do advocate information sharing usually restrict it to sharing within the corporation. However, some firms have found that sharing information with business partners, even competitors, has distinct advantages. Several researchers have studied the exchange of information within a particular industry, called "information trading," and their results sug-gest that such trading may yield competitive and economic benefits for firms. Over sixty high-tech firms, for example, have joined together in the Customer Support Consortium to share information and problem-solving strategies for their customer support functions. Managers at these firms have concluded that customers use products from multiple vendors and want to be able to call a single source to get answers to their questions. A multi-vendor support model requires that competitors—for example, Microsoft, Novell, and IBM—share their knowledge so that when a customer with an IBM computer and a Microsoft operating system calls Novell for help with networking, the Novell analyst can solve the customer's problem.[9]

Note that while we all share information at times, there are also occasions when it's inappropriate or illegal. Obviously, we shouldn't share insider infor-mation about company performance, competitive secrets with those outside our firms, or confidential personal information with those not entitled to it. Too much sharing may also lead to unwanted behaviors. For instance, when I was a partner at Ernst & Young, the firm had a policy against revealing partner incomes. The policy led to a culture of cooperation and information sharing; one didn't worry much about whether the partner who worked with you to sell a consulting engagement made more than you. Several other Big Six firms with which I've worked publicize partner shares or incomes internally so that each partner knows or can calculate other partners' incomes. This leads to many envious comparisons between partners and occasionally to information hoarding.

There are plenty of valid reasons why individuals may not want to share information. They may, for example, view information as being of unique value to their own careers. They may think certain information will reflect negatively on themselves or their part of the organization. They may be suspicious of what the recipient of the information will do with it. They may feel they'll have to spend time supporting the information if they share it. In short, the barriers to sharing are often deeply embedded in the information politics of an organization. In order for information behavior to shift in the right direction, a divisive political structure must shift, too.

In a recent study of information politics in twenty-five firms, for instance, I found several in which information was hoarded to preserve the importance and unique contribution of its creator or current owner.[10] In another study of the impact of a new electronic mail and conferencing system in a professional services firm, junior members were reluctant to use the system to share their ideas; they felt there were no incentives and plenty of potential negative consequences for doing so, such as other members taking credit for their work or shooting them down.[11] In the manufacturing industry, information about part stockpiles and shortages is routinely hoarded between parts and maintenance organizations, as one study on military avionics repair has illustrated.[12] And virtually every large organization has salespeople who hoard customer information (in order to keep some other salesperson from exploiting it), thereby furnishing inaccurate information about customer demand (which reflects well on the salesperson's performance or reserves scarce product inventory).

It seems that information sharing in companies is almost an unnatural act. Consider my own survey of thirty-five information managers, in which only one felt that "a lot" of information was shared across his organization, and almost half (forty-five percent) told me there was "little or no" sharing. It should be clear by now that in order to manage the communication or sharing of information effectively, those in charge need to set up standards for how employees decide what types of information to share, and with whom to share it. Managers should not only model the right behaviors themselves, they must also remove the organizational barriers to information sharing—be they political, emotional, or technological.

On a more positive note, two-thirds of the managers I surveyed reported initiatives underway to improve information sharing, including guides to the location and ownership of information, common information standards, and the creation of new staff roles to facilitate sharing. These managers are doing this not because I say it's a good idea, but because they—and the senior executives in their companies—know in their bones that improving a firm's use of information can make or break a business.

Handling Information Overload

When information is everywhere, as it seems to be in most corporations, the commodity in shortest supply is attention. When media, technologies, and information types proliferate, the only constant is our limited span of attention, especially that of decision-makers and those who need information to act. Unfortunately, businesspeople, who are generally both providers and users of information, have thought very little about how to attract attention to the information they create. As a result, most of it languishes on desks, in file cabinets, and (I hope) in recycling bins.

Some might say that unused information is not ignored; rather, it conflicts with managers' existing perceptions and biases. But cognitive science research tells us that we always look at information through some type of lens.[13] To overcome existing predispositions requires a higher level of attention than do the rare cases where the information receiver is a *tabula rasa*; but that's just reality in a world where we're constantly bombarded with sensory input. We almost always filter information when we successfully engage with it.

Nevertheless, information overload occurs everywhere in a business organization. Advertising doesn't engage customers, succeeding only through expensive repetition. Human Resources doesn't inform employees about benefit options or retirement plans. Senior managers present information about strategy or organizational change that doesn't catch anyone's attention or fancy. Perhaps the least engaging information of all is that which comes from the information systems organization—reams of dry-as-dust printouts that practically demand to be ignored and eventually trashed.

If we want to make full use of all the information generated by an organization, our perspectives and actions have to change dramatically. While information providers have previously viewed access to information as their primary goal, access is not enough. We all have access to far more information than we can possibly pay attention to (see Figure 6-1). New sources and media are appearing all the time, but the old ones (books, paper mail, newspapers) don't go away. Given the confusing array of options in most informa-

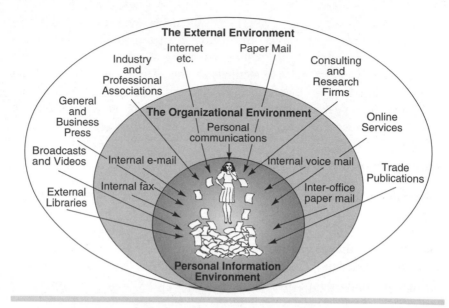

Figure 6-1. Typical Information Sources for an Individual

tion environments, we can't expect the poor user to find and separate out the really valuable information she needs.

We must communicate information in a compelling way that encourages the right people to recognize and use it. While this goal may seem obvious, such *engagement* is not a simple thing to accomplish. Most information transmission happens at the bottom of the "engagement hierarchy of information" (see Figure 6-2).[14] Even when providers try to make information more engaging—with appealing graphics, say, or a bulleted outline—the user generally only notices certain attributes of it. Rather than trying to read through a jargon-filled research paper, for instance, a field sales rep for a pharmaceutical company might retain a lot more information about a particular drug if he interviewed (perhaps even argued with) one of the scientists who conducted the original trials. Yet information is rarely presented so well that a user can move up the engagement ladder in this manner.

One current fact of organizational life: more information is communicated in read/view mode than in any other. Documents, reports, live and video-based presentations, television—and, unfortunately, this book—all rely on this mode of information transfer. Because reading and viewing require negligible engagement on the part of the information receiver, it's efficient—but not effective. We can "communicate" vast amounts of information through this channel, but each message has little chance of affecting anyone's behavior. That's because there's little emotional engagement with or commitment to the

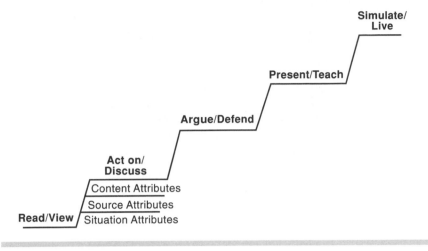

Figure 6-2. A Hierarchy of Information Engagement

information. Even when it is "received"—that is, the recipient actually reads it or pays attention when it's presented—it may not be acted upon.

Of course, some readings or presentations are better—or more engaging—than others, as Figure 6-2 indicates. We pay more attention to an entertaining speaker, and color documents are more pleasing to look at than black-and-white ones. We're also more likely to attend to a lecture from the CEO than from someone who has no power over us. But these make a marginal difference in engagement level; they don't change the fact that the information is passively received.

The content, source, and situational attributes that really do improve engagement—such as emotional interest, originality, and the perceived expertise of a speaker—are listed in the chart below. Most of them not only improve the transfer of information when read or viewed, but also enhance the more engaging approaches at the top of the hierarchy.

Secondary Engagement Attributes

Content	**Source**	**Situation**
emotion	perceived expertise	perceived consequences
brevity	power	comfort
visual appeal	personal appeal	who initiated
aural appeal	objectivity	individual vs. group setting
uniqueness	familiarity	voluntary vs. mandated presence
concreteness		

Polaroid, for example, started a new venture called the Graphics Imaging (GI) business unit to produce equipment and supplies for graphics professionals. Corporate headquarters gave Jane Linder, previously the corporate Director of Management Information, responsibility at GI not only for information management but also for strategic planning, business development, and new products and services.[15] She and the head of the GI business unit determined that if the unit was going to compete in an already-established marketplace, they had to adopt a new approach to market information.

Working with a consultant, Linder and the unit head decided that a "war game" would be the best way to engage GI managers. Linder and her staff designed the game, in which groups of GI managers would simulate various competitors. Each competitor would present its products and strategies to a group of potential GI customers, who would then discuss their reactions and select a supplier. Linder's staff prepared detailed background reports on each competitor, and team members paid attention to this information, since they needed it to present the competitor realistically.

These games were a great success. The teams engaged with the information to such a degree that some of the Polaroid managers began to mistrust those who were simulating the competition at lunch after the game! More to the point, the GI management team learned—and retained—how potential new products and strategies stacked up against competitors'. Linder and the division head have since gone on to develop engaging simulations for other types of information and management contexts, including scenario-based strategic planning, decisions about partnerships with other firms, and "concept engineering" for new products.

Still, Polaroid's innovative approach might not work for every organization or situation. First of all, preparing such an engaging exercise is very time-consuming. Linder estimates that it takes three or four times as long to design a meeting if the information is to be presented in an engaging fashion. Second, there's a higher level of risk. She notes that the planning team had to try to anticipate every contingency, including other managers' total refusal to participate. These difficulties mean that a much smaller amount of information can be transmitted using these more engaging approaches. Their use effectively implies that organizations must develop an information strategy to focus attention on a few key types of information.

Other organizations have attempted to use games for information engagement purposes, Springfield Remanufacturing being one of the most well-known. The company's CEO, Jack Stack, decided that his workers needed to engage with the basic financial information that describes any firm's success. Therefore, he turned the generation of his company's financial information into a game, which is described in his book *The Great Game of Business*.[16] The new-found ability of employees to engage with the company's financial performance measures led to changes in their behavior; for example, they stopped incurring unnecessary costs or purchasing new equipment at times when it would unduly affect financial reporting. This in turn led to a dramatic turnaround and many years of subsequent success for Springfield Remanufacturing.

The notion of engagement has many possible implications for information overload. It's obviously an underlying issue in debates about the value of interactivity in mass media. It could influence the ways in which external information providers communicate their information to customers. But the transition to a new approach will be hardest for internal information providers like information systems (IS) functions, which have traditionally presented technically dense documents at the bottom of the engagement scale. Indeed, it remains to be seen whether such a drastic reformulation of the IS role and style is even possible.

Still, focusing on engagement has done the most to stem information overload so far. Many companies talk about "fact-based decision-making," but it's seldom clear how they ensure that it happens. Most research indicates that it's far more common for managers to "decide with their gut' or "think on their feet" than to make a rational and systematic evaluation of information.[17] Even universities and business schools only occasionally teach students how much reliance to place on information vs. intuition, or how to draw conclusions and make decisions based on information. And when they do attempt to address these issues, it's generally within the narrow context of financial information use.

In my survey of thirty-five information managers in fifteen companies, only a third said that managers in their firms placed a strong emphasis on the use of factual information in decision-making. More than half did report, however, that their firms had undertaken initiatives to increase the use of information in decision-making, including standards for common information, profitability analysis systems to allow use of such information in making decisions, quality or TQM-programs, and a defined process for managing market information. Companies may get by on managerial intuition and luck for a few years, but over time the most successful firms are those that stay attuned to factual information—both from inside and outside the business—and use it to make decisions.

Dealing with Multiple Meanings

Organizations often overlook how quickly new meanings for key business terms can proliferate. Take this simple example: when a marketing manager starts focusing on distributors, he decides that distributors are in effect "customers" and need to be in a customer database. Because the distributor-oriented meaning of "customer" conflicts with a consumer-oriented meaning (and perhaps with the "official" corporate definition), he then creates a new customer database on a personal computer. And so, like a splitting biological cell, the meaning of "customer" starts to proliferate.

Multiple meanings for key units of information is an old problem, one that predates computers and most other forms of information technology. When a group of people tries to create categories or lists of information to be used by others, there have always been problems in the maintenance of meaning. Since the nineteenth century, international medical bodies have attempted to classify types of diseases (one such classification scheme is the International Classification of Disease), while individual physicians and country-based medical associations decide these categories don't work for their purposes, and so modify them or create new ones.[18]

This sort of information behavior has long been anathema for business information technologists. Indeed, it often has negative consequences. When alternative meanings proliferate, different managers will present different results at sales meetings. Or the CEO will ask for a list of customers and be told that it will take months to produce. Or the same customer will be sent multiple communications about a new product offering and start to think "this company doesn't have its act together *at all*."

Yet multiple meanings can also be a good thing. When a manager thinks of a new way to define a term like "customer," her innovation indicates an interest in better serving that business entity. And if she goes to the effort of creating a new database, it probably means "customer" was poorly defined (at least for her purposes) in the existing information environment. One might even argue that if a firm's employees are not attempting to proliferate meanings for key information entities, they don't really care.

The proliferation of meanings is so pervasive that I've formulated a general hypothesis: the more an organization knows about a term or concept relevant to its business, the less likely it is to agree on a common term or meaning for it. At American Airlines, for instance, there are several perspectives on what an "airport" is. For American's passenger-oriented marketers, an airport is any location where passengers want to go. To cargo-oriented employees, an airport is any place where cargo can be received or dropped off. To maintenance personnel, it's any facility at which aircraft maintenance can be performed.

At Union Pacific Railroad, various managers and employees find it hard to agree on what the term "train" means. The US Department of Agriculture has difficulty fixing on the meaning of "farm," and the Justice Department has multiple meanings for "trial." Such problems don't necessarily indicate poor information management; in fact, they signify a healthy interest in the topic.

But ultimately, there are times when multiple information meanings must be managed and controlled. For certain key information entities within an organization, it may be useful to adhere as closely as possible to one term and one meaning for that term. Many companies try to create this type of "enterprise" information or "global common" information. Before adopting it, however, an organization should be sure that it's willing to accept the negative consequences of a positive outcome—that is, employees using information that is less than ideal for their specific purposes. It must also be prepared not only to define common information, but to maintain it by monitoring and policing its use across the organization.

When Xerox Corporation set out to define common terms for key information entities, it first tried—and failed with—the traditional information engineering approach. IT managers then asked senior managers to address the issue, but they were unable to reach consensus. They did, however, decide that customer information was a good place to start, and recommended establishing a task force of middle managers who were close to the issue. Fifteen marketing and sales managers—and their IT counterparts—from around the world assembled to debate the issue. After they had agreed on a definition of "customer" (businesses that had already purchased products or services from Xerox) and defined a common customer number, they also defined eleven other customer-oriented terms, including "customer address" and "customer satisfaction." The task force then addressed how to "sell" these terms; eventually, a "commonality maintenance" group was created within Corporate Information Management at Xerox.

The Nitty Gritty: Getting Behavior to Change

To date, most approaches to influencing information behavior have involved information architecture. As I've already made clear, these efforts seldom succeed in changing behavior. But before suggesting some more positive approaches, let's review the reasons why architecture so often fails:

- Behavior change is rarely an *objective* of information architectures; at best, the goal of information architectures may be increased awareness on the part of employees and managers of the extent and costs of redundant, overlapping data; yet awareness does not in itself change anything.
- The *content* of information architectures does not lead to behavior change; it's generally incomprehensible not only to nontechnicians but often even to other technicians. There are also few tools for client-oriented discussions and negotiations about information requirements and structures.

- The *process* of developing information architectures inhibits change; stakeholders don't participate fully in their development— indeed, they rarely understand what the stakes of information architectures are—and therefore aren't committed to them when implemented.

I'm frequently amazed by how often technologists manage to shoot themselves in the collective foot. Even when information architecture *is* the right approach (see my discussion of the possibilities in Chapter 9), communication with those who'll be affected must be broad, frequent, and ongoing. IS professionals may not be the warmest or fuzziest types on board, but they have to talk with the people they're supposed to serve. And they need to think in terms of behavior, not electronics or programming code.

Developing measures of desired behaviors is crucial for any change process—architectural or otherwise. Appropriate rewards and controls have to be in place to reinforce the right behaviors and discourage the wrong ones. That means managers at all levels have to take enforcement seriously, and they have to administer rewards and sanctions consistently, not just distribute memos that tell employees what they ought to do.

In my experience, providing incentives to "do the right thing"—or at least to make it hard (or stupid) to do the wrong thing—is the most effective approach. Unfortunately, it's also the rarest. Although such incentives may exist in some organizations, they're not widespread or visible. If firms were truly managing information behavior, they'd have well-understood, clearly articulated incentives—for example, promotions, raises, even simple pats on the back—for behaving in the desired way. They'd recognize and reward their employees for acquiring, using, sharing, or otherwise acting upon information. They'd establish legitimate roles for information suppliers, hubs, or brokers. And they would value (and reward) decisions based on factual information, even if proven incorrect, more than "gut" hunches.[19]

Sanctions for undesirable information behaviors are more common, though they're hardly thick on the ground. Jack Welch, CEO of General Electric, has stated publicly that successful GE managers will not hoard information or protect organizational "turf." At one fast-food firm, the head of marketing told me that several marketing managers had been punished—that is, not promoted or given raises—for information hoarding. But when I asked the manager if these sanctions had been widely publicized, he said no; he was hoarding this information! If sanctions (not to mention rewards) are to be effective, they must be noticed and even institutionalized.

A few firms have begun to evaluate personnel on their information behaviors. At Buckman Laboratories, for example, a privately held chemicals firm based in Memphis, Tennessee, there are objective, quantitative measures of employees' information and knowledge sharing. The firm's 150 top sharers were recently invited to an off-site conference, where they were treated to a Tom Peters (the celebrated management guru) presentation, recreational activities, and discussions of how to institutionalize the sharing of information and knowledge. At the Lotus Development division of IBM—which sells Notes, an important tool for information sharing in itself—customer-support employees are evaluated partially on the basis of how well they share information; in fact, their ability to share accounts for twenty-five percent of their total work performance evaluation.

It's only when such evaluations are formalized that they can have significant, long-term effects on information behavior. The ultimate goal of managing information behavior, of course, is to create a positive information culture—one where it's simply the norm to "do the right information thing."

Indeed, you could say that the most positive information culture values and rewards teaching, mentoring, and all other forms of education that support the transmission of long-term knowledge. Most professionals, in particular, only absorb what they need to know—the unstructured knowledge of legal decisions, journalistic style, consulting approaches, medical practice, and so on—with the help of others who have been around longer.

Creating an organizational culture that values and provides opportunities for communicating "tacit knowledge" doesn't happen often. Today it's most frequently pursued under the banner of "organizational learning" at firms like AT&T, Ford, Intel, and EDS, all under the tutelage of Peter Senge's Systems Thinking and Organizational Learning Center at MIT. However, the devotees of organizational learning rarely relate their goals to the day-to-day management of information and knowledge. One exception is National Semiconductor, which pursues not only the cultural abstractions of organizational learning but also the concrete implementation of data, information, and knowledge repositories. As I discuss later in Chapter 10, National Semiconductor has seen the tangible benefits of effective knowledge transfer through the company's ability to open new semiconductor fabrication facilities more rapidly.

Individual vs. Group: Managing Behavior at Different Levels

Understanding how *individuals* handle information is at the core of all information behavior analysis. Indeed, at most companies information is usually stored and sought by individuals; the growth of personal computers illustrates the premium that employees place on handling their own information environments. But given the sheer number of individuals in even medium-sized firms—along with considerations of individual privacy and freedom—trying to "micro-manage" information behavior at this level is generally unrealistic and often counterproductive.

Most research on how individuals process information suggests that we're far from fully rational and exhaustive in our acquisition and use of it. Whether a particular item of information is applied to a decision depends on when we encounter the information, how it relates to existing biases, and whether we've already made up our minds.[20] Cognitive scientists call this the "garbage can" model of information processing; and rummaging around in individual garbage cans to try to improve the process seems fruitless.

There are at least two ways, however, that firms can validly address individual behavior. One approach is to issue policies, guidelines, and tools (from in-boxes and filing cabinets at the simplest level to sophisticated applications and networks at the most complex) to help individuals structure their personal information environments more effectively. Given the specter of excessive organizational control, I advise managers to emphasize how this approach facilitates information use—not to impose their own methods on others for the sake of keeping a "Big Brother" eye on employees.

Corporate management might also identify particular individuals within an organization whose information behavior they want to influence. These may be senior managers, or particularly active users, suppliers, or distributors of information, at whatever level they are found in the organization. This has been the implicit approach, for example, of firms that have devoted considerable effort to executive information systems.

At the *small group* level of behavior management, most research has focused either on how groups process information already available and arrive at a decision,[21] or on how information technology might be used to facilitate group tasks.[22] Advocates of electronic imaging have also speculated about how more efficient transfer of work-flow information might improve group-oriented work designs.[23] Occasionally, such concerns are embodied in small pilot or prototype groups that test concepts of a "model office." Yet few firms have systematically applied this knowledge across a broad spectrum of groups and their tasks. Because managers of small groups usually have only an implicit, intuitive knowledge of information behavior issues, they're not prepared to manage such behavior to make a group more effective.

But from my perspective, managing the information behavior of a small group is the most practical place to start. Companies should choose a small group of particular importance to its mission, and redesign how it works with information. For instance, how does a consulting project team acquire, analyze, and act on information about the client and the industry? How does an airline cockpit crew react to the information it receives about the flight? (This has been studied, but usually only in the aftermath of a disaster.) Perhaps most important, how does an executive team use information to monitor its operations and implementation of its strategies? In each of these small groups, information is critical to success. Yet for some unknown reason, few firms have undertaken close analyses of group-level information behavior.

Managers might also think about the *organizational* level of information behavior, even if this is quite a stretch. Academics, at least, have established that entire organizations can be viewed in terms of their ability to process information. For example, Jay Galbraith, a distinguished organizational behavior professor, has argued that some organizational designs (including structures, roles, and processes) are better suited to effective information processing than others.[24] This work on information processing, however, has yielded almost no practical recommendations.

In the real world, few firms have actually created new organizational designs to improve information processing. Those that have done so, such as Batterymarch Financial Management,[25] differ remarkably from other firms in their industries; Batterymarch has employed computers rather than people to identify what financial assets should be bought and sold, and therefore has relatively low costs. But Batterymarch hasn't been particularly successful lately, possibly because it has a contrarian investment strategy in a bull market. The negative results experienced by Batterymarch suggest that we don't know enough about information processing to design organizations around it—and certainly not to "hardwire" information behaviors into computer algorithms, as Batterymarch has attempted to do.

Researchers have also concluded that organizations can be viewed as having memories, intelligence, and learning.[26] Yet aside from acquiring technologies that would help to structure and transfer information, and despite some encouragement by academics,[27] firms have done little to achieve these concepts. For the most part, I believe managers should start more modestly with information behavior, addressing individuals and key groups before talking about transforming entire organizations. Senior executives can concentrate on setting a good personal example for information behavior, which will lead to more change than high-level pronouncements.

Finally, as firms become increasingly intertwined with other organizations in collaborative networks, we might all benefit from a better understanding of information behavior at the *interorganizational* level. Research on such information exchange has focused more on competitors than on collaborators, often addressing the economic cues and signals that firms send to and receive from competitors.[28] But such research plays out in actual companies in limited ways, since most managers usually just restrict sharing of information with competitors or the media.

Research on trading-partner information relationships generally focuses on the exchange of highly structured information through electronic data interchange (EDI). Though the successful use of EDI demands some openness in information exchange, most firms have only scratched the surface of what is possible. For example, Wal-Mart's information systems give suppliers access to store-level information on the volumes sold, inventory levels, even pricing and promotion figures for supplier products. This allows suppliers to replenish Wal-Mart's shelves continuously. As of now, few other firms give their trading partners such access to information.[29]

"My Computer Ate It": How IT Affects Information Behavior

Managers often make assumptions about how information technology will change what people do. For example, every day firms assume that because they've implemented an e-mail system, employees will be more likely to share information with their colleagues, simply because the technology is available. Similarly, companies—or at least the IS function—want to believe that executives will be more likely to use accurate and up-to-date information because workstations running executive information systems have been placed on their credenzas.

In fact, several research studies have addressed how electronic mail affects communication behavior.[30] It has become a (true) truism that e-mail leads to overly emotional messages, and that e-mail meetings somewhat reduce the role of hierarchy and position. What researchers have yet to prove, however, is whether e-mail use affects profitability, productivity, or even communications effectiveness. Though there exists little hard evidence either way, my suspicion is that e-mail is becoming a great time sink for managers and workers. At Tandem Computers, for example, field service personnel can send a "has anyone seen this problem" message to all other technical workers in the company. They usually find an answer, but at what cost in the time of all those people, who had to read and think about the message? Too often this sort of e-mail is a band-aid for poor information behavior.

It's also possible that too much e-mail has diminished, not increased, communications effectiveness. At Symantec, a Silicon Valley software company, managers were beset by frequent complaints from employees about poor communications. Of course, the company had e-mail; one Symantec manager was even accused of stealing secrets from his previous employer via e-mail (the charge was ultimately dismissed). Eventually, Bob Sykes, Symantec's Chief Financial Officer, decided on a strategy of "over-communicating." He decided to transmit important information he wanted everyone to know via company-wide meetings, letters to employees' homes, and voice mail—which has, according to a number of managers, improved communication at Symantec.

Still, we tend to address the problems created by e-mail with more technology (I call this a hair-of-the-dog-that-bit-you approach). Techno-utopians speculate that at some unspecified time in the future, intelligent agents and filters will solve e-mail infoglut. I would argue, however, that we'll always need to adopt behavioral solutions to this problem; in fact, we can do so today. Anytime someone sends you a message you shouldn't have received, send a polite but firm reply saying that you'd rather not receive such missives in the future. Ban the multiple cc:ed e-mail. Set a policy, as has Computer Associates, that e-mail is to be read and answered only at certain times of day. Start an education program on the use of different technologies for specific communications situations. With these steps, the overload problem will dissipate well before agents and filters leave the R&D labs.

Other studies of information behavior and technology relate to narrow areas—how, for example, a particular system's user interface affects the time users devote to system use. The results are seldom generalizable to real-world environments. We have very little useful, concrete information on how different types of technologies really change how people use information in their jobs. Until such research has been conducted, our assumptions about how information technologies affect behavior can only be intuitive.

But that doesn't mean examination of IT effectiveness is useless or not worth the effort. Consider the following communications issue, one that's unresolved in almost every organization today. Given the proliferation of technologies for communicating information—telephone, voice mail, electronic mail, fax, express mail, regular mail, teleconferencing—many employees who want to share what they know often need help choosing how to do so. In my survey of information managers, only a quarter felt that employees in their firms had a solid understanding of the technological options for information exchange; only a fifth believed their employees had little difficulty selecting the appropriate technology for a particular situation.

Even the most educated employees may lack basic skills for expressing themselves effectively. Though many firms offer remedial training in communications skills, the communication of information in its various forms is rarely treated explicitly. Needless to say, it should be.

Behavioral Management Tactics: Where to Start

Perhaps the most important component of information management is to make clear that information—and the behavior that promotes its effective use—is valuable (see the list below). Some companies now pay lip service to this notion with such statements as "information is an asset." Yet their actions, incentives (or lack

Tactics for Information Behavior Management

- Communicate that information is valuable.
- Clarify the organization's information strategy and objectives.
- Identify needed information competencies.
- Focus on managing specific types of information content.
- Assign responsibility for information behavior, making it part of the organizational structure.
- Create a committee or network to address information behavior issues.
- Educate employees about information behavior.
- Raise sticky information management issues with everyone.

of incentives), and real emphases suggest otherwise. Managers need to move away from platitudes, *communicating how much they value information* through any number of specific ways: for instance, requiring better external and internal information in planning documents; devoting more resources to the provision of information; giving information processes importance in the organizational structure; attempting to better capture organizational expertise and intellectual property; rewarding employees for being good information "nodes."

Too often the opposite message is sent. Library or information center budgets are the first to be cut in times of financial stress.[31] Information professionals, especially those with an information content focus such as librarians, receive low pay and have little status. Even in firms where employees are rewarded on the basis of what they know about the business, little attention is paid to how they disseminate their knowledge. Managers are observed making decisions based purely on intuition, and are censured only when they are wrong—not when they fail to use available information to make their decisions. Employees are sent multiple signals that their information behavior is irrelevant to the success of the enterprise.

The first tactic for managing information behavior is to reverse such negative signals. Employees must be convinced that what they do with information matters as much as the way they handle human or financial capital. Just as employees are rewarded for suggestions that save the company money, they should be rewarded for acquiring, forwarding, or applying critical information. The foreignness of these notions simply reflects the degree to which we have slighted information behavior in the past.

Effective management of information behavior also demands that an organization *clarify its information strategy*. Each individual should be aware of what the organization wants to accomplish through the use of information, and how it expects to accomplish it. These objectives should, of course, be tied to the overall strategic goals of the organization.

Focusing on the skills required by an organization—or *identifying the necessary information competencies*—is another useful tactic, and one that usually follows from a clear information strategy. Few organizations can be good at creating, using, selling, packaging, and distributing information—that is, everything. Therefore, managers must determine which skills will most help the company achieve its information-oriented goals. Some firms may decide to excel at the creation of information through research on products and processes; others may choose to purchase such information in the marketplace, concentrating on how to use or apply it.

Focusing on specific information content is a similar tactic, one that helps corporate citizens to focus their behaviors on key types of information. It's a little easier to start sharing information, for example, if we're told that customer information is the most critical. To try to change behavior for using all types of information is a bit overwhelming, even for the well-intended.

A good information strategy—one that is actually carried out—also relies on another tactic: explicitly *assigning responsibility for managing and improving information behavior*. Making such a managerial role or group part of an organization's structure can go a long way toward reinforcing the message that information behavior is valuable; but in the majority of organizations—even those with Chief Information Officers—no group holds such a corporate charter. As noted above, only a third of the information managers I surveyed said that anyone was responsible for information behavior—and that's probably a higher fraction than a sample of non-IS managers would yield.

The human resources function manages behavioral issues, the IS function manages information technology, finance manages financial information, marketing manages market information—and so forth. For any of these functions to manage or facilitate information behavior itself is rare. Therefore, *creating a committee to addresss information behavior* is yet another useful tactic. Managers from different functions might join together to form a permanent network or team, formulating policies and processes to assist in specifically managing information behavior.

The policies and processes could include determining information stewardship in each department; clarification of when information sharing and hoarding are appropriate; the specific behaviors called for when the company commits to managing by fact (rather than rumor or intuition); and recommended processes, such as defining information architecture and strategy in behaviorally sensitive ways, for information professionals.[32] The rules for such crucial information issues deserve a formal place in corporate procedure manuals, alongside the approved procedures for hiring personnel and spending the firm's capital.

Whatever its says in the rule book, *educating employees about information behavior* has to follow. Again, rather than mouthing platitudes, this only becomes a real tactic when managers make a concerted effort to do so. Educational activity in its simplest form involves teaching employees how to better find and use information. For example, one CIO at a large commercial bank considers it part of his organizational charter to improve the communications skills of employees. His department offers regular courses on communications skills, for students at all levels of the bank.

At a more advanced level, employee education might address information scanning (how to use libraries and databases), the need for fact-based management, and the use of competitive information. Such information-oriented skills can also be made a standard criterion in evaluating employee and managerial competencies.[33]

The trickiest aspect of institutionalizing information behavior management is that it raises the image of Big Brother and "thought control." Regardless of our individual political persuasions, most Americans are information libertarians—that is, we want freedom of thought, speech, and decision-making in the personal sphere. But in the corporate environment, the issue of controlling information behavior is more complicated, both ethically and politically. Employers presumably have some rights in this area. When IS managers, for example, are asked whether firms should monitor the content of e-mail messages sent at work, responses are almost evenly mixed.[34]

In pragmatic terms, total information freedom would be very expensive in the corporate environment. And whether individual professionals like it or not, there always have been plenty of restrictions on information behavior. Employees are often prohibited from disclosing information outside a firm, in either general or specific circumstances. In a more subtle way, most individuals are aware that their careers can prosper or suffer through appropriate or inappropriate information behaviors. Many times, however, the "rules" about appropriate use of information are entirely implicit and fall under the rubric of office politics.

Given the importance of information to firms' success, I also advocate the tactic of formally *raising the stickiest issues of information behavior management* with everyone. If employees are concerned about what constitutes appropriate information behavior, specific policies—or, at the very least, discussions of them—can be liberating rather than controlling. And on a larger level, such specific management approaches to information behavior can eventually yield a more open and trustworthy information culture.

Obviously, influencing information behavior and culture for the better is in its earliest stage. Only a few managers are even aware of the need to bring information behavior into the management portfolio. But nonmanagement is itself a form of management—a bad one, in information ecology terms. When individual employees must determine on their own how to identify, share, and otherwise behave toward information, it's unlikely they'll make the best use of what is undeniably an important competitive resource.

As I'll describe in the next chapter, one way to help employees do the right thing is to have an *information staff* in place that truly supports these efforts. Not just programmers and systems analysts, but information guides and content editors. Not just architectural blueprints—but human beings who'll patiently answer questions and lead people to the right sources.

Assessment Survey for Information Behavior and Culture

The greater the level of agreement with the statements below, the better an organization manages information behavior.

* My organization has clearly identified the types of information behaviors and overall information culture that it wishes to have.

* Employees are evaluated and rewarded on the basis of particular information behaviors— such as sharing or improving presentation.

* My organization has established and documented the information behaviors it wants to encourage.

* Training is provided to help develop desired information behaviors.

* We recruit and hire employees in part because of the way they currently (and potentially) handle information.

7

Information Staff

Systems personnel and researchers have
been looking at something they call
information, rather than
something that users call information.

Brenda Dervin, Ohio State University

The great secret of the computer revolution is that people now matter more to
information systems than ever—not less. People support information on computers by defining, analyzing, creating, maintaining, managing, and advising
on information resources. As any manager knows, without well-informed,
plain-speaking, *patient* information staff in place, a company's best-laid IT
plans will sink. The support structure of any information environment has to
focus on the people who add value to the information, particularly staff members like researchers, editors, guides, and other content interpreters. Ecologically oriented staff support structures therefore have the potential to deal with
information of any type, specifically targeting the unique needs of a business
organization.

Yet information professionals today are almost always synonymous with
technology experts. In terms of number, resources, and influence, technology
oriented staff have come to dominate the corporate landscape. While networks
of computers offer many benefits, they still can't think for us. Earlier enthusiastic hopes that IT could carry out higher-order information tasks—say, synthesis and interpretation—have faded. Computers by themselves are limited
to such relatively simple tasks as storing and retrieving, which means information must be supported by people.

In this chapter, I'll start by discussing the usual model for information support—a patched-together mix of the public library and computers—and later propose a new model that is based on the television industry. The library has been embedded in thinking about corporate information systems from the early days of paper-based records. But when information ecologists focus instead on the business value and uses of information, rather than on the technical tasks of storing and searching, the information staff of tomorrow will differ considerably from old-style librarians or IS analysts. These new information professionals will add value to information for users—and they'll carry out different tasks, such as pruning, providing context, enhancing style, and choosing the right presentation medium.

What's Wrong with Libraries?

Before the widespread use of computers, the corporate information environment most closely resembled a lending library. Files were kept on everything—customers, employees, divisions, products—and these files had to be stored for later retrieval. Many clerks would manually sort, label, and reshelve the files according to a consistent classification scheme. From time to time, someone would need to use the file, checking it out of the records department. Because the file often contained critical information needed by more than one person, its location was tightly controlled. (In some records departments today—patient records in health-care organizations, for example—the model still applies.)

In such an environment, information staff primarily focused on preservation of the information. This necessitated strict attention to processes for indexing, cataloguing, sorting, searching, and retrieving documents—all tasks that information technology can accomplish with greater speed than human clerks. Indeed, the library model of information management was merely augmented with the advent of the computer, not transformed. Despite the computer's ability to enable new forms of communication, develop new information sources, and decentralize the gathering and management of information, IT has largely been used to replicate the paper systems that preceded it. The "new" librarians became database administrators and mainframe computer operators. All information was centralized on a few machines, and access was, again, tightly controlled. Users could only get new information indirectly, through the assistance of a database programmer. And these computer-based librarians continued to focus on preserving information from damage.

Certainly, in the time of paper documents and limited information-processing capabilities, the library approach to information management made sense. Even today, some documents and files need to be treated in this manner. Key technical reports, trade secrets, insider financial information, employee records, and tax documents all represent information that must be carefully preserved and controlled.

The old library model had other strengths as well. For one thing, it emphasized human judgment and work, rather than techno-utopian visions of one giant computer "brain." The task of categorizing and arranging holdings within a library, for instance, is one that can only be done effectively by people. Libraries also provide staff to help users. In fact, a recent survey of managers to whom corporate libraries report found that one of the most important tasks of librarians is conducting searches.[1] Librarians have a place in a company's information staff, if only because their background—as compared to that of IS professionals and programmers—predisposes them toward face-to-face communication with users.

While the role of librarian may include information distribution, the discipline as a whole emphasizes information content. Librarians are more familiar with their holdings than are most other information professionals. They manage not only internal information resources, but also those that were obtained externally from the organization. Corporate librarians have begun to expand the scope of their work to include working more closely with business users and to provide competitive advantage with their services.[2]

Still, the vast majority of current information can no longer be profitably managed as if it were a library book. Information staff that envision themselves as essentially supporting a library, whether computer- or paper-based, end up ignoring or avoiding other important tasks. That's because:

Libraries are passive repositories of knowledge. Information comes in, and then doesn't go out until a user asks for it—a "pull" strategy for information distribution. While staff shouldn't "push" all information out to the user, they do need to make clear what information is available.

Librarians focus far too much on preservation. A sacred trust of any library or public archive is the preservation of the historical record for the benefit of future generations. But an unpleasant side effect of this focus is that librarians tend to view users as potential threats—thieves, vandals, or just awkward fools liable to spill coffee on valuable pages. One study of university librarians found they were more comfortable with tight control of their holdings, even if that meant scholars didn't get appropriate access.[3] The same is often true of corporate database administrators. These information "providers" will often go to great lengths to protect their information from outsiders (and some insiders), even at the cost of user access.

Libraries don't create or improve information. Instead they index, catalogue, and store information created by others; only rarely do they synthesize or restructure the information, since that task is left up to the user. But in an ecologically oriented environment, information staff must constantly create meaning out of the data that's acquired.

The library model typically assumes a physical repository. Librarians have long concerned themselves with how to display their collections attractively and efficiently. As one guide to managing "special," or corporate, libraries notes:

> Most special libraries have some customers to whom they circulate journals, but who never make personal visits to the library. In such cases, the circulation system undoubtedly saves the time of the reader, but all the advantages of display and exploitation of other stocks and services may be lost to the user who limits his use of library facilities to receipt of the circulated journal.

According to this library guide, the physical plant also improves protection of information holdings: "individual copies of journals may be entirely lost whilst on circulation, or they may be marked, illegally copied or mutilated before they are returned to the library."[4] However, information and xerographic technologies have made physical repositories somewhat obsolete. And few managers or employees in Western firms take advantage of library resources today, for many different reasons. The most obvious: nobody's got the time. A leisurely browse through the corporate library at lunchtime—for many, lunchtime itself—has faded into history. Even the rare few who still consider library time important enough to somehow wedge into their schedules are often reluctant to do so, for fear that being caught reading on the job could put a quick halt to a climb up the corporate ladder.

The Limits of Current Support Staff

Aside from corporate librarians, the people who support information technology are often referred to as the organization's information staff. Such technologists do have a role to play, but they aren't the only—or often most appropriate—staff members for supporting all of a company's information needs. In fact, when top management limits its view of information staff to IT professionals, they're cutting off all sorts of other, nontechnical ways to leverage information use. Before I get into what these nontechnical approaches might be, let's look at the usual roster of information staff.

Technical Staff

Despite all the money spent on technology, the people required to support IT often cost more than the equipment itself. The expertise and skills required to set up and manage even a simple system are extensive. Given that these IT people are such an expensive resource, they tend to dominate the corporate information environment—sometimes for the good, since even the most technical roles have information-oriented components. But more often than not, the technical focus of the various roles described below usually distracts everyone from the human aspects of information use.

Programmers. This job title may mean many things, but the common thread among programmers is their focus on software. Programmers adapt, maintain, enhance, or create computer software. In that role, they typically are responsible for the user interface to computerized information. A subset of programmers are database programmers, the folks who specialize in writing the specialized software that will search and retrieve data in databases. A database programmer usually works closely with database administrators (see below) to protect the data, while still providing specialized access for users.

Systems Analysts. This title also covers a wide array of positions, but systems analysts are usually concerned with design and analysis of computer systems on a more macro level than programmers or database administrators. Systems analysts are usually charged with making the entire system perform as expected, which includes responsibility for design, hardware selection, network selection and design, and oversight of programming. Typically, a systems analyst begins work as a programmer and then is promoted. Systems analysts do play a big part in supporting information, for better or worse, when they define requirements for a system. This phase usually defines (often quite indelibly) the information content and structure within the system. Only rarely, however, would a systems analyst attend to information requirements that don't involve a computer system.

Database Administrators. Large computer databases require more than just initial design and infusion of data. They must be maintained, protected, and, inevitably, adapted to new needs. These are all the tasks of database administrators, but their primary charge is always the preservation and protection of the data that has been entrusted to the database. Consequently, they are the gatekeepers—or "new librarians"—through which any changes to the database must pass.

Information Resource Managers. This role is to database administrators as systems analysts are to programmers. Information resource managers design the high-level structure of data within the organization and try to influence all technical support staff to respect the overall data architecture.

System and Network Administrators. These technical staff members handle day-to-day maintenance of the existing systems infrastructure. That means managing user access across the system, enabling user accounts, troubleshooting any problems, backing up data, warning users of potential problems, and informal user training. Though systems administrators have little to do with adding value to information itself, they have the most contact with users of any of the technical staff.

Other Information Workers

While technical staff are necessary for maintaining and implementing IT, few organizations have workers that are specifically charged with helping employees determine their information needs, particularly when the information is not on a computer. The "information provider" roles that do exist are currently organized along functional lines. Just as librarians are useful additions to any information staff, the various providers listed below have their place. But even if these managers handle all the information within their small slice of the world, they don't have the expertise or authority to manage information in the organization as a whole.

Management Accountants. These professionals spend most of their time explaining, detailing, and compiling information for the rest of the organization. The information they focus on usually relates in some way to financial performance, but may extend to other types of performance. Management accountants either support specific business projects or inform the organization about performance status and issues as an ongoing task. McKinnon and Bruns argue that this group is well-positioned to take on a broader information provision role within organizations, but today their expertise rarely encompasses nonfinancial information.[5]

Records Managers. This staff role first became established in the era of file-folder-based customer information and has grown now to include both paper-based and electronic records. Records managers focus on creating, storing, retrieving, and using records without the loss of any vital data within those records. From a cultural standpoint, these managers are particularly concerned with preserving information, and are therefore less likely to enhance effective use of current information.

Business, Market, or Financial Analysts. The corporate world is filled with analysts who are really information specialists. They may analyze information about the business itself, the market, cash flows, or any of a hundred other things. The common thread between all analysts, however, is that they assemble, analyze, and create information to support specific business decisions. These decisions may range from "Should we buy or rent our offices?" to "How should we price the shares of the Australian subsidiary?" to "What happens if we hire five new salespeople?"

Business analysts are quite common in some firms, such as investment banks, where they analyze and make recommendations about buying or selling securities or stock. However, in many industrial firms analysts aren't as common as they once were; they've been viewed as "overhead" or the province of corporate staff, and so have been pared back. Like other information providers, the analyst roles that still exist are often functionally structured, so the analyses they perform remain trapped within functional boundaries. In addition, business analysts typically work in an ad hoc fashion. They don't usually see themselves as helping to build information systems that will exist beyond them or the current problem they're solving. And they do little to build up or influence the information architecture of a firm.

Individual Managers and Workers. Every member of an organization who uses or modifies the information environment is also part of the support structure. This includes almost all managers, who both use the information system as customers, and communicate to other managers who see them as part of the information system.

As I made clear in the last chapter, every information worker's behavior can contribute to an effective approach to information management. Individuals must learn not only to get help from others but also to manage their own information environments effectively. To be sure, information support shouldn't just be "do it yourself"; but it also shouldn't be palmed off as someone else's responsibility. Well-managed information support groups will inform the organization how information providers can specifically help users; but they'll also make clear what tasks individuals have to handle for themselves.

Which sounds good in theory, even eminently rational. Realistically, however, making such a distinction in information support requires a certain level of training on everybody's part. The missing piece here, of course, is ensuring that individual workers have the appropriate skills to perform their individual tasks. Otherwise, how can we expect beleaguered, confused, and threatened workers to take on the right level of information responsibility? This question indicates where ecological managers might begin rethinking how information support staff can provide the right kind of help.

What Else Do We Need from Information Staff?

Over the last year or two, I've been conducting a very informal survey in executive education and MBA classes wherever I go. I ask students to list for me some of the characteristics that the ideal information support structure in an organization should have. Their answers aren't surprising; in one form or another, the characteristics they suggest are all things that managers and academic researchers have thought of before. What still surprises me, however, is how consistent these characteristics are across groups of both

MBA students and executives. Almost all of them say that the ideal information staff should have:

- a broad business understanding and knowledge of the organization's structure and function;
- knowledge about the diverse sources and uses of information in the organization;
- facility with information technology;
- political savvy as well as the ability to exercise leadership;
- strong interpersonal skills;
- a strong orientation toward overall business performance, rather than a narrow allegiance to internal functional goals.[6]

Given such consistent answers, why do so few information staffs, in practice, display little more than technical expertise? I asked these same MBAs and executives to rank the functions within organizations according to how well they met the ideal. The functions rank, on the average, as follows: marketing, strategic planning, management accountants, information services, and librarians. Ironically, that means those most responsible for an organization's information requirements are the least prepared for it.

Some real-life information support groups do meet most of these criteria. In particular, the Rapid Response Network within McKinsey and Company's Organizational Performance practice provides a good example of the desired traits, as I'll discuss in more detail in Chapter 9.[7] The group responds quickly to requests, using both technology and print resources. Its information providers understand the company 's consulting business well; in fact, some are former consultants. The Rapid Response Network synthesizes existing information sources and occasionally creates new information. These information staff members primarily focus on adding value, an orientation that is facilitated, in practical terms, through billing these costs to clients. If this group has any shortcoming, it's that staff concern themselves only with organizational consulting (although other such groups are also emerging at McKinsey). In formulating the ideal information support structure, there's always a trade-off between broad information coverage and having people on hand who know one set of topics particularly well.

Based on my consulting experience and research, one thing almost everybody wants is a single interface to a wide range of information sources and skills within the organization. Depending on its scope and the organization's size, the ideal information staff might include one person or several information professionals who specifically help users access everything from transaction data and computerized databases to external reference materials, to internal and external experts, to opportunities for networking both inside and outside the organization, to rumors or other "soft" information. Instead of the user having to track down, negotiate, and develop this network on her own, internal "customer" liaison staff would locate all of it, at least in a particular information domain.

Clearly, the ideal information staff not only passively accepts user requests but also actively develops information sources, channels, and programs for users who don't yet know they need the information. In a sense, ecological information professionals become evangelists, constantly attempting to recruit new members and provide new services to those members, even before they ask. They are familiar—but not obsessed—with key information technologies. Most important, such providers are highly responsive when users do ask for information, and understand its business context. In other words, their *raison d'être* is adding value to information.

Making Information Meaningful: The Primary Staff Goal

Unfortunately, few current information professionals even know what makes information meaningful, let alone specific ways they might add value to it. While there has been a great deal of research done on the value of IT investments, those studies only focus on evaluating the economic impact of computerized information.[8] Here I'll discuss what makes information itself valuable, not the value of particular information technology investments.

I'll confine myself, however, to the economic value of information in business organizations. Although some information is priceless ("The meaning of life is. . .") and some can't be quantified with a price tag ("I love you"), advice on how to add value to such intangibles can be found in other sources—say, the work of theologians, artists, therapists, and philosophers. Far be it from me to suggest that such sources have no relevance to business; but the words of prophets, poets, and priests are beyond this book's scope.

Back on the solid ground of business and economics, Richard Saul Wurman, a noted information designer, argues that data must be "imbued with form and applied to become meaningful" as information.[9] Imbuing and endowing information with meaning in this manner is the first part of adding value. And needless to say, only humans can do this effectively.

All information is not created equal; some types are more valuable than others. For example, while it's useful for a company to know that a competitor has made a competing bid on a contract, knowing the actual number in the bid is even more useful. Wurman defines information as that which "reduces uncertainty."[10] In other words, we primarily use information to make decisions and, one hopes, to succeed. This sort of definition is helpful to someone trying to calculate the purchase price of information, or to compare the value of one set of information to another. Of course, these calculations are still based on highly subjective criteria.

McKinnon and Bruns suggest a more process-oriented way of evaluating information.[11] They propose three characteristics that define the value of information to managers: timeliness, accuracy, and relevance. The first two certainly make sense; and we know information is relevant if it's useful to the manager who receives it. But what specific characteristics make information relevant? Managers faced with having to create "relevance" are right to be confused by this question.

In order to clarify just how information staff might better help confused users, I propose six characteristics that determine the value of information in business organizations: accuracy, timeliness, accessibility, engagement, applicability, and rarity.[12] Obviously, all of these characteristics are interrelated; they're part of information ecology's entire web of components, and can affect everything from strategy to politics. In the previous chapter on information behavior, I introduced engagement as the key to capturing user attention. But the ideal information support staff will pay attention to and manage all of these characteristics.

Accuracy

Information must be accurate to be perceived as valuable and to be used with confidence. At the most basic level, accuracy refers to the lack of simple errors in transcription, collection, or aggregation. This is a binary sort of accuracy; it's either right or wrong. But information staff should also consider other things that affect accuracy, such as resolution of measurements. Consider two trucking firms that use a global-positioning system to keep track of the location of their trucks. One firm only makes routine deliveries from one city to another, so it only needs to know three things about a truck: is it in route, at a stop, or at base? But the other trucking company, which takes many special orders, needs to know where its trucks are within a few miles so it can reroute them immediately as calls arrive.

In addition, no matter how accurate measurements and data are, if the manager who receives the information doesn't trust the source, then the data is of questionable accuracy—whatever information professionals may argue. For most managers, this kind of reliability is what matters most. McKinnon and Bruns point out that managers go to surprising lengths to develop multiple information channels to corroborate and build trust in the information they do have.[13] In general, information takes on such "cognitive authority"[14] in the same way that any relationship builds trust: by consistent, reliable performance over time. Support staff can therefore improve the accuracy of the information they provide by: (1) finding out from users what sources they value and trust; (2) regularly assessing the accuracy of key sources; and (3) instituting a data-quality program for key transaction data.[15]

Timeliness

In many instances, information must be up to date to be of any use at all. The definition of timeliness is very situation-specific. For strategic planning, information that is several years old can still be considered timely for plotting and predicting trends. For a production manager, however, production levels may have to be updated hourly to be useful. The need for timely information is one reason why so much is passed directly from person to person, whether it eventually appears in a computerized database or not. As McKinnon and Bruns observe,

> It is difficult to imagine that an accounting system could ever be the primary information system used by a manager. Accounting measurements and reporting take time, while things observed directly or communicated less formally provide a basis for instant evaluation and action.[16]

Managers are typically aggressive in seeking out timely sources of the information they deem critical. That means one of the most productive activities of an information staff is *not* to waste time developing formal systems—on computers or otherwise—that deliver information too slowly.

Accessibility

If the information is too difficult or time-consuming to obtain, it may not be worth the effort to use. In today's computerized environment, access usually refers to connectivity, or the ability of one computer to access data on another computer over a network. But connectivity only refers to physical access; it makes no guarantee that the actual end user of the information will get what he or she wants from the information. Much research on managerial information use suggests that accessibility—real accessibility—is a primary criterion in determining what information managers use.[17]

Certain forms of information are more cognitively accessible than others. Support staff might consider putting information in document form, or turning raw data into a narrative "story." At the very least, they can leave information that originally comes in these forms alone, rather than trying to restructure (and reduce) it for a computer-based system.[18] Access involves not only being able to get both your hands and your mind around information; an information system must be structured in such a way that you can understand it, and retrieve what you need from it, without having to work with piles of data you don't want. As Wurman points out, "accessibility is made possible by the discovery of a structure . . . unique to a specific subject that allows readers to find what interests them and feel no guilt about ignoring what does not."[19]

Engagement

Information, no matter how valuable it is otherwise, must be noticed to be useful. The information's impact is a measure of how it engages a potential user through its format, medium, presentation, or other means. As I emphasized in Chapter 6, how engaging information is has become increasingly important in an era of information overload.

Engagement is also the least generalizable characteristic of information. Each organization, even each employee, pays attention to different things. Information that's thoroughly engaging to one company may seem completely unremarkable at another. Good salespeople, for example, know they must tailor their presentations to their specific audience. They may be selling the same products with the same benefits and features, but they present the information differently for different customers. That means good information support staff may have to be salespeople as well as evangelists, thinking of clever ways to "sell" the right information to the right user.

Applicability

When information can be directly used to solve a business problem or support a business decision without extensive rearranging or further analysis, it is applicable—which obviously makes it relevant to the user, as well as valuable. For instance, in their study of managerial information habits, McKinnon and Bruns asked managers to describe a good report. Almost uniformly, these managers said good reports "relate directly to the managerial tasks of those receiving them." Unfortunately, no one who has worked in a large organization will be surprised by the managers in this study who also complained they routinely received stacks and stacks of reports that had nothing to do with the tasks they performed.

Certainly, the disorderly nature of managerial jobs and their consequent information needs doesn't make information applicability any easier. Shocking as this may seem to techno-utopians, management is simply not the kind of structured, contemplative work that relies on formal information systems.[20]

As Mintzberg points out, "The classical view says that the manager organizes, coordinates, plans, and controls; the facts suggest otherwise." Managers have broad goals, but rarely any detailed plans; instead, they rely on openings and opportunities—which means most managers rely on short, open-ended, face-to-face communications to create change.

Quite obviously, a formal executive information system is not going to provide applicable information for the typical manager. In order for support staff to improve the applicability of information, they need to focus on facilitating communication, the transmission of "soft" information,[21] and network-building throughout the organization and the external environment. Information requirements won't be determined in brief interviews or structured discussion, but rather through longer-term observation of day-to-day managerial behavior.

Rarity

Given that information often conveys power—and that information environments are inherently political—rarity may make all the difference to a given piece of information's value. Information theorists are fond of saying that information is a unique resource because it doesn't lose value if given to others. But while it's true that not all information has to be rare to be valuable, if the information can be obtained and used by others easily, then it may well have less value to me and my company. If I don't have some privileged access to or special skill in creating that information, then the advantage I gain from it is bound to be short-lived.

Here's where it pays for an organization's information staff to be politically astute. If rarity is an issue, then that places a premium on internally created information. In areas defined as critical by an information strategy, for example, staff members might create information from scratch in such a way that no other organization could get it. They might also restrict broad access to information that would lose its value once circulated.

New Tasks for Information Staff

Sounds good, you say. But how, exactly, does one change the characteristics of information and increase its value? Table 1 lists some of the tasks staff might perform—pruning, providing context, enhancing style, and choosing the right medium—and which of the six characteristics they affect. It's not exhaustive, but it does indicate which tasks will probably be critical in the future. In general, pruning has the greatest potential for adding value across the board;

Table 7-1. Key Information Tasks

	Tasks			
Attributes	Pruning	Context	Style	Medium
Accuracy	■			
Timeliness	■	■		
Accessibility	■	■	■	■
Engagement	■	■	■	■
Applicability	■	■		
Rarity	■			

improving information accessibility and engagement, on the other hand, might be the most useful focus for support staff.

Information Pruning

Information would be generally more useful if everyone who managed it wrote short stories for a hobby. The critical challenge for the short story writer is, of course, keeping it short. Every word must count and move the story along. G.K. Chesterton even coined a phrase for what writers must continually do: "murder their darlings." That is, even if the digression is smart, beautiful, and witty, it's still a digression and must be ruthlessly expunged, no matter how quirky or personally interesting. Similarly, information managers must relentlessly prune the obsolete, the irrelevant, and the inaccurate from key sources and media. To do so, of course, they must know the business environment and the objectives of their audience. They must also be empowered to act as *information editors*.

Information managers often seek to prune information in an automated fashion. This usually takes the form of date-oriented pruning: information older than a specified time period is deleted or trashed. But this is a particularly mindless approach to pruning, since some useful information must be kept available for years. Instead information editors must prune with an eye toward the quality of the information (very difficult to assess through automated means), the level of access thus far to it, and the centrality of the information to the purposes of the enterprise.

Pruning can be done at the beginning of an information life cycle as well as at the end. For example, in Ernst & Young's knowledge networks for its consulting practice, an editor responsible for each network constantly peruses unstructured knowledge bases, documents from client engagements, and internal seminars to decide what knowledge should go into the network's "official" knowledge base in Lotus Notes. The technology allows monitoring of document access, so those that aren't used after several months are removed and archived. Useful documents are kept on the system for as long as they remain in demand. Since the editors are consultants who rotate through these information staff positions, they have a good sense of what information will be useful to those in the field.

Adding Context to Information

Contextualizing information is a powerful way to increase both the interest of an audience and the audience's propensity to act on information in a certain way. Adding context usually involves detailing the source of the information, the comparative information available, and the previous history surrounding this information. Consider a monthly expense report sent to each departmental manager. Even if the data within that report are the same every month, staff can influence how much attention managers pay to it. Indeed, these managers might act very differently on that information if they knew whether their department was the only one over budget; the company's main competitor had fifteen percent higher expenses in the same department; or that for the last five years no one had ever referred to the expense report.

Including such comparative information lets managers know how they stand relative to some other group or standard. Knowing that sales are up tells us little; knowing that they are expanding twice as fast as the competitor's sales is quite useful. And if you have to tell the boss that sales are down, it helps if you can point out that the rest of the industry also had lower sales. On the other hand, benchmarking attempts to "raise the bar" beyond a competitor's performance to the best level currently existing anywhere. Therefore, support staff might add useful context through a number of comparisons— say, comparing performance with that of competitors, other divisions within the company, previously set goals, previous performance, and best practices/benchmarks.

Providing historical context for information usually includes a discussion of all the people that have affected current business dealings. That's why companies try to assign the same salesperson to the same customer over time. The personal relationship and trust they build certainly matters; but even more significant, the history of that relationship is stored in the salesperson's head. For example, a long-term salesperson will know how often this customer expects to be called, how much they'll complain about a late order, and whether they may be a contact for other business.

As any sales manager will attest, it's difficult to transfer such history from one salesperson's head to another. And maintaining the historical context of information has been severely threatened by the fluidity and mobility of today's work force. If the information is only in the heads of a few people, and they keep moving on or getting replaced, how can it be preserved? For precisely this reason, information professionals often fail to provide historical context. It can only be transferred to computer or paper with considerable effort by the person with the knowledge. While there's no single answer to this problem, managers might begin by recognizing its importance. And by identifying certain information support staff members as key "historians," especially in sales and other relationship-building areas, the organization may do a better job of maintaining a sense of history.

Most information gains context, of course, through voice-to-voice or face-to-face communication. Many researchers, including Mintzberg and McKinnon and Bruns, have found that most of the communicating managers do is face-to-face, or at least over the phone or other unstructured channels. Yet some organizations have made the mistake of trying to eradicate this sort of communication because it is "inefficient" or "unmanageable." Michael Hammer and James Champy's well-known book *Reengineering the Corporation* epitomizes this view by stating if "people in different parts of the organization have to telephone one another frequently or send a lot of memos or e-mail messages, that probably means a natural process has been inappropriately broken apart." Hammer and Champy also claim that "if people's cubicle walls and their computer screens are papered with Post-it notes reminding them to fix this or look into that, the processes in which they're involved are probably broken too."[22]

These are not symptoms of problems; they are a necessary part of any job with even a moderate level of complexity. The CEO of Intel, Andy Grove—widely regarded as an excellent manager of an excellent company—has office walls that are papered with Post-It notes. Managers who somehow eradicate this sort of behavior (and human nature being what it is, I'm not sure that's even possible) will only succeed in cutting off a vitally important source of information that can't be transmitted in any other way.

One reason to prefer messy Post-it notes and informal conversation over more "efficient" information transmission is that nobody is an automaton, particularly any employee doing a skilled job. Few of us are solely "information processors" at work, the equivalent of RoboCops who discuss only what's relevant to actual business decisions or the task at hand. Techno-utopians may dream of managers and support staff who operate mechanistically, but I've never seen anyone—whether in a reengineered corporation or not—who fits that description. As Guje Sevon and James March, two organizational behavior experts, point out, "The persistence and pervasiveness of idle talk makes it relevant not only to understanding everyday life but also in improving managerial behavior and to designing management information systems. Gossip cannot be easily ignored."[23]

Support staff would do well to remember, of course, that much of information's context is difficult to control. The communicator of information only creates one part of the context; the audience also brings its own. For example, the external cultural environment or the social background of the audience affects how any information is interpreted. The job of the information professional is to try to assess that context and tailor the information content accordingly. In today's era of diverse and globalized work forces, providing cultural and social context should not be overlooked.

Enhancing the Style of Information

The *New York Times, New York Post, Newsweek, Sports Illustrated*, and *National Enquirer* may all carry the same story, but the style in which they present it will engage very different audiences in different ways. Depending on how it's presented, information's style is defined by wording, facial expressions, emphasis, staging, and other communication choices. It can also be affected by the use of literary devices, such as analogies or metaphors. As journalists, artists, and politicians know, style can make information especially engaging by appealing emotionally to an audience. However, emotions are not supposed to play a part in the business realm. American businesspeople, in particular, like to think of themselves as making decisions that only require analytical and deductive reasoning. They don't want to believe they've been swayed or affected by their emotions. Yet while facts are important components of an information ecology, how managers use both head and heart to make sense of them is just as important.

Irrational or semi-rational decision-making happens every day in every organization. A large professional-services firm, for instance, had long planned to sell a particular business unit to its own managers. Much careful analysis had gone into the reasons for divesting the unit, the manner in which the sale would be accomplished, and the calculation of the selling price. The deal was to be closed on a Monday morning. The preceding Saturday, however, the CEO of the firm played golf with the CEO of a large company that had once employed the unit to be divested. The client CEO noted several times during the game that the unit had done good work for his company, and that the relationship with the subsidiary had aided the relationship with the parent. On Sunday, the professional service firm's CEO canceled the sale. He knew about all of the careful analyses, but selling off this perceived jewel just didn't feel right to him.

Fact-based decision-making has its uses, and I certainly don't mean to throw the baby out with the bathwater. But denying that people ever respond to information emotionally is useless, naive, and counter-productive. Many current information professionals, for example, resist improving the style of information because they assume style somehow interferes with the facts, or is a waste of time. This is only true if you don't care whether the facts are ever received or used. "I put the information out there, and it's easy to find if you want to," insisted a librarian I once interviewed. "It's not my job to put on a dog-and-pony show; we are all supposed to be professionals here."

Nothing could be further from the truth. Enhancing the style of information is one key to making it valuable. A compelling presentation commands respect for the information embodied; an off-putting one courts dismissal. In either case, style is very much at issue, because an inappropriate style can doom the most important information to the wastebasket—or the wrong emotional response. Just as a doctor would never crack a joke when informing parents their child is critically ill, information staff shouldn't anger nontechnical users with arrogant responses to questions or by proffering jargon-dense "support" files. It might help to view fact-based rationality as not a lack of style per se, but rather a particular style that appeals to a particular audience.

Enlightened information professionals don't hide behind one style for all occasions but will embrace various styles for specific situations and audiences. Support staff should consider the following approaches:

Variation. Vary styles consciously—a humorous memo for internal managers, a "slick" multimedia presentation for key customers—to indicate different attitudes and concerns about the same information. IBM managers realized, for instance, that when all information is presented via slick transparencies, the audience stops paying attention. The CEO of Bear Stearns, the successful brokerage company, wraps his executive messages in rambling philosophical letters to employees.

Interactivity. Make sure users have the option and chance to interact with the information. If every form of communication in your organization consists of passive messages—be they e-mail or paper memos that always end up in the circular file—much less relevant information will get through. At Union Pacific Railroad, information providers wanted to get train crews to access company information on train-based personal computers. The interactive hook they provided was to let users monitor and plan their pension and vacation balances on them. While on the computers, crews also ended up checking scheduling applications and even online policy manuals.

Staging. In presenting and packaging information, think beyond formal business surroundings such as conference rooms with overhead projectors. Depending on the topic, try a more creative or less formal "stage" (like a company picnic or a memo attached to an e-mail contest) that may better suit the information. At General Motors, for example, executives are most comfortable with three-dimensional visual information, perhaps because they are used to seeing models of new vehicle designs in this form. GM's information managers therefore attempt to make information as graphically appealing as possible. Once they even built a market model in Lego blocks to allow managers to walk into and touch the displayed information.

Dramatization. Heighten the emotional impact of information, rather than purposely subduing it. Ask an especially charismatic manager to present complicated numbers at a meeting—complete with notes and silly slides of his dog. Or have the art director create a compelling multimedia presentation to illustrate the latest reorganization. Obvious as this may sound, making certain information more noticeable—that is, dramatic—means it's much more likely to have a lasting impact.

Choosing the Right Medium for Information

Style is, of course, very much connected to the medium of presentation. Information support staff today have a wide range of options for the communication of information at their disposal:

- video display or conference
- teleconferencing
- overhead or slide-based presentations
- hard-copy reports
- e-mail
- face-to-face communications
- phone calls
- faxes
- snail mail: internal or external service

Aside from how (or whether) they appeal to the emotions or dramatize information, each of these media have different strengths and weaknesses, and are applicable in different situations. Fax and express mail, for example, presume time-dependence. Detailed budget reports would be well-suited to hard copy or even diskettes, while announcement of a new strategic direction may be more suitable for a full-color video.

Researchers in this area have tended to focus on the "richness" or "leanness" of various communications media. "Rich" media convey more information about the feelings of the participants. Face-to-face communications, for example, are rich; electronic mail is lean. Except it's not that simple. Several researchers have shown that rich, highly nuanced communications can take place in a lean medium like electronic mail.[24] The discussion of media richness also implies that a single communication will take place over a single medium. But some firms have discovered that multiple distribution channels are necessary for certain types of information. As I discussed in the last chapter, Symantec "over-communicated" the most important information through both verbal and written means.

Information support staffs need to bear in mind that neither providers nor users of information have a well-developed sense of what media are appropriate for what purpose. Some employees who do want to share a unit of information may need help in choosing how to do so. In my survey of thirty-five information managers in large organizations, only a quarter felt that employees in their firms had a good understanding of the technological options for information exchange, and only a fifth felt that employees had little or no difficulty selecting the appropriate technology for a particular situation. Helping those who possess information to select the appropriate medium for sharing it, then, is an important means of adding value.

Deciding between broadcast and narrowcast channels for information is also linked with the medium of presentation. Information professionals now have several broadcast choices, especially given the availability of computers and multimedia networks. In addition, computerized control of faxes, e-mail, and even telephone messages allow information staff to narrowcast a message to just one person. Excessive use of broadcast media to reach only a small audience not only wastes time, but also reduces the attentiveness of the audience to that broadcast channel. As in the fable "The Boy Who Cried Wolf," if an irrelevant memo is sent to a particular department enough times, then the employees in it may stop paying attention altogether to the memos.

As Shown on TV: A New Model for Information Staff

The notion that making meaning is an information professional's primary goal—not to mention the specific tasks of pruning, adding context, enhancing style, or choosing the right medium—represents a radical departure from the status quo. Tinkering with just a few of these value characteristics or tasks probably won't change the overall support structure much; indeed, some of them clearly conflict with the old library model of information support. That's why I believe information staffs need to adopt a new model, one based on the television industry, as well as new roles to perform some of the value-adding tasks described above.

A television network faces many challenges and performs many functions that information professionals should embrace. The TV model is high on customer orientation, high on innovation, and low on technological focus. Television executives, like business information professionals, continually wrestle with strategic and tactical information conundrums.[25]

Consider Coopers & Lybrand's Knowledge Network, the accounting company's main internal information service for knowledge of best practices. C&L's Network is a good example of the TV model in action, even down to the use of terminology. The Network was explicitly modeled after cable television, with several dozen different "channels" that broadcast information on the overall industry, C&L practices, and regional and country business trends. Each channel has several different "shows" sponsored by experts in the area. Each show runs for a week. "Talk shows" are discussion databases on a wide range of specific topics related to C&L's services. The Network's subscribers receive other types of programs tailored to their specific interests. And many viewers receive customized stock quotations on companies in which they are interested.

Andy Zimmerman, who manages the Knowledge Network, closely monitors ratings of its shows, programs, and the entire Network. In at least one area, tax information, C&L also sells program access to its clients. Internally, more than 7,000 professionals use the Network each week; more than three-quarters of C&L survey respondents had used it to prepare a proposal or answer a client question. Yet managers correctly view the technology that supports it as just an adjunct to the overall approach.[26]

While I agree with Newton Minow's 1970s comment that television is often a "vast wasteland," the industry has been fantastically successful in gaining viewers and changing their information behaviors. The average American watches between four and five hours of television per day. Perhaps that's the only statistic necessary to document the medium's success. In a nutshell, here's why I think the TV industry's approach to information provides a much more useful model than the old public library:

Television managers are obsessed with usage and users of their information. The TV industry lives and dies by two questions: how many people watch? Of those who do watch, how important an audience are they to advertisers? This is the industry that developed "PeopleMeters" to monitor how many people are in the room and whether they're facing the TV. If no one is watching, then advertising revenues go away. Television is all about building a loyal audience whose needs are met on your channels. TV executives must focus on the information their customers really want, not on what they say they want, or on what is good for them.

Content is critical on televsion. Television networks attract viewers by offering appealing content—and in general, the more emotional or dramatic, the better. In the US, the "big three" broadcast networks and PBS attempt to offer content that is of wide interest, while cable TV stations incorporate both broadcasting and narrowcasting: you can watch either ABC or the Artichoke Lovers Channel all through one medium. In addition, TV executives know they have more options than just creating their own original programming.

They can also buy old *Star Trek* and *Cheers* episodes; take over programs that aren't working on other networks; repackage other content like live opera performances or beauty pageants; or pay someone else to create new content. As a consequence, they have a much wider, more flexible, and more diverse set of options when scheduling programming for their channel.

The television industry hasn't let technology get in the way. The television industry employs a lot of slick high-tech, from morphed computer graphics to satellite feeds. Yet technology is not the primary focus of TV managers or consumers. The industry employs a mix of technology, some of it ancient (coaxial cable), some of it cutting-edge (fiber optics). And most consumers couldn't even tell you the brand of their set-top box. They don't care who makes the box or its microprocessor, only what is on the channel—and since that's what matters to advertisers, that's what matters to TV executives. There are, of course, companies attempting to turn set-top boxes into computers; this may have technical advantages, but it's unlikely to replace the current focus on content.

The TV business bundles its information effectively. On television, information comes in easily understood bundles of programs and channels. Programs last for a specified period of time and normally revolve around familiar characters and themes. The various channels of information have a consistent, clear, and publicized definition. Viewers know what to expect on various channels, and they typically get what they anticipate.

Television distributes through multiple means. In the early days, the airwaves were the only distribution mechanism. Now, however, you can receive a television station over the air, through cable, or through a satellite dish. The industry's goal is to get its programming to us through any means possible.

New Support Roles in the Television-Type Organization

Today's companies still need librarians, database administrators, LAN managers, and all of the other traditional information professionals currently running the networks. But in the future, these roles will be more easily outsourced, which will free up people to focus on information and content issues. Equifax, a leading credit bureau, already attributes a recent focus on doing more (and making more money) with its credit information to having outsourced commodity IT roles.[27] It has started a variety of new businesses, including giving point-of-purchase credit references for stores that want to issue new credit cards, and checking of physician and employee applicant credentials.

The new staff roles already emerging at companies like Equifax and Coopers & Lybrand mirror those necessary for running a successful TV network. For example:

Information Innovators. Like screenwriters, a support staff's creative "talent" will search for new information and new ways of presenting it. These providers may build new databases that support direct sales, or may provide a list of Internet hotspots that list clues to the financial status of competitors. Whatever their approach, their job is to help solve business problems through the effective use of information, or to open up new opportunities.

Content Editors. These folks start with information that has already been compiled, then adapt it for the audience who needs to use it. They will focus on making information meaningful through pruning, adding context, or any of the other new support staff tasks. Information providers who can take raw data or information and convert it into interesting and relevant programming for a specific audience are becoming increasingly necessary to company bottom lines. This is already occurring in the burgeoning CD-ROM industry, which frequently repackages old information in new ways.

Content Directors. These information managers will "direct" an ongoing series or genre of business "movies." They'll create, borrow, or repackage content in a particular domain of the organization, be it marketing or R&D. Like a film director, a content director is given a budget, a target audience, a "script," colleagues like information innovators and content editors, and responsibility for completing a project. He or she must build the script into a product the audience likes, under budget and on time.

Information Producers. These executives work with a particular part of the business to understand its information needs and to somehow meet them. Information producers have to sell their product to someone—generally, top management—and then assemble all the elements of the team to make it happen. They're the chief "rainmakers" of an information support staff, and like film producers, they have all the power, take all the risks, and should get most of the rewards. An information producer will build new channels for marketing or other areas, always keeping an eye on the overall strategic mission of the corporation. He or she is the person most likely to know, and work well with, all the other executives in the organization.

Chief Content Officer. This manager oversees the entire information environment of an organization. Like today's network executives, these managers will have responsibility for allocating information resources among producers and projects.[28] While there are now many CIOs who control, at least to some degree, IT in their organizations, there are very few who have dominion over all information content. As with the many changes required by information ecology, transforming the CIO into a CCO involves not only management pronouncements—or even active support—but day-to-day actions that demonstrate why effective use of information, not technology, solves business problems.

By this point in the chapter, it should be clear that this new model of information support will probably be resisted by both the powers-that-be and traditional information staff. Just trying to focus on information, rather than on technology, will be a difficult battle. And creating the support staff of the future presents a number of other management challenges. For one thing, cross-functionality is critical. So is the development of new staff roles, like editors and directors, that add value to information. Information consumers will also have to change how they manage, share, and work with information throughout the organization. Yet even in the face of such challenges, some corporations have been experimenting with more ecologically-oriented information support staffs. Take, for example, Hallmark.

Improving Information Access at Hallmark Cards

At Hallmark Cards, as at most organizations, managers want timely access to the right information. But all too often, that information resides in different areas of the business in multiple databases. Or the database containing a given piece of information is connected to a specific application supporting an operational function. Because such databases typically involve complex data structures, access is even further complicated; the requester needs access not only to the data but also to the algorithm creating it.

In light of these problems, the Hallmark management information systems organization worked with business areas to address the information problems of users. In March of 1991, these information support staffers launched an initiative called DIAL—Data Identification and Location. The objective of DIAL was to design a new process for timely information provision by facilitating access to the best data sources. The DIAL project team was composed of eight individuals, four from management information systems and four from the business areas of Finance, Research, and the Hallmark and Ambassador card divisions.

For the next four months, the DIAL team identified problems the different business areas had with data access, explored alternative approaches, and developed recommended solutions. The team realized fairly quickly the potential value of creating a new staff role—that of information translator or liaison—ideally located within each of the main business areas. Such a translator would bridge the gap between management information systems and users, and provide the organization with the ability to take better and more cost-effective advantage of the data already available. Various users had already made clear, in fact, that in order for data to be truly useful to them, it had to be interpreted according to the specific business context.

By the end of the DIAL project, the team recommended that senior information managers establish this new role, with the title of "information guide," in the four business areas. Six months later, their recommendation was accepted. The information guide role was officially adopted to serve within the business area as the primary point of contact for assistance in locating data (not information, unfortunately). This would begin with responsibility for determining where data resides and for identifying appropriate steps to access the data.

The guides met twice a week for the next two months to define their responsibilities further and to resolve issues they were encountering in gaining acceptance in the business areas they served. For example, potential users didn't understand their roles at first and the distinction between information guides and programmers or database analysts. Through these meetings, the group defined the role of the information guide as the single point of contact for data requests within the business area. They viewed their mission as consisting of four components:

- Support the user base: clarify user needs; assist users in locating and accessing data; educate users; and request security authorization.
- Identify strategic data opportunities: track the number of requests received for specific data items and make the most frequently requested data more accessible for users.
- Build the infrastructure: determine system, database, and network requirements necessary to support all guides and users.
- Monitor resource usage: keep track of the number of requests received and the users accessing master files and databases.

Ten information guides are currently at work within Hallmark. The guides are in the process of developing an "information map" through a tool called the "card catalogue" to help find where data sets are located. The card catalogue enables guides to cross-reference a variety of Hallmark information sources and databases through the use of keywords. They are also developing data-entry screens to add to, store within, and access the library. Ultimately, they hope to create an automated dictionary that will provide user friendly access by data element and category.

The role of the information guides has steadily grown in importance at Hallmark. Given the volume of information requests, the guides now realize a large part of their job is to identify training requirements for users on FOCUS (a database system) and other tools so that they can make their "customers" self-sufficient as soon as possible. There are also several libraries at Hallmark, but the guides view their job as getting access to corporate data on computers, not through library information.

In addition, the new position of "data manager"—or the most knowledgeable individual in a business area about a specific data item—now complements the guide role. The data managers outnumber information guides by a factor of ten, largely because they hold other jobs and are perceived to be doing information work in their spare time. Frequently, data requested by Hallmark workers crosses product lines and needs to be aggregated at a division level or broken out at product level. Data managers assist by developing a common definition agreed to and understood by all business-area users. Even a simple term like "card" can have various meanings when cards are a company's main business—does it refer to a card under development, one already approved for sale, or one already on sale?

Hallmark's innovative, yet still data-focused, approach to support staff indicates why information professionals need to create hybrid organizations that balance computers and human information providers. The ideal information support staff will look to the future more than to the past, engage users rather than transfer facts, make more money than it spends, and innovate more than it preserves. As the next chapter on *information processes* emphasizes, support staff will also be the ones to define just exactly who does what—and how a process might be improved—to prevent bottlenecks and breakdowns.

Assessment Survey for Information Staff

The greater the level of agreement with the statements below, the better an organization manages its information support staff.

✳ A specific group or groups within my organization is charged with managing information of all types.

✳ Our organization has a mechanism for coordinating the activities of groups that manage information.

✳ Information providers are taught, through a regular and consistent program, how to add value to information.

✳ At least one information staff member helps users assess their needs and access multiple types of information.

✳ Our organization has evaluated its information management structure within the past five years.

Information Management Processes

Our vast, unapplied deposits of corporate knowledge and
information have little power when they're tucked away in
reports, file drawers and databases. Organizations today do
not lack information. They lack the tools to get the right
information to the right people at the right time.

From the Electric Power Research Institute

I've spent much of the past decade telling managers that they should view
work as a process. Once you've thoroughly described a process such as order
management—including its various subprocesses or steps—you can then
improve it incrementally or change it radically. Information management is
no different; it is a structured set of work activities that comprise the way in
which companies capture, distribute, and use information and knowledge.
Viewing information management as a process may seem elementary; yet to
date, few organizations have taken such a systematic approach. More important, identifying all the steps in a given information process—all the resources
involved, all the people who affect each step, all the problems that arise—can
point the way to changes that really make a difference.

A process perspective meshes well with information ecology. Defining
information management as a process emphasizes both measurability and
improvement, which matches the ecological emphasis on description and evolution. Defining a process also typically involves naming somebody to "own"
it. Process management requires a process manager. When an executive takes
charge of information management, it sends a signal to the organization that
this is an important area to get right. A process manager can play a large part
in enforcing the cooperation needed among various parts of the organization.

And not only do processes have owners; they have an identified set of customers. As in other business areas, focusing on customer needs and satisfaction will make information management more effective.

Finally, a process orientation helps introduce a cross-functional approach—that is, the ability to draw on the methods, tools, and techniques of a variety of information-oriented functions in a company. As I discussed in the previous chapter on support staff, the groups involved in managing information within organizations are many and diverse. Yet only rarely do they cooperate in a cross-functional, integrated approach to information management, one of the keys to an effective information ecology.

There are two basic ways to look at information processes. First, we can discuss *the* process. For those just beginning to consider the distinct demands of information management, it's useful to identify the basic activities that generate such demands. When we take this view—and it's the one I'll follow in this chapter—we create a generic process model that applies to the many specific information processes within an organization.

Second, you can analyze more specific business processes that are particularly information-intensive. Processes like market research, IT management, financial reporting, and product configuration take place within the context of other business areas, but are primarily about information management. You could therefore illuminate the general topic of information management by focusing on these specific instances. But since studying more traditional processes depends heavily on the details of, say, the marketing or financial organization, I've chosen not to view the information management process from this angle.

For our purposes, I'll describe a generic information management process that has four steps: determining information requirements; capturing information; distributing information; and using information (see Figure 8-1).

Of course, it's also possible to define the information management process—or any process—in other ways or with a different number of steps.

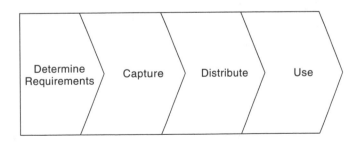

Figure 8-1. The Information Management Process

Standard Life Assurance came up with eight steps, which I list in Chapter 3. Or consider IBM's definition of its "Market Information Capture" process, which includes seven steps for information management:[1]

1. *Requirements management*. Matching users needing information with suppliers of information; obtaining the information requirements of the people who need the information; and getting mutual commitments from suppliers and users.
2. *Information asset plan*. Classifying the information up front—according to security level, how long it should be retained, and how it should be protected.
3. *Information systems plan* (optional). Planning for storage and dissemination of information (electronically or on paper).
4. *Acquisition*. Getting the information.
5. *Analysis*. Analyzing the content of the information to establish confidence level, reliability, and quality.
6. *Dissemination*. Distributing the information to those who need it.
7. *Feedback*. Asking receivers, via surveys, if the proper information was received and distributed in a timely fashion, and whether enough training was given to use the information.

Coming up with a generic process model for information management will always depend on a particular organization's interests, problems, or business. In IBM's case, the third step for an information systems plan appears because the company envisions offering and distributing electronically stored information via computer in an "Information Warehouse." Multimedia presentation of information would be available on workstations (including image, graphics, video, voice, text), and such an approach needs to be accounted for in their model.

Still, almost every information management process has to define an organization's information requirements in some fashion. This is the first of the four steps I'll discuss in detail below and perhaps the most important challenge confronting information managers.

Step 1: Determining Information Requirements

While a great deal of time and ink has been lavished on how companies should define their information needs, results have been underwhelming at best. In fact, most organizations have made little progress since the introduction of Critical Success Factors as a method in the early 1980s.[2] This method involves deduction of information requirements from the factors that "must go right" if the business is to perform well. But managers aren't always aware of the correct factors; and, in any case, how to translate "what must go right" into information needs isn't obvious. Even more disconcerting is the failure of formal information systems to adapt to users' needs in providing critical information.

Determining information requirements is a difficult problem, because it involves identifying how managers and workers make sense of their information environments. To understand the topic properly requires a variety of perspectives—political, psychological, cultural, strategic—and corresponding tools, such as individual and organizational assessments. Yet this information process step has been defined too narrowly and rationally in the past. Many have assumed that management is a straightforward process of defining a problem and finding information to solve it; that managers understand their requirements; that they gather only the information necessary to make a decision; that buying the right computers will solve all of an organization's information problems.

Here's how this step most commonly proceeds today: A third party, such as a vendor, consultant, or systems analyst, goes to managers and asks them either what information they need, or what their "critical success factors" are and what information is required to monitor each factor. Some of these third-party folks do employ more subtle means of eliciting what they want to know. For example, an IT consultant might ask a manager, "When you return from a two-week business trip, what information do you seek out first?" Even so, in order for this all to work, the manager must already be astute about her information requirements, or at least well aware of the general factors that drive the business.

In any case, decades of managerial research have shown that determining information requirements is much more ambiguous and complex than that. Mintzberg has argued since the 1970s that formal information systems don't serve managers well, because of characteristics of the systems themselves, the nature of the organizations in which managers work, and the nature of the managerial (indeed, the human) brain.[3] Other researchers have also found that managers often gather information for symbolic purposes; that they care as much about "gossip" as they do about formally required information; and that there's often only a tenuous link between the information gathered and the decisions supposedly based on it.[4]

It sounds like Step 1 of this process is the most subjective of activities, and that it's impossible for any third party to understand what information a manager truly needs. Yet some more recent studies suggest just the opposite: that managers in different business situations have highly predictable information requirements.[5] Some might even argue that asking information managers what they need usually comes far too late in the process. As Peter Drucker notes:

> In the West, all the emphasis is on the *answer* to the question. Indeed, our books on decision making try to develop systematic approaches to giving an answer. To the Japanese, however, the important element in decision making is *defining the question*. The important and critical steps are to decide whether there is a need for a decision and what the decision is about. And it is in that step that the Japanese aim at attaining consensus. Indeed, it is that step that, to the Japanese, is the essence of the decision.[6]

According to this argument, the real issue is not identifying management information needs but making sense of the business world. Drucker and others, such as Karl Weick, a distinguished and thoughtful researcher of organizational behavior, believe that a great deal of "sensemaking" has to take place before the problem is adequately defined.[7] We've all heard about Japanese firms that budget a much higher fraction of product and system development time for determining information requirements; in many cases, there's apparently a real payoff, since these firms then spend less time on design changes.

All of these approaches to dealing with information requirements appeal to me. For one thing, it's clear that information managers should focus on defining the problem and current situation, acting as descriptive "naturalists" in an information ecology. "Sensemaking" should be undertaken early in the information-requirements cycle, and should include considerable debate about what the problem really is and how it might be framed. Of course, deliberation and sensemaking shouldn't simply mask inactivity and lack of creativity. But Joint Application Design sessions, a method for determining information requirements that essentially locks users and suppliers in a room with a facilitator, are an example of such a useful debate when they move beyond just the design of computer systems.

In addition, information analysts should play a key role in defining information requirements, a role that hasn't traditionally been expected of them. To begin defining information requirements, these analysts need to "shadow" managers, day in, day out, in order to understand managerial tasks and information needs from the ground up. Based on such observations, the new analyst will be knowledgable about soft information as well as hard, formal as well as informal, noncomputerized as well as computerized. You may recall that at Standard Life Assurance, the UK company I discussed in Chapter 3, that information managers interviewed senior executives to understand how they used competitor information. Documents, these managers found, were less effective for informing executives than face-to-face briefings. They also identified a need for synthesizing information on competitors, which had previously been gathered separately by each function.

Ecologically minded managers should make a real effort to define useful soft information. Computerized systems naturally incorporate hard financial statistics, operational performance data, and other quantitative or highly structured information, but as Mintzberg points out:

1. Hard information is often limited in scope, lacking richness and often failing to encompass important noneconomic and nonquantitative factors....
2. Much hard information is too aggregated for effective use in strategy making....
3. Much hard information arrives too late to be of use in strategy making....
4. Finally, a surprising amount of hard information is unreliable.[8]

In fact, soft information—everything from news to ideas to gossip and rumors to best practices—supplies the context and richness that makes hard information more valuable. As I emphasized in the previous chapter, making information meaningful (not maintaining computers and networks) should be the primary goal of a company's information support staff.

Effective information systems also call for "requisite variety," a term borrowed from cybernetics research. The idea here is that an information system's sources should be as varied and complex as the environment the system seeks to represent. Indeed, many managers already wrestle with the continuous tension between identifying immediate business requirements to drive system development and the tendency for change in the business to make those requirements obsolete. The requirements we highlight today won't sufficiently provide solutions over the long haul.

The crucial need for variety in an information system can help us understand why there are so many *ad hoc*, idiosyncratic requirements for information in a large organization, such as those generated by senior executives and managers involved in marketing, strategy, or competitive analysis.[9] In order for an information-management-process model to have any real value, it has to reflect the turbulence, volatility, and complexity of markets, workplaces, and the human mind.

One greeting card company has done a standout job of defining its information requirements. The treasurer's office at this company, which kept track of the firm's investments, determined that it needed a real-time system to capture and deliver key information about events that could potentially impact the firm's portfolio. At the outset, however, a team created to address the need raised basic questions: what constitutes key information, for example, and how should boundaries be drawn around it? And from what sources should key information be derived? No sooner were the questions posed than users began to squabble over the answers given by management.

One executive argued, for example, that information on world politics and governmental stability from Henry Kissinger's consulting firm should be sent to all managers; others believed the information was both too expensive and too far removed from the day-to-day value of the portfolio. The nay-sayers won in this case, thanks largely to cost and copyright issues. At the same time, top managers could tell that the system's potential users—senior executives and mid-level financial analysts—and the company's systems planning department were not even close to understanding each other.

To resolve the situation, the CFO added consultants, system planners, users, and internal information specialists to the original design team; he told them to reach consensus on information requirements and then to build a system to meet the agreed-on specs. After an initial failure with the critical success factors method, the team adopted what it called a "soft systems" approach to development: one that accounted for the various "world views" of users and incorporated their perspectives into the system—not simply as input, but as an element of systems design. Soft systems analysis maintains a connection between information requirements and those who need the information throughout the design process. By melding both hard and soft information—daily updates from world financial markets as well as the text-based comments of country managers—the team came up with a rich picture of the systems environment, and has also created a system capable of dealing with *ad hoc* requests and imprecise information.

Step 2: Capturing Information

Once managers have defined the necessary information for a process, they have to get their collective hands on it. Although this is the obvious next step in any information management process, capturing information is really an ongoing activity, not something that can be dispatched once and for all. Therefore, the most effective processes explicitly incorporate a system for continuous acquisition. This step consists of several different activities—scanning the information environment; categorizing the information into a relevant structure; and information formatting and packaging—which I'll describe separately below. Again, these activities aren't necessarily sequential; for example, scanning should be done according to predefined categories, but may end up suggesting new categories as well.

Scanning Information

Effective information scanning—a critical part of any information management process—relies on a combination of automated and human approaches. Automated search systems have become increasingly sophisticated; just consider the new search engines that seem to blossom every week on the World Wide Web. And customized systems in various organizations promise to construct personalized newspapers based on predefined categories of information interest.

Some organizations have made electronic scanning and distribution the hallmark of their information strategy. At Chase Manhattan Bank, for example, CIO Craig Goldman announced that he intended to "put information intermediaries out of business." By filtering information and selecting what to pass along, he said, he was convinced such intermediaries, both inside and outside the bank, were doing the overall organization more harm than good. In their place, he wanted a delivery system that could provide all relevant information and news alerts directly to bankers.

This turned out to be a taller order than even Goldman envisioned. While a new electronic system was the immediate goal, like so many initiatives that affect an entire information ecology, this one also had to account for human factors. The strategy called for massive integration of internal and external data, the participation of a wide variety of information service vendors, and a first-time attempt at a team-development approach —any one of which, alone, would have presented a daunting challenge.

But the system ultimately delivered in 1994, called CIX (for Chase Information Xchange) was worth the effort. Aware that some resistance to the new technology was inevitable, Goldman believed that "if I have to have my bankers press more than two keys, the system will not work." The bankers who now use CIX, which is based on Lotus Notes, e-mail, and search tools, have already found it to be exceptionally valuable. Within a single application, they're able to get information and communicate it to colleagues within the bank; the system also features automatic storage and retrieval.

In many other companies, librarians are the information scanners, backed by an effective use of information technology. Toshiba's libraries, for example, excel at both scanning and distribution.[10] In 1984, the Japanese electronics company merged three R&D libraries, focusing their activities on information capture and delivery. The firm's explicit emphasis on "environmental scanning" is now designed to identify information valuable to senior management. The actual work is performed by a team of fourteen information professionals—systems developers, librarians, network specialists, and managers—who collaborate to synthesize the information into a single concise report. This combined support staff carries out twenty-four-hour scanning of all major news wires and broadcast media, as well as every important industry and business publication. From this base, librarians and managers create a daily report that is disseminated among 600 high-level users throughout the organization. Later, relevant journal articles, government reports, and other valuable documents are indexed on this system, organized by subject, and archived on laser disc on the company LAN.

When my colleague Larry Prusak visited Toshiba on the day an IBM/Apple alliance was announced, he saw the value of this combined human-electronic scanning approach firsthand. The information team quickly acquired all the public announcements about this key industry development and proceeded to analyze quotes, reportage, and other media discussions. They then selected the materials that best illuminated the meaning of the IBM/Apple story for Toshiba, and distributed these to the right people.

The Toshiba process is aided by features that eliminate "noise" in information capture—repetitive appearances of wire service stories, for instance—and perform automatic English language translations. It's also continuous, with librarians and editors working in shifts around the clock to produce about thirty stories a day. These stories are widely read, in part because they are kept brief: the day's leading story is typically two pages long.

No one pretends that this is an inexpensive operation; although the technology used is not extensive, buying so much external information, then scanning and formatting it, can be tremendously costly. When asked how they justified the costs of such an extensive scanning system, however, Toshiba managers expressed surprise: "It's like heating the building," one high-ranking executive said. "We have to have this."

Electronic scanning typically adds little value to information other than filtering. Human analysts, such as Toshiba's librarians and managers, are the real key to scanning; they can add context, interpretation, comparisons, local implications, and many other types of value—all of the characteristics I detailed in the previous chapter on the ideal support staff. Information intermediaries, which Chase Manhattan's CIO dismissed as creating more problems than they solve, are considered invaluable at Toshiba. There, information providers believe any important event generates a profusion of stories. While Chase Manhattan's CIX system seems to do a good scanning job, once again, Japanese managers may have a better overall grasp of information ecology. Toshiba's top management, as well as its innovative support staff, knows it takes time, experience, and editorial judgment to pick and choose the most effective business stories.

Too often at American companies, information scanning isn't really considered part of the support staff's job; it's just supposed to "happen"—and though it sometimes happens, managers often don't end up with the information they need, particularly if it's ad hoc, unstructured, and humanly "soft." In general, organizations derive information from three sources:

- *outside expertise:* published materials or other formal sources like conference presentations;
- *cognitive authorities:* individuals or institutions that have gained credibility in a given field—for example, the information and data analysis empires that have arisen over the past decade;
- *inside scuttlebutt:* your own organization's grapevine.

The latter category is the most controversial and problematic for traditional information scanners. Some, especially IT empire builders, reject it out of hand as an inaccurate source. But as Mintzberg rightly points out, hard information is also frequently inaccurate. Firms should obviously take care to avoid legally problematic soft information like personal slander or speculations that would be admissible in court. Yet scuttlebutt can also be a useful source, especially once support staff focus on making information meaningful. Here's where formally acknowledging the role of a good information editor can make scuttlebutt valuable rather than a liability.

The very best scanning environment, of course, is one in which everyone does scanning and then shares captured information with others. No matter how much value a Toshiba research library adds to information, no centralized scanning group can ever compete with an entire organization of scanners. Drucker has noted, "People will have to learn to take information responsibility both for what they need and for what they owe."[11] Effective scanning is yet another example of desirable information behavior. It's quite possible that a Japanese company like Toshiba, which explicitly incorporates scanning support teams, may also foster a better information culture; yet effective scanning, on both an individual and organizational level, isn't only a Japanese phenomenon.

At Choice Hotels, CEO Robert Hazard keeps a box on "lodging trends" in his desk. Each day he scans relevant sources and makes notes on index cards, which he reviews after work and eventually puts in the box. He also clips and files relevant articles. According to one writer, "He and his team of executives constantly fire articles of interest back and forth with accompanying notes: 'Hey, Jerry, did you see this? How does it relate to your area?'"[12] Such informal scanning and sharing—the strength of American business style, if you will—should become more pervasive everywhere.

Categorizing Information

When we create categories, we structure the "blooming, buzzing confusion" of information. Cognitive scientist George Lakoff notes that categorization "is not to be taken lightly. There is nothing more basic than categorization to our thought, perception, action, and speech."[13]

Yet while creating the right categories for information definitely affects how well it's captured, traditional information managers have a tough time with this activity. Categories are always arbitrary, although some are more useful than others; you might sat they should be "MECE"—"mutually exclusive, collectively exhaustive." But even if technologists insist their approach to categorization is objective or rational, categorization schemes are never value-neutral; they advance one view of the world at the expense of another, whether it's techno-utopian, political, or cultural.

Ecologically minded managers, whether they like it or not, know how hard it is to predict what categories of information will be useful for a business. Even when they choose the right categories, their usefulness is often brief; the information environment they attempt to structure changes quickly. I've already noted that the more an organization knows about a topic, the greater difficulty it has in agreeing on category names and their meanings. Take the Internet's Usenet, which categorizes all information under the bizarre headings of computing, science, recreation, news, society, talk, miscellaneous, and alternative.[14] The scheme may have been appropriate for the interests of Usenet's initial users, but it's now quite skewed.

Categorization remains a quintessentially human activity. People define initial categorization schemes, mediate between others with differing views, monitor the capture process for evidence that new categories are needed, and finally update the categorization scheme at frequent intervals. Like scanning, to do it well is a labor-intensive process.

Teltech, a small company in Minneapolis, devotes substantial attention to categorization. The company's "knowledge engineers" are always refining its categorization scheme—called a "thesaurus"—by observing the behaviors of users and adding new terms or synonyms when necessary. (I present Teltech's approach in detail in the next chapter.) McKinsey also devotes considerable attention to categorization. The consulting firm has developed a set of "knowledge categories" and a thesaurus that help to structure the firm's databases, expertise directories, and collections of client documents.

In order to make appropriate decisions about how information is categorized and stored, managers must begin with some basic questions:

- What business function will be advanced by the proposed categorization/storage scheme?

- What individual information behavior will be optimized by a given categorization scheme and storage mechanism?
- What information is to be categorized, and does it have any structure that lends itself to a natural categorization?
- Can the organization "borrow" an existing categorization scheme (SIC codes, the Dewey Decimal System) without substantial damage to the information management objective?
- How will the categorization scheme be maintained and updated over time?

As these questions indicate, categorization is connected to many components in an information ecology: strategy, politics, behavior, support staff, architecture. But a process approach is useful here, precisely because it helps tease out the many different elements involved.

Formatting and Packaging Information

According to Edward Tufte, what you see is *always* what you get. Tufte, a multidisciplinary scholar who has made the visual representation of information his life's work, believes that the packaging of information determines how much it's accepted and used. "Visually attractive graphics...gather their power from content and interpretations beyond the immediate display of some numbers," says Tufte. "The best graphics are about the useful and important, about life and death, about the universe. Beautiful graphics do not traffic with the trivial."[15]

Packaging goes on every day in the information business. Because of their appealing style and concise presentation, I reach for *The New York Times* or *The Wall Street Journal* to find out what's contained in the government's latest population study rather than slogging through the study itself. A conference with a doctor, who provides appropriate context and (we hope) a reassuring emotional tone, tells you a lot more than you'd probably glean from looking at the X rays of your damaged knee. Even lawyers, long infamous for burying arcane information in obscure language, are quickly catching on to the idea that more clients are to be made and kept by delivering information in understandable packages and formats.

In Chapter 7, I detailed the ways information support staff can help make information meaningful, such as providing context, enhancing style, and choosing the right medium—or package. When considering packaging as part of the information management process, analysts can also recommend whether information should be bundled with other products and services. For each class of information user, providers should ensure that the bundle of information, products, and services accompanying the whole package will most effectively meet the information need. For that reason, information companies are beginning to offer services along with information; firms like Dun & Bradstreet and Dialog are exploring the sale of consulting, systems integration, and overall information management services. Teltech offers database services that are assisted by a "knowledge analyst"; the customer (at a remote site) and the analyst can jointly view a search on the computer screen and widen, narrow, or recast the search after seeing initial results.

Documents are one of the most obvious and useful ways to package information. "Information" is a bit of an abstraction, one that doesn't resonate with many managers. Ask them what information they use and need, and they'll stare blankly. Managers know what documents they use, however, and which ones they value and like. Documents have structure and context, and they exclude enough information so that what remains is digestible. Focusing on what documents an organization needs to manage often leads to a much more fruitful discussion than looking more broadly at information requirements. One of the reasons Xerox calls itself "The Document Company," in fact, is that top management believes documents will become a much more important information unit in the future.

A company's existing documents don't always have the right format, however. Packaging information became a major issue at NYNEX, the regional telecommunications firm, where the Information Resource Center (IRC) produced a thirty-to forty-page daily report called Telecommunications Alert. This print document reproduced news stories of perceived relevance to the firm. The Alert drew on a vast resource base and was widely distributed throughout NYNEX's New York headquarters. But after an extensive review of the IRC's operations, outside consultants found users didn't care much about this ostensibly useful document.

While the user group as a whole voiced interest in receiving articles on a wide range of topics, their actual behavior suggested otherwise. Most wanted their news in more individually targeted units, rather than an aggregate product for everyone. What they were actually doing, it turned out, was ripping out the one or two stories that piqued their interest or related to their area and discarding the rest. Even for those executives whose interests covered an exceptionally broad range, the volume of stories was overwhelming. They were simply unable to read or absorb more than a fraction of the Alert's information, because they didn't have the time or ability to place such a wealth of material in any sensible context.

In this case, the company's emphasis on scanning information wasn't paying off. Unlike the librarians at Toshiba, who apparently do quite a bit of condensing, enhancing, and contextualizing of the stories they disseminate widely, NYNEX's information support staff weren't taking enough of an editorial role to make such an expensive system useful. As a result, the IRC's managers decided to change the news delivery function. NYNEX now has an editorial staff that adds value to external information, and the stories are sent individually (via e-mail) to the subscribers who request them by topic. Perhaps the greatest test of this service will be whether it survives NYNEX's planned merger with Bell Atlantic.

Meanwhile, at Dean Witter, efficient and effective document access is a critical for the company; like most brokerage and banking firms, its professionals make heavy and repeated use of documents obtained from an internal central library. Up until 1992, however, the documents were managed individually, and there was no means of on-line access.

To remedy the situation, the company's senior administrative executive chartered a team of systems, library, and administration officials to create a new system. The team started by identifying certain "core documents" that had to be easily accessible. Like good information ecologists, they also determined what tools were necessary to index and store information, what additional resources would be required, and what political barriers would have to be overcome. In 1993 the firm had a CD-ROM "perfect information platter"— a collection of all core documents— made, which is updated monthly and kept on a local area network server. Dean Witter was able to substantially reduce its library staff while greatly increasing broker satisfaction.

Step 3: Distributing Information

As the discussion of information capture indicates, distribution is the next necessary step in the process, one that's very much connected with how information is packaged. Every company is replete with information that could be invaluable to the firm's managers. But few, if any, of the people who need it know where it is or how to get it. The information often isn't in one place, but in diverse locations throughout the company, some as obvious as the shelves of the corporate library, others as obscure as the anecdotal memory of a bashful employee.

The distribution step involves connecting managers and employees with the information they need. If other steps in the process are working, then distribution is more effective: defining an organization's information requirements helps increase awareness of what information is available; the right format makes it easier to distribute. Other components of information ecology also affect distribution, to wit:

- an effective *information architecture* guides information seekers to what they need;

- certain types of *political structures*—like federalism—make distribution across functions and units more feasible;
- a firm's *technology investment* directly affects distribution.

Perhaps the most high-level, general decision managers need to make is what distribution strategy to employ. Will information be pushed to or pulled by its users? A push strategy is typical; some central provider decides what information is to be distributed to whom, "pushing" it out to their desktop—sometimes electronically, more frequently on paper. The best argument for this strategy is that people don't know what they don't know.

A pull strategy, on the other hand, assumes users are the best judges of what they need, and also that information is best distributed at the time of actual need. In order to pull the right information, users must be motivated to seek and retrieve it; they can't be passive receivers of information someone else deems important. Corporate libraries are generally unsuccessful examples of a pull strategy—so much to read, so little time—but new technologies like the World Wide Web, which allow easy document storage and retrieval on individual desktops, have made pulling information more feasible.

Hewlett-Packard, for instance, has explicitly adopted a pull strategy for information distribution.[16] The company's corporate information systems group has developed an electronic document management system that incorporates such information as the corporate personnel directory, policy manuals, and competitive intelligence information. The information is downloaded to local servers every night. The corporate librarians at HP have assisted in indexing the information. Document usage is also measured by librarians and the departments that "own" the documents in order to determine how long to keep them in the repository. An initiative is underway to convert the system to a World Wide Web–based approach, because the Web is not only easier to use but also corresponds to how HP personnel already access external information.

Of course, many firms adopt combinations of push-and-pull distribution. They push some information on users, and allow other types to be pulled. The most logical information to push out is maps and guides to information that allow other sources to be identified and pulled. This lets people find out what they don't know; then they can pursue only the information in which they're particularly interested.

Defining the distribution step of the information management process can also help clarify which of many information media is most appropriate. Over the past several years I've asked management and executive groups in informal meetings whether they get their critical information from computer systems. Rarely do they say yes—even IS executives. In fact, a survey of corporate managers found that CIOs were the least likely to get the information they really needed from a computer.[17]

Information professionals often describe computer distribution of information as the most timely. Certainly, once it's entered into a computer, information can move across networks at a rapid clip. And computers distribute certain types of information extremely well, including information that is highly structured, updated frequently, needs to be sent to multiple sites at once, distributed to far-flung geographic locations, or kept in an electronic repository for pull by users. However, getting information on the computer in the first place is the real issue. McKinnon and Bruns, in their study of information use at manufacturing firms, found that managers often don't rely heavily on computerized information because it's relatively slow to portray performance results. If a manager wants to find out, for example, what happened on the third shift, he'll usually call or seek out the shift supervisor rather than checking the computer.

Like so many aspects of information ecology, the best distribution systems for information are often hybrids of people, documents, and computers. McKinsey's Rapid Response Network is an excellent hybrid model. One of the company's consulting practices helps clients with issues of organizational structure, change, and effectiveness. The leaders of this practice decided that a key aspect of its success involved distribution of information and knowledge from McKinsey's previous engagements and from external sources. These managers created the Rapid Response Network (RRN), which was set up in 1991. (I participated in this practice while working at McKinsey, but left shortly before the Network was created.)

The RRN consists of a small core group of consultants and librarians; a network of consultants willing to offer advice remotely; and a computer database of practice documents and other useful information. Consultants seeking organizationally oriented information call the RRN's core group, which then takes the request, interprets it, and puts the resulting information into the right format. Documents are sent either electronically or by courier to the requester, who may also be referred to an on-call consultant for further discussion. McKinsey's Rapid Response Network is committed to responding to any request for information within one day. The RRN also works to identify its "key documents" so as to cut down on the volume of information maintained. This very successful approach to electronic distribution would not succeed if either its human or its technological elements were missing.

The Electric Power Research Institute (EPRI), a California-based research center funded by electric utility companies around the US, has implemented another successful distribution system. EPRI's work was of little value to its sponsors when those sponsors couldn't easily access it. To address this problem, EPRI managers decided to build EPRINet, an electronic repository and dissemination system. The network is now used heavily by sponsors in searching for and retrieving documents.

EPRI's situation also points to the other key distribution issue: to whom information should be distributed. Many managers assume that the most important direction of information dissemination is always up—to senior managers. Yet senior managers may not be able to act on specific information, and the person who really needs those numbers or that competitive intelligence may be much lower in the organizational hierarchy. Many firms are discovering that their "executive information systems" should really be called "everyone's information system."

This is particularly true for information about the performance of business processes. In a study of the management of business process information, Mike Beers and I found that even firms that lead in process quality and management sometimes distribute information to the wrong place.[18] Within the IBM field service organization, for instance, managers have long had a process orientation and paid attention to measurement. Initially, however, support staff aggregated information and reported trends only to senior management. While field service managers found the information valuable, they weren't the ones who could act on it directly by resolving process difficulties, such as service calls that didn't solve the customer's problem. Not until handheld computers used by service technicians were programmed to require greater levels of detail on process performance and problems—*and* the information was redirected back to the service front line—did these reports really improve service performance.

At the Ritz-Carlton hotels (a firm that, like IBM, has won the Baldrige Quality Award), daily performance information on 720 processes is collected centrally, but is quickly disseminated out to the workers and process managers who can act on the information. The information is also used for performance evaluation of individual workers. At Ritz-Carlton and in most of the other firms Mike Beers and I studied, top executives decided that process managers only needed aggregated performance information.

At AT&T Universal Card, another Baldrige winner, each of 123 process performance measures are collected and analyzed daily, at the individual and organizational level. While this is a large number of measures, most of them are collected not for purposes of aggregation at headquarters, but for use and analysis by those who perform the daily work processes of the company. All of the process performance information is available on-line through a system called U-KNOW. All Universal Card employees can determine how their teams are doing on daily process performance by pressing a few keys on any workstation in the company.

In general, organizations have a variety of stakeholders to whom information needs to be distributed: investors, regulators, customers, and members of the communities in which they are located. This has always been true for companies, but new situations and technologies now require new decisions about how much to communicate. Many firms, for example, are currently wrestling with the issue of how much information to disclose to investors, investment analysts, and the press. Some recent research and policy has suggested that both companies and investors would be better served by the disclosure of more information, particularly nonfinancial information.[19]

Indeed, organizational learning occurs not only through capturing information, but from distributing it to others. At venues in which information is exchanged, it's usually necessary to give information to get it. Many firms are concerned about giving away information, but companies that hold back may also not receive much information in return.[20]

Step 4: Using Information

The information management policies of many organizations are reminiscent of our approach to disease. We spend enormous resources to develop new, high-tech medications, yet patients frequently don't take or complete their prescriptions. Like medicine that is never taken, information is no good until and unless it's used. The use of information is clearly the final step of any information management process; but even researchers and managers with a process orientation have largely ignored it.

Market research is the only exception. The Marketing Science Institute, an association of researchers and practitioners, has put "improving the utilization of marketing information" at the top of its list of "10 research priorities for the 1990s."[21] Academic researchers have focused on the development of measures for information use; the different perspectives of information creators and users; and how information is used in specific research projects.[22] They've also looked at the use of research in social and political policy, though politically oriented managers don't seem especially concerned with their findings.[23] Ironically, this research itself is difficult to use, since the researchers' books and papers are academic in style, and loaded with difficult jargon—not the first time potentially innovative ideas generated by academics have failed to reach a larger audience.

At one level, information use is highly idiosyncratic; whether an individual worker seeks out, absorbs, and digests information before making a decision often falls into the shadowly realm of the human mind. I've already suggested some of the complex psychological and cultural issues at play here in Chapter 6. Still, a process orientation can help ground these messy factors in specific initiatives. There are several pragmatic ways Step 4 of the information management process can be improved: through measurement; symbolic actions; the right institutional contexts; and the incorporation of information usage into performance evaluations.

One key approach is to garner support —preferably of a contractual nature—before actually doing any information gathering or provision. This helps both in legitimizing the work ("Gee, if Strategy is paying for your services, you must be onto something"), and in ensuring that the customer truly wants and plans to use the information. At Bell Atlantic, users can "buy" information services from the firm's Strategic Planning Department or seek an outside vendor. Prior to the start of each fiscal year, the person in charge of Bell Atlantic's Strategic Planning canvasses various departments and units and signs them up—or not; sometimes outside vendors win the bid. But even when the work goes outside, the annual discussions are far from wasted; they have helped Strategic Planning to learn what kind of information is desired, and users to formulate their own requirements.

Measurement

While it's difficult to assess individual information use it's relatively straightforward to measure use—or at least intentional access—from the provider's standpoint. Good librarians have always measured information requests, and good information systems managers have long measured the number and computing power of the machines they support. For electronically based information, it's frequently possible to measure "hits" or accesses on a database or document repository. McKinsey, Coopers & Lybrand, Sequent Computer, and Hewlett-Packard all monitor information and knowledge use in this fashion.

When top managers know how frequently a company's stored information is being used, they can do the equivalent of what television network executives do when they assess Nielsen viewership ratings. Material that's not frequently accessed can be dropped or modified. Popular material can be analyzed to determine why it's so heavily used. Of course, popularity isn't the only criterion for distributing information; few people find corporate policy manuals thrilling bedtime reading, but most still want access to them on-line.

Information managers may also want to know who exactly is accessing material; senior executives or highly paid knowledge workers often make a disproportionally large number of hits. However, the "who" of database access is difficult to determine technically and may also involve ethical issues; in these cases, voluntary surveys may be the only recourse.

Symbolic Actions

Symbols shape behavior in any organization, and they can be used effectively to stimulate greater use of information. Symbols cover everything from executive example to rewards and prizes to mission statements and high-level pronouncements about values.

At Texas Instruments, for example, top managers set out to inculcate better usage of "best practices" information across business units. In order to stimulate such behaviors, the company held a "Share Fair" at which the objective of information and knowledge sharing was evangelized. There was also an award ceremony involving an important symbol: the "Not Invented Here, But I Did It Anyway" award, given to both the provider and the user of a good idea. In this case, the winners shared an idea about semiconductor fabrication across two divisions. A senior vice president spoke at the meeting and presented the awards.

The Right Institutional Context

Regular management meetings provide the most common context for information use. Every firm uses financial information systematically—or at least every successful firm does—because these bottom-line figures are discussed at each meeting of the board of directors. Adding other types of information to the board's agenda is a powerful way to emphasize its importance. At General Motors, for instance, Chairman John Smale found on his taking the job that only financial information was presented to the board of directors on a regular basis. He added regular reports on vehicle quality, health and safety data, market share by segment, production by plant, profit by car line, and return rates on GM investments to the board's agenda.[24] Although it's difficult to prove, I'd hazard a guess that better information use has had something to do with GM's revival over the past several years.

Other firms have emphasized specific types of information use in regular internal meetings. American Airlines senior managers convene every Monday morning to discuss the past week's operations and service. Dell Computer's top executives meet on Friday afternoons to go over how information is used in customer service. As a result, both of these companies lead their industries on the items monitored.

Performance Evaluation

Information use can be further institutionalized through performance evaluation and personnel-oriented rewards and punishments. At Asea Brown Boveri,

for example, managers are evaluated not only on the outcomes of their decisions, but also on the information and decision processes they used to make
them. At the British oil company BP, the Information Strategy Group gives
an annual award for the most innovative and valuable use of information
and/or information technology. The award is presented by a firm director and
is well publicized by internal newsletters.

I've already discussed rewards and punishments in the context of information behavior and culture. Yet information usage can also be measured and
improved like other processes. This essential step has been neglected in the
past, but I believe it's better to make good use of a poor information environment than poor use of a good one. Ultimately, the entire information management process is only as good as its information use.

Improving the Information Management Process

Over the past decade, literally hundreds of firms have attempted to improve
their processes. First using total quality and continuous improvement
approaches, then more radical, reengineering-oriented methods, a wide variety
of processes has been addressed. However, information and knowledge-oriented processes have seldom been the focus of rigorous improvement programs. This is true, I believe, for two reasons. First of all, most managers
simply aren't aware of the importance of these activities—even if information
and knowledge work is at the core of key revenue-generating activities like
R&D and Marketing. Second, these activities are hard to address in process
terms, because their practitioners are typically autonomous, independent
knowledge workers.

To try to find out more about this phenomenon, I and two colleagues of
mine, Sirkka Jarvenpaa of the University of Texas and Mike Beers at Ernst &
Young, studied thirty efforts to improve knowledge and information work
processes.[25] These ranged from publishing processes to capital investment
decision-making to fund-raising work at a university. We came to several conclusions about how to improve this type of work:

- Top-down reengineering approaches don't work well in knowledge and
  information professional settings. They don't involve enough worker
  participation, and they seek to deliver radical, measureable improvements in processes that are difficult to quantify.
- The old approach to knowledge and information work, which might be
  summarized as "hire smart people and leave them alone," is also unlikely to deliver desired improvements in coordination and productivity.

- A participative approach to information and knowledge work processes that emphasizes outcomes, not detailed work steps—along with external factors like common physical location and working in teams—will probably deliver the best results.

In other words, to improve information processes, we should adopt approaches that are ecological. We should emphasize constant improvement over time, the key roles played by people, and the use of multiple interrelated factors. I'd even argue that "process ecology" is a potentially valuable concept, but that's a story for another book. In this one, I'll now leave the world of processes to focus on how information architecture, if carried out from a new ecological perspective—one that may make traditional IT professionals uncomfortable—can be a powerful tool to improve information use.

Assessment Survey for Information Management Processes

The greater the level of agreement with the statements below, the better an organization manages its information processes.

✻ My organization has created a generic model for the information management process that it hopes to implement.

✻ Information management process steps—such as determining information requirements, capturing, distribution, and use—have been assessed in a systematic manner and improvements undertaken.

✻ We can measure the performance of key information management processes.

✻ Specific information-intensive processes—such as market research, product configuration, and customer management—have been improved or reengineered.

✻ Key information users have played a role in designing how information processes should function.

9 ⋮ •

Information Architecture

> If you carefully listen to most data processing managers or
> CIOs talk, what you'll most likely hear is how well their high-
> tech networks handle data. It's a bit like hearing high-tech
> architects brag about their houses; they're so enthusiastic
> about the designs, they forget that families will have to live
> in them.
>
> Michael Schrage, The Wall Street Journal

Throughout this book, I've hammered away at traditional approaches to information management—the techno-utopian view that all human needs can be
"engineered," structured to fit into a computer, designed via an architectural
blueprint. In the above quote, Michael Schrage, who is both a journalist and
an MIT researcher, describes, in a nutshell, how overemphasizing technology design often ignores the real human issues of information use.

Yet information architecture has its place, especially if this component of
the information environment is considered just that—one of several other interrelated components. Information architecture, in the broadest sense, is simply a
set of aids that match information needs with information resources. A well-
implemented architectural design structures information in an organization
through specific formats, categories, and relationships. Information architecture
often links information behavior, processes, and support staff to other aspects of a
firm such as business processes, organizational structure, and physical location.
From the perspective of information ecology, architecture includes not only engineered models but also maps, directories, and standards. These aids may be automated, document-based, or in the mind of a single expert.

One of the best reasons to think architecturally is that information is broadly dispersed throughout organizations. It arrives at a firm from many sources, is

used in a variety of places, and then gets stored in a variety of media and formats. Not surprisingly, workers often have a hard time accessing information that already exists somewhere within the organization. One survey estimated that managers spend seventeen percent of their time (six weeks a year) searching for information.[1] If access is so difficult, it's no wonder companies waste millions of dollars duplicating information that already exists.

The answer, of course, is not just to reduce the number of information sources; sometimes information is only valuable if it can be assembled from diverse sources and locations. At an international airline, for example, a marketing analyst picked out a dissatisfied customer at random in an effort to identify customer service problems. This (former) customer became disenchanted with the airline, but managers only "got it" after sifting through information sources in a variety of formats: flight departure records, official complaint records, lost luggage reports, and correspondence with the airline CEO. By considering these diverse information sources, the analyst was able to report that this customer would have had a very high "lifetime value" for the airline if he hadn't become so unhappy with service. Not only did the airline's architecture of customer information become apparent from this effort, its confusion indicated a real place for improvement.

Any information provider can improve the value he or she adds to information by making it more accessible. Information architecture, by guiding a user to information's location, greatly increases the likelihood of successful use. And information already obtained can be more easily reused. When users know what information is available, they're less likely to purchase, obtain, or create the same information again—which, of course, also decreases the costs of acquisition and storage. While few firms have ever calculated their costs in creating or purchasing information, large organizations often have problems with redundant information.

At one fast food firm, managers realized they definitely needed an architecture of market information. Ostensibly, the company seemed to be putting the right emphasis on information. Its group of forty market researchers prided themselves on being able to answer almost any question anyone in the company might ask on a market, product, competitor, or store location; when these researchers were busy, questions were passed onto the firm's advertising agency. Each year, researchers answered more than 4,700 questions. However, research results weren't stored or saved, except in individual files. If the same question was asked of a different researcher, a new search would be undertaken. The total absence of information architecture in this environment made for a very inefficient, highly redundant set of information processes.

In this chapter, I'll discuss the best ways to approach architecture from an ecological perspective. In particular, I'll detail how IBM and American Express have developed successful information maps, and Teltech has created a structure for categorizing expert information. To my knowledge, such innovative efforts are much broader than any ever described. That's because these companies have primarily emphasized changing information behavior, not creating "elegant" data categories, models for the future, or high-powered computer systems.

Is this more than you bargained for with information architecture? Some organizations may find my recommendations a bit extreme, especially those ruled by traditional IT advocates. But if you only want to manage computerized data, then you're not addressing most of the information needed by your organization. If you only intend to create models of the future, then you'll provide users with no guide to the current information environment. If you don't expect that your architecture will change how employees use and manage information, why bother with it?

Why Most Architecture Won't Change Behavior

First, the bad news. Despite the potential of information architecture, it has a checkered past in real organizations. For decades, most architectures have only dealt with computer-based information; their primary purpose hasn't been to create better information access but to serve as the design specifications for computer systems and databases featuring non redundant central storage of data. As a result, they often seem highly abstract and detailed, which means few users can understand them.

Information architecture, as traditionally conceived, represents the worst of "top-down" management; it often assumes that some authority within an organization has the right to design and implement an information environment in his or her own image. Yet ironically, many information architectures are never completed or take too long to implement. As a director of information management at Xerox told me:

> We tried information architecture for twenty-five years, but we got nowhere. We always thought we were doing it incorrectly, until we finally realized that it was the wrong approach. The initiatives were driven by IM rather than by senior business managers; they were always abandoned in favor of specific systems development projects—the new order processing or billing system—that yielded more obvious benefits. And when we used the information architecture-oriented approach in a business process reengineering context, the high levels of detail distracted managers from the real process change issues in the business.

For all these reasons, information architecture to date has rarely led to change in anyone's behavior—and, ultimately, behavior change has to be the real objective of any information-management initiative, be it installation of a new computer system or a new sales technique. Most managers want everyone who uses information in a business to do the following:

- use common terms to describe particular information elements;
- acquire information for decision-making or further analysis from approved reference sources, rather than creating new sources or using outdated or unofficial sources;
- employ defined processes to create or use particular information;
- adhere to certain information norms for access and sharing.

To be sure, systems personnel may handle information in more technically oriented ways, and traditional information architectures may "speak" to them. But while it may be useful for information users to understand the behaviors expected of information systems creators (and vice versa), any information architecture should clearly delineate the behaviors expected of the two groups; each has only limited interest in the other's actions. In fact, in many cases it may be desirable to create separate versions of the architecture for technical and nontechnical groups.

In general, information architects must determine what types of behaviors they hope to elicit from what specific group or workers. Individual firms will have different change objectives, depending on their strategies for the business and for managing information. But as I've already discussed in Chapter 6, there are three basic reasons why most architectures fail to affect anyone's behavior: (1) information architects rarely consider behavior change to be the main *objective*; (2) the *content* is incomprehensible to most users; and (3) the *process* of developing information architectures inhibits change.

At best, the goal of traditional information architectures may be to increase employee awareness of how much redundant, overlapping data costs. For example, one railroad firm justified their high-level architecture for computerized information in this way. Yet awareness in itself doesn't necessarily change anything, a lesson the railroad firm learned the hard way. Despite the architecture, information users continued to create their own information categories and repositories. One marketing manager said, "I've heard about the information architecture, but it's for IS to help them manage their own business."

The true objectives of most architectures are achievement of technical efficiency through avoidance of replicated data, or the specification of an applications architecture, that is, given the information we say we need, what applications systems should we develop to provide the information? But even these objectives mean systems developers will have to change their own behavior—starting up new projects, abandoning others, and building systems that provide the information elements specified in the architecture—although most information managers never make such expectations explicit. In any case, these technical objectives are usually meaningless to users.

Then there's the content issue. Traditional information architectures are generally incomprehensible not only to nontechnicians but also to technicians who didn't create them. From IBM's Business Systems Planning on up to information engineering, architectures have featured complex and voluminous flow diagrams and matrices. No business manager could or should be expected to make sense of such detail. Data-flow diagrams for complex systems often resemble circuit diagrams for microprocessors. Even the names of information architecture tools are either far too abstract (entity-relationship models) or downright unappealing (CRUD matrices).

As my former Ernst & Young colleague Jim McGee has noted,[2] information architectures of the past have allowed for few client-oriented discussions and negotiations about information requirements. In architecture for buildings, clients and architects often have their most meaningful dialogues about the sketch, which comes much closer than blueprints to communicating how the new structure will look. In information engineering, there are only blueprints.

One client-oriented tool is the use of "principles" to define information architecture, which I describe in Chapter 4 on information strategy.[3] Principles can be an effective bridge between strategy and architecture, and have been widely employed with some effectiveness. The best versions of principles-oriented architectures often reflect how organizational and individual behavior must change. If the architecture calls for common information, principles should clearly specify what part of the business requires the same information, which information will be common, who will oversee keeping it that way, and why commonality is necessary in the first place—all in understandable language.

But information architectures that stop with principles won't address the models, standards, and existing information inventory needed to manage an organization's information fully. For one thing, architectures rarely include motivational content for encouraging behavior that is consistent with the architecture. They could incorporate rewards or incentives—or controls or enforcement—but almost never do. Some architectures imply incentives, such as the promise of timeliness, integrity, or accuracy if information is used in a specified way; yet leaving users to guess the implications of such a system will lead to frustration more than anything else, not to mention all sorts of missed opportunities.

Finally, consider the inadequate process for developing most information architectures. Too often, architectures are created by a small cadre of the information elite. Some architectural efforts involve interviewing managers to elic-

it their information needs, but a one-hour interview doesn't constitute sufficient participation or inclusion of all key stakeholders in the process. What's
more, the managers who are interviewed may not know their own information requirements; the analysts or assistants who supply them with information
may be much better sources.

Many senior executives are unaware that an information architecture even
exists or is being created in their company; when they are aware of it, they don't
see it as critical to accomplishing their own objectives. If senior managers aren't
attuned to information architectures, it's unlikely they'll support incentives for
behavior that complies with the architecture. Furthermore, if executives don't
send out signals that the information architecture is important to them and to the
organization, few politically sensitive employees will be motivated to change.

Given architecture's potential—or at least its prevalence in most IT
shops—you'd think senior managers would care about where all those IT dollars go. Yet most executives don't understand the business consequences if an
organization lacks an information architecture or has a poor one in place—or
what problems can be resolved by an effective one. The technical explanations of most systems designers—data redundancy, sloppy applications architectures, minor problems with data integrity or accuracy—don't constitute a
compelling case for senior managers. They might view their inability to predict quarterly financial results accurately for the investment community as
more pressing. However, rarely do information architects incorporate actual
or potential business problems into their designs.

As with so many computer-oriented approaches to information use, architecture will get nowhere without a consideration of human behavior and moti-
vation. This may sound obvious, but information architects need to
communicate with those whose behavior is to change frequently, continually,
even after a new architecture has been introduced. When they're developing
the architecture, they should also identify key personnel "change roles,"
including target users, initial and sustaining sponsors, and other managers who
can help implement the necessary changes.

An ecological approach to information architecture calls for good measures of desired behavior; that's the only way to tell if a given architectural
blueprint really reflects how people use information, or successfully maps a
new way to do something. Any new architecture has to make appropriate
rewards and controls explicit; also, some type of enforcement arm for admin-
istering both must be in place.

Of course, all architectures are not created equal. I'll spend the rest of this
chapter discussing various forms of information architecture—from traditional information engineering models to more innovative information mapping—
along with guidelines for their effective use.

Information Engineering

Because information engineering has so dominated information architecture in the past, let me address first—and quickly dispense with—this particular form. In Chapter 2, I made clear why a machine-engineering approach, especially one coupled with a managerial desire for control, can be so ill-fated. But despite all its problems, information engineering does have some value. It's particularly well-suited to the specification of databases—the primary purpose for which it was designed—and when done in moderation and with concern for human use, it can be highly beneficial.

The heart of this sort of architecture is the so-called "affinity matix" which is a chart consisting of the data entities required by the organization along one dimension and the processes or activities that make use of the data along the other.[4] The cells of the matrix are often used to note whether the activity creates, reads, updates, or deletes the data, leading to the charming term "CRUD matrix." In addition, information engineering often includes modeling of sources, uses, and flows of information entities through an organization or process. As such, it's highly reductionistic, seeking to reduce information to its atomic components—usually data elements and small business processes or activities. Information engineers almost never attempt to model information that can't easily be put on computers.

Needless to say, there are many pitfalls here to avoid. Attempting to model an entire enterprise is perhaps the most misguided goal of a machine-engineering approach. In fact, this goal was once so pervasive that information engineering was synonymous with the term "enterprise modeling." But unless you're modeling a very small enterprise, describing all the information used by all the processes in an organization will take a very long time—several years in many cases. Even if you're lucky enough to work for top managers that will grant you this much time to tinker without demonstrating economic benefit, your organization will undoubtedly have changed substantially by the time your model is completed. In other words, you will have modeled an organization that no longer exists.

It makes much more sense to model either a particular class of information (and the processes that make use of it), or a small part of the entire organization—ideally a somewhat self-contained part. At American Airlines, for example, information engineers modeled particular processes like airplane maintenance and spare parts management. They also modeled relatively small businesses, such as the Sabre Travel Information Network, which distributes computers and reservation systems to travel agencies.

Partisans of information engineering may object to cutting up the enterprise in this manner, arguing that the whole point is to identify subject-area databases that can be shared across multiple applications. "Clusters" of cells in entity-relationship models signify, they claim, that a database needs to be built with those particular information entities. Some modelers act as if clustering happens naturally—or supernaturally, through the equivalent of a Ouija board—but obviously it's a function of ordering items in rows and columns. Most modelers already have a sense of what databases need to be constructed; they work backward to shape entity-relationship models that fit their preordained conclusions, rather than waiting for clusters to emerge out of the mysterious ether of the organization.

The quality of an information model, then, is closely associated with its brevity. *The model itself should fit on one or at most two pages* (with twelve-point type or larger). Otherwise, nontechnical managers will get lost in the details. And the terminology should mirror that used by businesspeople in talking about their business. Data modelers often adopt abstract or foreign terms (for example, "PROD_ID" to mean product name) in order to specify each information entity. *Avoid such technical jargon at all costs.* A number of participants in architectural efforts have told me they were unable to recognize information and processes they use every day in their work.

Last but not least, *the behavioral objective of an information engineering exercise should be clearly stated*, both by all those participating in the system's development and within the architecture document itself. At American Airlines, for instance, managers in a business unit wanted to identify the nature and extent of information redundancies and overlaps. Information engineers created a one-page model in which they hoped such redundancies would be addressed in meetings reviewing the unit's information systems; they hoped one manager would turn to another and say, "You do a demand forecast? So do I; let's cooperate on it." Because there were no impediments to such understanding at American, the desired behaviors did occur.

Information Mapping

From an ecological perspective, identifying what information is available today and where it can be found is a much better use of architectural design than attempting to model the future. Information mapping is a guide to the present information environment. It may describe not only the location of information, but also who is responsible for it, what it is used for, who is entitled to it, and how accessible it is.[5] The most obvious benefit of mapping is that it can improve access to information. If a map can tell me, for example, where to find information about product performance under conditions of extreme cold, I'm much more likely to find and use it.

Mapping can also illustrate shortages and redundancies. In some areas of an organization there may be too little information; in others, the same information may exist in multiple locations, creating opportunities for efficiencies in purchasing and maintaining the information. Maps can help managers assess how adequate the existing information base is for meeting current and future needs. And they can enhance information quality by identifying key information attributes—for example, the source, age, storage medium, and accessibility. Finally, mapping can improve information behavior and culture. Constructing a map tells the organization that information is a significant resource meant to be shared. If done properly, this gives some credit to those who "own" or maintain the information. And just listing information sources probably increases communication.[6]

Even if the benefits of information mapping seem clear, however, it hasn't been a popular activity in the past. Most of the substantial mapping efforts have occurred at the national government level; for example, a substantial information map was created at the US Department of State.[7] Several federal agencies in Canada have also mapped their information. As for large private sector organizations, IBM, American Express, and Hewlett-Packard have led the way in initiating or completing information maps.

The simplest map is a listing or directory of information resources. This listing can be automated or paper-based; it is a collection of "information about information." Perhaps the best example of this type of map is IBM's *Guide to Market Information*, which I'll describe below.

Information listings are most useful when they contain a wide variety of information types. Neil Burk and Woody Horton, the creators of the information mapping concept, suggest that information maps should incorporate "sources, services, and systems" (see Figure 9-1 for a simplified version of such categories). This figure illustrates that the term "map" need not be interpreted literally. The idea is to give information users some clues as to the whereabouts of information. If the above chart of "sources, services, and systems" by location is applicable, it doesn't have to include geographic coordinates.

A Guide to Information at IBM

Now let's look at how IBM's *Guide to Market Information* came to be.[9] In 1991, the company began to identify and improve broad, cross-functional business processes. One of the original processes identified in this initiative was "Market Information Capture"—actually, both the capture and distribution of market-oriented information. As a result, IBM formed a group—the Market Information Capture team—to take on this responsibility, create a

Locate Resources in Terms of Users, Suppliers, and Managers

Organizational Units / Information Resource Types	Organization Branch X			
	Unit A	Unit B	Unit C	Etc.
Sources				
Services				
Systems				

Figure 9-1. Information Resource Types in a Map
Source: InfoMap, F. W. Horton, C. Burk, 1988

directory for information, and promote and support a council to help establish information requirements.

The first task of the team was to define the market information capture process itself. The team identified three necessary steps, the first being "base lining," which meant increasing awareness of what information was available within IBM. The second was to ensure that the collected information was indeed the right information—the information requirements step that's so crucial for any information management process. The third step was to define the roles and responsibilities of internal customers and suppliers of market information, which basically involved improving the support staff structure. All three steps continue to be essential aspects of market information capture at IBM today.

Several problems prompted the company to address market information capture in the first place. One was redundant information. In a typical scenario, a hardware development group within IBM would hire an outside consultant to report on computer needs of customers. Then another IBM group, perhaps in software development, would hire a different consultant to get the same or similar information. Such information often wasn't shared, at least in part because employees didn't know that it already existed within the company. Another problem involved the purchase of external information that was never really used. Research departments would spend funds allocated in the budget for information that didn't have a specific purpose but that managers assumed somebody might want. In many cases, however, no one had ever asked for that kind of information.

There was a widespread perception within IBM that "we don't have enough information." But the market information capture team found that the *amount* of information wasn't the problem. Rather, there was probably too much information: collected but unneeded—or collected and needed but not used, because its existence or location were unknown.

Therefore, to respond to the question "What information is available within IBM?" the team created the *Guide to Market Information,* a proprietary "catalog of catalogs." The *Guide* lists available marketing information, a nontechnical description of the information, the person or organization responsible for the information, how to contact that person or organization, and whether the information was created within IBM or bought from an outside supplier. The types of information listed are proprietary research, internally developed databases, internal electronic bulletin boards, libraries, and external databases and reports that IBM frequently uses. The *Guide* serves the following purposes:

- It increases awareness of what information is available and who is knowledgeable about information.
- It promotes sharing of information and synergy across the organization.
- It helps pinpoint what new information is needed.

In 1991, over 1,600 first-edition copies of the *Guide* were printed and distributed within IBM. By 1992, the company printed 5,000 copies of the second edition, which is 470 pages long, to meet increased demand. Both editions were priced at cost and sold out. In its 1993 third edition, the *Guide* became available on workstations and in hard copy. Its popularity reflects the obvious need for an information directory within IBM.

The *Guide* lists specific IBM contacts (person, department, or help desk) and the electronic address for that contact, in addition to the description and listing of the information source. IBM employees who find a desired piece of information in the *Guide* can then call a person who is knowledgeable about the information. The listed IBM contacts add value to the information. They help the requester of the information determine whether it's appropriate or not prior to acquisition. Also, these contacts act as an informal network of references to other sources and people that may have pertinent information.

Even so, in compiling information for the *Guide,* the marketing information capture team found that employees who had information sometimes were reluctant to share it. Some originally feared they would be overwhelmed by the demands to support the information and wouldn't have time for their real jobs, since no support structure existed for this purpose. Being listed in the guide was voluntary; IBM management issued no directive requiring information to be listed. Fortunately, collecting contacts for the 1992 edition was easier than collecting it for the first, since by then IBM employees had begun to realize the benefits of information sharing. Those listed in the *Guide to Market Information* have now started to accept that responsibility as part of their jobs.

Geographic Maps at American Express

In addition to a listing or directory of information, maps may relate information to some other basic dimension, such as geography. The best way to present a company's geographical distribution of information is graphically. On the World Wide Web, for example, there are many hypertext maps in which clicking on a particular region of the map yields information sources in that area. At American Express, Myrna Rae Johnston, an information manager, created a geographical map that pinpoints the company's information processing centers. (See Figure 9-1 for a portion of American Express's international map.)[10]

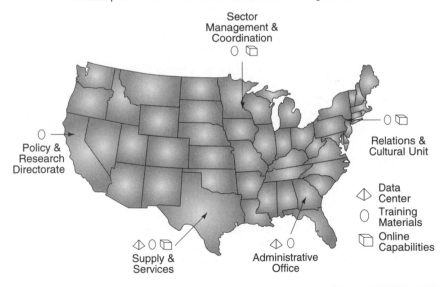

Figure 9-2. American Express Information Map

Slapping a few labels onto a preexisting map may sound easy; but even though Johnson was only attempting to map sources of mainframe computer information, the process was difficult. Her experience at American Express indicates why even the best of architectural efforts also involve information politics, behavior, processes, and strategy.

First Johnson had to receive the right facts from the finance, public relations, corporate secretary, archivist, and human resources departments. Then organization of the map turned problematic. In her words:

> It was an interesting aspect of our international operations that pointed to the best way of organizing the map. This came to light as I was comparing legal entities with financial entities, and discovered that in many countries (Spain, for example), revenue had to be booked from each of the major products into a separate legal entity. This meant that there were three incorporated subsidiaries in Spain (Travelers Cheque, Card, and Travel). The same was true of many South American countries. The implication was that, for a map to be consistent and meaningful across the firm, I would have to extrapolate the business *functions* of the entities, rather than recording the business *names* of the hierarchy. For example, although each country with an American Express Bank location had a legal subsidiary, branch banks all reported into the Network Banking *business* group within a region (North Asia, South Asia, and so on).

Johnson also faced bureaucratic problems as she prepared her map:

> The most nerve-racking part of the project was what I would call the "disapproval cycle." Because no one had responsibility for or "owned" the information, no single executive could approve it. The corporate office could approve only the corporate headquarters piece, and each of the five organizations could approve only their part.
>
> Several people got cold feet about the project, including the communications manager, my own senior executive, our CIO, TRS's lawyers, and even the formerly helpful vice president in Corporate Communications. Her thought was that, if we had never done a chart of the company before, then there must be a good reason for that. The senior executive and CIO were of the opinion that the project should be seen only by other TRS Technologies staff, as opposed to the usual distribution to TRS management. This grew out of a political concern that, because we were only a little piece of the organization, the effort could be viewed as anything from wanton spending to political usurpation. Perhaps most uncomfortable of all were the lawyers, because they really had no way to verify the type of information presented by the map.
>
> In the face of these reservations, I decided to send the draft directly to the Office of the Chairman of American Express, and left several electronic mail messages for the Corporate Secretary. The CEO's office was extremely

cooperative, thought it was a wonderful idea, and had a list of ideas for how it could be used within the organization for everything from project planning to new-hire orientation. As a result, the cold feet warmed up—although the lawyers still demanded I get all approvals in writing. . . .

Based on my experience in mapping a company as complex as American Express, I would make the following recommendations to others attempting similar tasks:

- Get buy-in from the top before you start, so that you can avoid cold feet later (temporarily ignore the lawyers, unless they're enlightened about information sharing).
- Determine your audience (what are they going to use the map for, and how much detail will they need?).
- Review all available bits and pieces of information (legal, financial, business, organizational, etc.) before deciding which type of information to pursue and where to make a cut-off.
- Decide what distribution and format channel you will use, so that the people you contact can visualize what you're doing and can be "bribed" by the outcome.
- Track your sources in a hierarchical form; you can use it later with the corporate lawyers (as in, "where did you get that piece of information"), for other projects in which you may want a source of higher-level knowledge, and for acknowledgment of cooperation in your mapping project.
- Make sure the software used for your draft is compatible with that of the graphic artist who will later design it (assuming you are creating a computer-designed product).[11]

Any budding information ecologist would do well to heed Myrna Rae Johnson's sage advice. In addition to her guidelines, I suggest some other specific tactics to keep in mind when mapping information:

Include pointers to people. As I've emphasized over and over again, the most valuable information in organizations resides within people. Therefore, maps should include pointers to those who possess information so that they can elaborate on it, provide context and meaning, and generally make the information more engaging for the recipient. IBM's *Guide to Market Information* is especially good at providing pointers.

Select a domain to map. In large organizations, all information around the entire firm can't be mapped in one project; such an objective would likely fall prey to the same problems encountered in enterprise information engineering. Therefore, information managers should settle on a particular domain to map, one that is ideally driven by the company's information strategy. The domain might involve a particular type of information, such as customer, product, or competitor; a particular business unit, function, project, or process; even a particular time period or location.

Drive detail with usage. Obviously, there is a great deal of information within any organization, and a map's level of detail could quickly become overwhelming. Don't go into great detail until there's some indication of demand for that kind of map and its associated information. Information providers should start with a rudimentary map, circulate it to their users, and only develop the map further if begged to do so.

Stick with institutional sources. Given that much of the information in organizations resides within the minds and file cabinets of individuals, managers may be tempted to map individual-level information. However, mapping at this level raises many difficult issues of information ownership and usage rights; who owns, for example, the information brought by an individual into a company from another company where he or she once worked? Maps should be restricted to sources, services, and systems at the institutional level—at least until such difficult issues are resolved. Indeed, Myrna Rae Johnson's ordeal with the American Express map indicates how sticky even institutional ownership of information can become.

Plan on frequent revision. The categories, sources, and uses of information change frequently; consequently, providers need to keep revising information maps if they expect them to be useful. Again, updating should be driven by usage; there's no reason to update a map that nobody uses. More important, because a map requires frequent revision, it also needs a stable institutional home—that is, an owner with the responsibility and resources for maintaining it.

Consider automation—in moderation. Information maps aren't just about computers and computerized information; but these tools may still be usefully employed by information architects to create a map. Certainly, a simple directory of information can be more easily revised and updated if it's in database form. And as noted above, hypertext-style lists and maps can be very useful in organizing an information environment. Hewlett-Packard is using Lotus Notes not only to store an information map but also to deliver requested information to users.

Other Types of Information Architecture

By pursuing the idea of architecture as an aid to matching information needs and resources, I hope to show how this traditional IT realm can expand, grow with the times, and offer more viable options. One key element of architecture that's familiar to IT advocates is the standard. In technology architecture, standards ensure that dispersed computers and networks can interface and communicate. In information architecture, standards enable broad access to information and easy interpretation and use.

At Xerox, some divisions have created a standard for strategic planning documents. The company specifies a standard format so that decision-makers can easily find the information they require. Professional firms have long produced client documents in standard formats, partly to bring a consistent identity to the firm, partly to enable reuse. Automobile companies and others who depend heavily on product design for their success have also created standard formats for design documents. These initiatives aren't new, as I made clear in the previous chapter on information processes; yet they're increasingly becoming the focus of information architects.

The World Wide Web

Indeed, one of the most important standards in information architecture involves documents. For more than a decade, standards for how documents are displayed on computers have evolved. The resulting Standard Generalized Markup Language (SGML) format has allowed different types of computers to display documents in the same way. A header is a header, a paragraph is a paragraph, a footnote a footnote.

But a subset of SGML is now beginning to revolutionize information distribution and display. The use of Hypertext Markup Language (HTML), which allows display of simple text and graphic information across the Internet, has created the World Wide Web. Parts of documents can be linked to other related documents anywhere in the world. Since its creation in 1992, the Web has become the fastest-growing segment of the Internet. Commercial organizations, nonprofit groups, governments, and individuals proliferate new Web pages at an estimated rate of one per fifteen seconds.

For information ecologists, the Web is a fascinating development. It illustrates how relatively simple standards for information formatting, search, and entry can blossom into a fantastically complex array of documents. A great part of the Web's appeal lies in its simplicity; documents are easy to construct and to access, and technology doesn't get in the way of use.

The World Wide Web is also an excellent example of an "emergent" or "bottom-up" architecture. Its structure changes every minute and is an artifact of millions of decisions made by individual page designers about the content of their documents and the links they construct to other documents. On the Web, no one individual or group decides who has valuable information to display. Bottom-up architectures lead to a strong emphasis on information marketing and attractive, innovative displays; functions like Netscape's "What's New and Cool" become critical. This type of architecture also creates a real need for maps and search tools that lead users to desired information; thus far on the Web, these tools have lagged behind new pages.

Emergent architectures based on the Web are beginning to appear within organizations as well. Computer and high-tech firms are the pioneers in this regard; Hewlett-Packard, Sun Microsystems, Sequent, and Sematech are among the organizations developing internal Webs for their proprietary information. Sequent's, for example, is called the Corporate Electronic Library, and contains proposals, white papers, discussion highlights, and externally sourced documents of relevance to the company. Almost overnight it became the primary place to look for information that could aid the sales force in selling Sequent computers.

Structuring Expertise at Teltech

Another form of information architecture emphasizes skill and expertise databases. Many companies have experimented with these, though they're difficult to establish and maintain. The categories for expertise change frequently, and it's sometimes difficult to decide which skills may be relevant to business situations. When a skills database was being created at AT&T Bell Labs, for example, developers wrestled with the issue of whether foreign language and liberal arts backgrounds should be included in it.

But consider Teltech, the Minneapolis company that maintains a network of experts and external databases to answer clients' technical questions, and has developed a successful knowledge "thesaurus." When clients call Teltech for access to experts, they seldom use the same terms experts do in describing their work. Therefore, Teltech has to translate for clients in order to connect them with the company's available expertise. This function is performed by knowledge analysts in combination with Teltech's on-line search and retrieval system, the "KnowledgeScope." The KnowledgeScope includes a thesaurus of over 30,000 technical terms. It is maintained by several full-time "knowledge engineers," who add 500 to 1,200 new concepts per month to the database along with removing outdated ones.

Each technical term has a preferred usage and several possible synonyms. For example, the term "polymer" in chemistry might have synonyms like "copolymers," "olefins," and "hydrocarbon polymers." Because customer satisfaction is essential to the company's business, Teltech's main goal is to include the terms used by clients in the database. Each day the knowledge engineers receive a list of terms sought unsuccessfully in the database by analysts or clients accessing the database directly. Many of the unsuccessful searches are due to misspellings, but valid misses are added to the database. Only the knowledge engineers are able to add new terms or concepts; but the company's knowledge analysts, who work directly with clients, often suggest new terms through electronic mail or face-to-face conversations with the engineers.

Until 1994, Teltech's approach to structuring knowledge was hierarchical rather than thesaurus-based. Its previous database was called the Teltech "Tech Tree" and had several key knowledge branches or categories, including scientific/technical, medical, and chemical information. However, both clients and analysts found it difficult to navigate through the tree, and new terms tended to be added at inappropriate levels. Teltech's information managers have found the thesaurus much more satisfactory.

The company also maintains a database of expert biographies, which is linked to the thesaurus through keywords. During recruitment for the database, each expert is asked to fill out a detailed biography form. Teltech then constructs a set of keywords that link each expert to the concepts in the thesaurus. A textual description of the expert is also created, which can be read in whole or in part by knowledge analysts as they describe an expert to a client, or as the client accesses the biography directly. The expert biographies are updated annually to reflect new expertise and new terminology. Further, new experts are always being added to the database.

Teltech's efforts in creating a structure for expert information are instructive. If information is to be captured and leveraged, it must first be categorized. And Teltech's thesaurus approach looks promising for many situations and types of firms, since information is usually communicated and sought in words, and words are the primary unit of information in a thesaurus. Once again, even the most technically sophisticated IT approach has to rely on how human minds—not computers—handle information.

Architecture as Part of the Ecological Web

Clearly, not all information can be squeezed into an architectural model. Yet this most technological of components, when effectively employed, illustrates how all elements of the information environment are interrelated. Since architecture is the last component of the internal information environment I'll be discussing here, walking through how it's connected to the other elements can illustrate the entire ecological web.

Decisions about where to begin an architectural design should be driven by a company's information strategy. For better or worse, information politics may also affect how architecture is used; if the dominant political structure isn't very democratic, attempts to map information, create directories like IBM's *Guide*, or structure expertise are likely to fail.

Good architectures are essential for efficient information processes, especially those steps dealing with access, capture, and distribution. Architectures are typically created by the information staff, and may include references to people who provide support for information. And architecture can and should change information behavior and culture. If it doesn't do so, in even the smallest way, then all the technical elegance in the world won't solve an organization's information problems.

Once we leave the information environment behind—as we're about to do in Chapters 10 and 11—we can see how architectural decisions are also linked to a company's organizational and external environments. For one thing, architectures are guides not only to internal information but also to what's gathered from external markets, particularly the information market.

For another, in the organizational environment some architectures are directly related to a firm's technology investment, as the American Express example above indicates; its information map was primarily oriented to IT capabilities rather than information itself. But architecture can also incorporate specific aspects of the business situation—for example, a map can provide pointers to business units, product groups, or geographic locations. And an organization's physical arrangement is likely to affect a map's scope and range, as well as the distribution of information across a corporate "geography." The next chapter on the organizational environment not only covers these three components, but also underscores the many connections between technical efforts and human actions.

Assessment Survey for Information Architecture

(The greater the level of agreement with the statements below, the better an organization manages its information architecture.)

* My organization uses a planning approach to identify the non-computer-based information we need and have.

* Non-technical managers and employees can understand our computer-oriented architectural efforts.

* We have created information maps to guide individuals to the location of needed information.

* Our information architectures include pointers to the people who possess the information or who are knowledgable about its use.

* Our architectural objectives are driven by explicitly-stated behavioral objectives.

10

Connecting to the Company:
Information and the Organization

Success in information management is
5% technology, and 95% psychology.

Tom Peters, *Forbes ASAP*

Alhough I devote most of this book to the internal information environment of a company, an ecological approach also has to account for the complex organizational environment—a company's overall business strategy and structure; what it has already invested in technology; and the physical arrangement of its various offices, units, and manufacturing facilities. Ecologically oriented managers ask, "What about an organization affects—and is affected by—the way it manages information?"

Bear in mind that the relationship between a company's organizational context and its information environment works both ways. That is, the organizational environment can guide or motivate a particular information environment, just as that information environment can enable or constrain the organization. Information managers used to assume that business strategy, for example, always drove information strategy. Yet after more than a decade of strategic thinking about information and technology, it's clear that both can open up new strategy options. Reengineering efforts, in particular, indicate that information and technology can make new process designs possible, or disable their implementation. In any given organization, the direction and strength of the relationship between the organizational and information environments varies, but it's never a one-way street.

How an organization uses and is affected by information is a broad issue, one that can't be fully resolved here. In this chapter, I'll discuss the three components of the organizational environment that I believe are most relevant to information ecologists: business situation, technology investment, and physical arrangement. Up to now, these business factors have rarely been viewed in the context of information management.

Business Situation

This organizational component is perhaps the most critical to motivating change in information use. I would also generalize that if an organization wants to make a major change in its business situation, it will need to change its information environment as well. In other words, if it intends to change either its information or business situation, changes in one will probably lead to changes in the other. We can't always anticipate how the relationship between a company's business situation and information environment will shift over time, but acknowledging that such changes *will* happen can help organizations weather turbulent business conditions.

I'll address several elements of a company's business situation in this section: business strategy; business processes; organizational structure and culture; and human resources. I don't claim that these elements completely characterize any company. I won't be discussing, for example, an organization's financial condition, which is obviously a key aspect of its business situation. My main purpose is to indicate how business issues—which senior managers often don't connect to the specifics of a company's information environment—can crucially affect the success of information management initiatives. I hope that other information ecologists will be sufficiently motivated by this chain of inferences to explore different aspects of the business situation and their relationship to information.

Business Strategy

Just as physics is "the queen of the sciences," we often view strategy as the absolute monarch of business management. Business strategy is, of course, the stated direction of the organization with respect to markets, products or services, and financial results. Strategic goals are usually framed in general language, and avoid mentioning any means of implementation, including the use of information. Yet any strategy has specific implications for a firm's information environment. Take, for example, a few common strategy options from the recent management literature. According to one theorist, a strategy of "hypercompetition" in fast-moving markets implies an information environment that includes: (1) high levels of attention paid to competitor information; (2) high quality and quantity of information about product development; (3) a managerial willingness to change information strategies frequently; (4) information gathering and analysis in four arenas: "cost/quality, timing/know-how, strongholds, and deep pockets."[1]

Another recent study of strategy options suggests that firms should choose between three mutually exclusive alternatives: customer intimacy, operational excellence, or product innovation.[2] While I have doubts about how exclusive these strategies really are—firms often need to do a bit of each—the strategic emphases do dictate different information environments.

Customer intimacy obviously suggests a heavy emphasis on customer information. This kind of intimacy involves not only transaction or quantitative information on the customer, but also the rigorous management of *qualitative* customer information—from birthdays and children's colleges—to movie or music preferences—to the business strategies of your customer's customers. A company that emphasizes operational excellence, on the other hand, will be most concerned with information like product quantities, quality, costs, and prices; suppliers and the goods and services they supply; and logistical entities such as shipment date and billing address. Because operationally focused companies need to coordinate their core business processes, sharing information across functional boundaries is a key characteristic of their desired information environments.

Finally, companies that specialize in product innovation will have an entirely different information environment. Because R&D and engineering information is often best transmitted face-to-face, this form of information exchange should be carefully considered and factored into this kind of company's information strategy. It almost goes without saying that these managers should focus on product design and specification information.

Such generic strategy alternatives and their related information environments illustrate that business strategy should—indeed, has to—influence information strategies and tactics. The specific strategies of some firms or industries are even more directly linked to effective information use. In health-care organizations, for instance, many top managers now want to build, generally through acquisition, an integrated network of primary- and acute-care facilities that meet all the health-care needs of a patient or an insurer. Under this strategy, common patient information becomes the glue that holds a health-care network together. While most institutions in this industry still have highly fragmented information environments, many are trying to knit together an "electronic medical record" through the use of either integrated application packages or "frontware" on workstations that can access multiple applications and databases.

Many banks are also growing through acquisition and want to adopt an integrated perspective on a customer's financial dealings. Because of competition from those outside the traditional industry, banks now need to offer their customers a more comprehensive package of services and must be able to recommend appropriate offerings. But this strategy in the banking industry can't be easily accomplished through front-end integration. The rigorous and transaction-oriented information environments of banks create a need for more integrated application and database designs. As a result, several banks and vendors of software to banks—including BancOne, EDS, Hogan Systems, and Westpac Financial—have attempted to create fully integrated customer-oriented applications and data architectures. Thus far they have all been unsuccessful, but some firm will eventually make the necessary breakthrough. In any case, the information vision is quite clear.

Or consider the personal computer business, which is highly dynamic and complex. The industry is increasingly moving toward a "lean production" strategy, in which customers are offered multiple configurations, and a system is built to order rather than to stock. Such a business strategy calls for an information environment that emphasizes forecasts of system and component needs for the future, as well as highly integrated logistical and order-management information. Therefore, most firms in this industry are implementing SAP, a highly integrated set of applications and data. Some firms, such as Compaq, are also devoting considerable energy to forecasting demand through complex simulation models.[3]

It should be obvious by now that business strategy influences the information environment. But what about the other way around? Information environments can drive strategy, too, especially in the realm of core competence.[4] When an organization has core competencies in information-related domains—that is, institutional skills involving some aspect of information management—it may find itself pursuing strategies that leverage those competencies. In practice, this can mean the simple extension of an existing information-based business. Senior managers of an advertising agency, for example, which excels in the creation and presentation of information designed to persuade others, may conclude that they should also be in the market research business. A firm that manages multiple types of information for its customers, such as Dun & Bradstreet, continues to build or acquire information-oriented businesses.

But a company's information competencies may lead to a more radical strategic shift, too. When a firm in the agricultural chemicals business, like Monsanto, becomes good at managing information about agriculture, top management may decide to enter the new business of selling agricultural information as well. Similarly, Citibank executives decided in the 1980s that since the company was successful at managing financial information for itself, it should also begin to manage information for its customers. In this case, however, Citibank's business strategy—clearly driven by the internal information orientation of CEOs Walter Wriston and John Reed—wasn't implemented well. Citibank overpaid for some businesses like Quotron; in other areas, the company was ahead of its time, such as in its frequent-purchase information system marketed through grocery chains.

Whether business shifts happen naturally or radically, particular strategies are often related to particular information environments. In a limited sense, we've known this ever since information systems planning was first linked to business strategy in the 1970s. The only difference today is that the information environment, as I've presented it here, forms a much broader, more complex ecological web than any information systems plan.

Business Processes

As I've already detailed in Chapter 8, how work gets done depends heavily on the availability and quality of information. Adopting a process perspective on work implies that information is shared across functional boundaries within a firm. Coordination across processes also requires consensus on key information elements; that way, "customer" or "product" will mean the same thing to everyone involved throughout the process. Firms that structure work along process lines also frequently believe in measuring and improving those processes. Therefore, process management requires information environments in which decisions are based on facts rather than on intuition or rumor, and where process-performance measures (cost, time, quality) are important information entities.

Many companies that have decided to reengineer or improve their processes find that they need to change basic aspects of their information environments. I would even argue that the recent popularity of reengineering has motivated the most change in information environments, or at least the most managerial lip service paid to the idea. And it *is* a good idea, although few firms really understand how to create such change.

General Motors is one of the few. At GM, process improvement and reengineering work have focused on, among other things, the new car development process. Like other automobile manufacturers, GM wants to decrease the time it takes to develop a new car model, as well as to ensure that the design and features of new cars reflect market preferences. Therefore, GM managers emphasize the use of market research within the new car development process. Specifically, GM has defined what it calls the Dialogue/Decision Process, which structures the analysis and use of market information throughout the cycle of new-car development.[5]

Or take Xerox, where a radical initiative to redesign the order-management process became the impetus for major changes in the information environment. The firm's goal was to move most aspects of order management to the customer site so that even complex orders could be designed, priced, and submitted in real time with the customer. From an architectural standpoint, however, the necessary information was fragmented across multiple applications, databases, and document repositories. In order to make it accessible, Xerox is now constructing what it calls a "Shared Electronic Library" of order-related information.

Information environments can also lead to new demands on work processes. Many of the organizations that now have the largest and most ambitious reengineering initiatives underway originally began by addressing problems in their information environments. For example, at the US Internal Revenue Service, managers realized in the 1980s that major changes were necessary in the systems that processed taxpayer information. Some systems were several decades old, were unreliable, and could no longer be economically maintained. After several years of systems architecture and development work, and an early reengineering success in the Collections department, IRS managers became convinced that more process changes were necessary to take advantage of the new systems. The organization is now spending several billion dollars on new systems and processes that receive all returns electronically, allow for rapid translation of new tax codes into information systems, and can better identify tax frauds.

On a more pragmatic level, many other firms end up making process changes because of specific applications packages they've adopted. Some megapackages like SAP provide very broad applications that cut across business functions. One manager described SAP as "business integration in a box." However, in order to take advantage of the common data and integrated applications from such packages, most firms need to better coordinate their business processes. Many consulting firms now offer reengineering services in conjunction with SAP configuration and installation.

Organizational Structure and Culture

These days, it's fashionable to claim that organizations are becoming flatter. Because of spreading information technologies and the shrinking number of middle managers, information is supposedly flowing both vertically and horizontally, becoming more pervasive and democratic—an appealing notion for everyone but middle managers.

I'm not persuaded. I see layers added to organizations as often as I see them removed. I don't see many low-level workers having intimate electronic chats with CEOs. And there are still lots of middle managers, or at least individual contributors who more or less manage themselves and are paid a middle manager's salary. More to the ecological point, in working with several hundred companies over the past fifteen years, I've never encountered one that reorganized, flattened itself, or embarked on cultural change because of the availability of information technology. In fact, I don't believe organizational designers are comfortable enough with information technology to make it a major part of their grand schemes.

What I do see is that organizational changes lead to IT changes—or that IT can make organizational changes possible, even when they're undertaken without the technology in mind. I first noticed this at DuPont's Textile Fibers division in the 1980s. The division was one of the first to adopt early retirement incentives in an effort to downsize; but because there was little experience with such programs at DuPont and elsewhere, the firm had no means of predicting how many employees would take "the package." At Textile Fibers, many more managers—almost half of the division's middle tier—opted to retire than was anticipated. At first the division's executives panicked, wondering how work could get done if everyone left at the same time. But the division had recently installed an e-mail system, and employees began to rely heavily on it to replace traditional reporting structures. The division's executives now claim they might not have survived the loss of so many managers without the system.

At best, the relationship between organizational change and information/technology change is a fluid one, with shifts on one side rippling to the other, back and forth over time, creating incremental improvements. At Lithonia Lighting, the leading supplier of industrial lighting fixtures, top management decided to recognize an organizational change that had already place. After several decades of relying on an internal sales force, the firm had shifted to using independent agents, most of whom primarily sold Lithonia equipment, to distribute its products to construction contractors and suppliers. Lithonia managers—particularly Charles Darnell, the CIO and head of the High Technology Lighting division—realized these agents now provided a critical link in their business, and began to give them access to Lithonia's computer-based information. Then, as part of an IT planning project, a new "organization chart" was drawn with agents at the center of the information flow (see Figure 10-1). While the company was still organized internally by products and functions, the new chart forced Lithonia managers to look at their business in a new way. If agents were really at the center of the organization, then they needed more and better information about Lithonia's products and processes than they had been getting. The chart led to a new round of changes in Lithonia's information environment, such as the creation of new

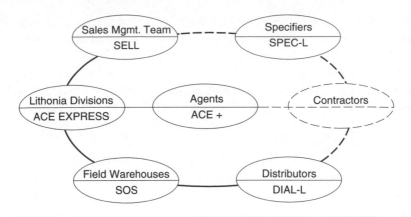

Figure 10-1. Lithonia Lighting's Organization Chart for Information Flow
Note: Words in capital letters in ovals are Lithonia information systems applications; dotted lines are planned connections.

systems that allowed direct access by agents to Lithonia's inventory, pricing, and ordering systems.[6]

Human Resources

People are what the organizational environment is really composed of, and no diagnosis of an information ecology is complete without an understanding of the type of people in it. I've already discussed specific information behaviors in some detail; but an organization's general approach to human resources can also determine whether information initiatives succeed or fail. Perhaps the most important human resource characteristic is the general emphasis placed on information. Are managers and employees analytical? Do they seek out information before making decisions or taking actions? Is attention paid to internal communications, whether they involve an organization's strategy, products or services, or other people? Are employees aware of what is going on with competitors, customers, and the rest of the external environment? Are they "information heat-seekers?"

We all know people in organizations who deserve this characterization. They seem to know something about almost everything, and almost everything about something. They are frequently sought after for their knowledge and opinions. These people weren't born knowing everything (though they may have learned early on the value of education and intellectual stimulation). It takes hard work to achieve this level of awareness. If an organization is going to recruit and retain such individuals, it must recognize, evaluate, and compensate them accordingly. It must also persuade everyone else that "informational heat" pays off.

I once consulted for a professional services organization that was slowly losing billable hours. Managers finally decided to ask customers why they were requiring fewer services over time. "Because you don't know that much about our business, and therefore you don't add a lot of value," was the gist of what most of them said. Therefore, this firm revised its business strategy, placing a new emphasis on absorbing much more information about clients, and thus adding more value to its services in the form of industry, process, and competitor knowledge. The firm established a large "Information Center" to gather and distribute such information. Managers began to specify what materials the firm's personnel should read. They even had new value-adding business processes designed.

Their strategy, however, was only as good as their people. Many professionals in this firm weren't interested in absorbing more information. They didn't want to read in their spare time; they wanted to play golf. Several partners told me that "they can't make me do this," and implementation of the strategy began to wane. One was overheard saying to a colleague, "I haven't read a business book since college, and I'm not going to start now." At a company with such recalcitrant professionals—who probably don't want to change because in the past they've been given few incentives to do so—managers may only be able to implement such a strategy over a long period of time, through a series of new hires and retirements.

Technology Investment

Companies can and do spend millions of dollars on new information technology, even when the exotic new computers, workstations, or latest database applications do little to improve information use. However, when an organization's technology investment is viewed from an ecological standpoint, IT *can* make a real difference. While my model of information ecology largely stresses components other than technology, it would be senseless for me to maintain that an organization's IT doesn't affect its management or use of information. Certainly, there are ample sources on the topic of IT architectures and capabilities,[7] and I won't review them here. In considering a company's overall technology investment, I'll discuss only the attributes that matter most to an effective information ecology.

In the messy real world, of course, information managers are often stuck with the clunky or outmoded systems they inherit from their predecessors; while these managers may have some money in their budgets to make changes, they can't often redesign systems from the ground up. Still, one key to effective investment in this resource is the use of *appropriate* technology—

technology that's no more complex or powerful than necessary. Despite a great deal of media hype to the contrary, you don't need the latest technology to have a strong information environment.

One firm attempting to use appropriate technology is Verifone, a fast-growing company that leads the credit-transaction equipment (card swipe) industry.[8] The company's CIO, Will Pape, notes, "If you're just using e-mail, there's no reason to have a Pentium. You don't need a Ferrari to drive to the supermarket." While Verifone's highly distributed business model means that employees rely heavily on IT for communications and information distribution, these applications, and the individual productivity tools used in almost all firms, don't require the best processors and largest disk drives. Some Verifone employees do have high-powered personal computers, but they must justify their acquisition with applications that truly demand such power. Not coincidentally, Verifone has one of the richest information environments for a firm its size, and has been very successful financially.

The use of appropriate technology has many benefits for information-oriented firms. Most important, monetary and support resources are freed up; ideally, these can be devoted to new information staff rather than to technology. In addition, familiar technologies are easier for users to understand, meaning they'll put their energies into content rather than trying to master a new technology. Finally, when the right machines and programs are in place, managers send the message that good information technology and good information use are not equal.

As with other aspects of the organizational environment, a firm needs to assess how its technology investment supports or retards its overall information strategy and desired information environment. Since most companies have already invested, for better or worse, in information technology of some sort, the real managerial task may be getting other aspects of the information environment to align with the IT. The following general guidelines should be kept in mind when investing in new technologies:

A high degree of network interconnectedness facilitates the exchange of information in organizations. This involves local area network connections to each desktop; wide area networks to all major company locations; high bandwidth connections for graphics, document images, and video; and the availability of portable networking for workers in the field. For example, Hewlett-Packard's corporate Information Systems organization states that one of its primary goals for 1996 is "To provide HP employees working outside their traditional office setting or in distributed teams with information technology-enabled work environments that are highly productive and intuitively simple." However, a specific organization must decide how much bandwidth and interconnection is economically justifiable.

Knowledge and information workers require personal computers or workstations on each desktop. In addition, operations staff require easy access to such workstations, while field personnel benefit more from portable computers. One aspect of the configuration of such workstations should be local storage so that individuals can effectively manage their own personal information environments. Note that most workers don't like devices such as "X-terminals" or "network computers," which lack their own disk storage.

Effective information management increasingly involves providing network access to internal information repositories with many CD-based databases. Access to external information services and databases requires the ability to dial out either at the desktop or through a server. Heavy users of CD-based information should have their own drives.

The effective management of organizational information environments increasingly demands network management software. The capabilities of these tools make it possible for individual data environments to be backed up and software distributed easily around the organization.

An increasing number of sophisticated software packages can help manage and distribute qualitative or document-based information in organizations. Lotus Notes is perhaps the best-known of such tools; while merely implementing Notes won't create an environment of information sharing, it will facilitate sharing and effective use where these behaviors already exist. Other tools, like Sandpoint's Hoover, extract information on specified topics from external databases and bring it to an individual's personal computer or workstation. Tools like grapeVINE (from grapeVINE Technologies) help to structure internal discussions of specific topics, such as competitive intelligence. Finally, individual information users may benefit from "organizer" or "personal information manager" software.

For external information access and communications, use of the Internet is increasingly becoming a necessity. Perhaps the greatest current value of Internet access is the ability to send mail messages around the world easily. But employees can also use the Internet to search databases, transact electronic commerce, and discuss business-oriented topics.

For some companies, the World Wide Web can be a new means of organizing and accessing information. The Web, of course, is a hypertext-based, technology-independent means of displaying textual, graphic, and audio information over the Internet (or an "intranet"). The externally oriented version of the Web is interesting enough; perhaps even more exciting is the growth of Web-based architectures within companies. The Web offers a model for how we will display and access internal corporate information in the future (and increasingly in the present). Many companies already have their own internal Webs, only some of which are accessible to the outside world. Just as we can now navigate through Web servers all around the world, we can navigate through the wide range of information available in large organizations.

From a behavioral standpoint, the Web also encourages "browsing" and experimentation, which—judging from the rapid growth of the Internet—people like to do. Since each Web user creates her own links to information, its structure addresses the primary problem with most information architectures—that no designer can ever anticipate all the diverse information needs of an organization. Last but not least, the Web's architecture is based on documents, an information format that people feel comfortable with and understand.

Physical Arrangement

This third and final organizational component may be the most ignored aspect of an information ecology. Yet research suggests that it's often quite critical to an effective information environment. What I mean by physical arrangement is where individuals and groups are located in relation to others with whom they work. This component also consists of the physical structures—building layouts, offices, furniture—in which people work. Finally, it includes the physical appearance and dispersal of information.

Few generalizations about information apply more than this one: we exchange information with those whom we see—face-to-face—frequently. There are many reasons why we like communicating face-to-face:

- it's easy—it doesn't require writing a memo or an e-mail message, or even looking up a phone number;
- it's often unplanned—I see you, and I remember that I had something to tell you;
- it's "rich"—it allows transfer not only of words, but also facial expression, vocal tone, body language;[9]
- it builds trust—when I see your face, I feel more comfortable exchanging sensitive information.

This fact of organizational life has great implications for communication and information management. It's clear that people who are removed from each other in physical space are unlikely to share much information. Still, that in itself doesn't doom all forms of remote communication. First of all, there are probably differences between types of people and their willingness to communicate through other means. Scientists and engineers, for instance, are probably more likely to communicate electronically and through documents than sales or marketing personnel. That's partly because of the kind of people scientists tend to be, the nature of their work, and possibly because they've had access to the Internet far longer than most other professionals. Even here, however, researchers have found that scientists and engineers communicate primarily through face-to-face contact, and that the likelihood of communication drops precipitously with distance between their offices.

Obviously, people who need to communicate regularly should be physically near each other. Indeed, a number of companies have recently manipulated physical location to influence information exchange. At Chrysler, as at so many US automobile companies, top management wanted to increase the speed of new-product development. In this case, the company has pulled it off on several recent development projects, including the Neon and Cirrus/Stratus. According to Chrysler managers, perhaps the most influential factor in increasing development speed was locating design teams together in Chrysler's Technology Center. The firm's "platform teams," as they were called, were able to communicate easily across organizational boundaries when they saw each other frequently. Other research has suggested that product-development groups with high levels of collaboration—face-to-face and otherwise—achieve higher levels of productivity and development speed than those without it.[10]

Apple Computer has also made a new R&D center the focus of its improvement efforts. At Apple, managers decided to put all researchers and product developers into a new six-building campus. However, the building designers believed it was important to provide both private space and public space for workers—so that they could both generate ideas and then share them. Building architects describe this as a "cave and commons" design.[11]

When 3M built a new facility in Austin, Texas for its electronics division, the building was designed to increase the likelihood that people would run into each other in the course of the work day. No desk is more than five minutes away from any other desk. Functions are intermingled. Work spaces (for example, chalkboards and informal meeting areas) are placed next to restrooms. 3M managers give partial credit to the building design for reducing product development time by an order of magnitude.

And at IBM senior managers made a locational change to facilitate better information flow between customer service and manufacturing. They moved the company's personal computer support help line from Atlanta to Raleigh, North Carolina, where the computers are manufactured. Their objective was to make better information connections between customer-service employees, who received calls on problems with IBM computers, and the design and assembly workers for those computers. IBM managers credit the move with quick improvements to a computer battery door and to more informative error messages.[12]

Some firms make explicit attempts to pull workers together during the day to exchange ideas. In a study of Japanese pharmaceutical firms several years ago, I noticed that several had what they called "conversation plazas" or "talk rooms" to which researchers were encouraged to go at a specified time each day. Apple's new R&D facility has a cappucino bar for this purpose.

Location can also increase cross-functional information sharing. At a Steelcase facility in France, two teams developed new products of similar complexity. One team was isolated in a separate facility; it had no contact with the rest of the business. The other team had its own space within a building occupied by other Steelcase employees, and the team had contact with the rest of the organization at lunch, in halls, and other typical meeting places. The product-development time was about equal for the two teams. But it took the isolated team three times longer to get their new product into production. Steelcase managers hypothesize that the integrated team saved time because its members were able to discuss engineering and manufacturing issues with coworkers as the new product was being developed.

Important business capabilities like new product development or customer service, then, frequently benefit from co-location. Research by consultants Andrew Bartmess and Keith Cerny, who have studied several plant location decisions, bears this out.[13] Bartmess and Cerny focused particularly on one organization—Seagate Technology—that moved only manufacturing functions to the Far East. Seagate lowered its labor costs, but lost the ability to communicate easily between design and manufacturing. This firm suffered substantially in the marketplace from its poor new product-development performance. A firm in the semiconductor equipment industry, Applied Materials, chose to move first sales, then design and manufacturing, to Japan. Putting these functions in close geographical proximity to one another helped to make Applied Materials a market leader in that highly competitive environment.

Of course, a common location need not always be permanent. Several firms have found they can put employees together on a temporary basis to increase information sharing. For example, managers at National Semiconductor often need to transfer semiconductor fabrication facilities, or "fabs," from one part of the world to another. After much trial and error, National's managers have learned there's one basic factor that improves fab production in new locations: time spent by the receiving location's managers in the company of workers running an existing fab. When the receiving and contributing workers spend less time together up front, the new fabs are plagued with difficulties. When they spend more time together, the transfer of capabilities runs more smoothly. Researchers have also documented the positive connection between common location and technology transfer in other high-tech firms.[14]

Ford has used a temporary common location for essential workers to good effect. The company's new product-development strategy emphasizies developing "world cars"—models that can be sold in a number of markets-and involve designers and engineers from all over the globe. Product-design teams are initially brought into Ford headquarters in Detroit to define the project, get to know each other, and develop working relationships. After this initial phase, which typically takes about six weeks, these team members return to their home countries and collaborate electronically.

This combination of common and dispersed locations is consistent with other research on electronic communications. Some face-to-face contact is often necessary to establish a human context for collaboration before electronic communication can proceed effectively.[15] Interestingly, other research suggests that high levels of electronic communications also increase the amount of face-to-face communication in an organization.[16] In either case, all managers intrigued by the possibilities of telecommuting need to remember that face-to-face communication still matters.

Many firms are designing "virtual offices" by replacing or augmenting physical offices with technology. Sales, customer service, and technical support personnel are being consigned to "the field," armed only with a portable computer and a cellular phone. Some of these efforts are well-planned projects; they are designed, quite pragmatically, to free up autonomous workers from office bureaucracy and excess commuting time, or to increase "face time" with customers. But other virtual offices are poorly disguised attempts to reduce physical real estate costs, with little thought given to why field employees may have trouble working in isolation. It's likely, for instance, that sales and service workers who have no offices will be less likely to transfer their learning about customers to other functions within an organization. Although it's too soon to assess how successful, even under the best of circumstances, virtual offices and telecommuting really are, I hope designers of future work environments will combine virtuality with the rich communications made possible through face-to-face contact.

In practical terms, many organizations are geographically dispersed, and employees must communicate electronically. For example, Verifone's philosophy is to locate employees near customers, not other employees. The result is a "virtual company," but CIO Will Pape believes in supplying these otherwise isolated workers with a good information environment. He notes:

> The traditional role of the CIO is to provide data. I do not simply provide data, but rather, I provide information that has already been interpreted. In this way, every one of Verifone's senior management has an identical view of where the company is in order for them to adjust their individual plans.[17]

Every day he writes an information summary of key events, financial achievements, and corporate developments and beams it out to the Verifone community via e-mail. In such a dispersed organization, Pape argues, information providers must constantly seek to add value to data through context, interpretation, and filtering. In other words, when we can't ask the controller down the hall why the cost of goods sold was up last quarter, someone else has to provide the information.

Common location is not the only physical factor that affects an organization. Both common sense and many research studies[18] suggest that office design influences information exchange. Unfortunately, there seem to be few firm guidelines for anyone who wants to design the ideal office environment for a particular type of work. Some firms like Hewlett-Packard prefer "open" office environments, at least partly for reasons of information exchange; others prefer more private offices, at least for certain managers.

Maximizing communication, in fact, isn't always the only—or most productive—goal for information management. A study of software developers, for example, indicates that including some space for quiet concentration led to productivity increases of eleven percent.[19] But even these increases may be achieved at the expense of the software's fit with user requirements. For now, all I can recommend is careful thought about what type of communication you intend and how the office environment might affect it.

One other aspect of physical arrangement that influences information management is the actual distribution of information throughout the organization. We typically expect to find information in repositories that are specially designed for its display and storage: computer screens, file cabinets, bookshelves, in- and out-boxes. Yet there are many other alternatives for the effective display of information. Many firms, for instance, have begun to place television monitors in halls and stairways. They hope that employees will "tune in" to a broadcast while walking by and will learn about the company's stock price, latest new product, or reorganization.

NEC's research facilities in Japan and New Jersey offer one of the best examples of physical dispersion of information—one that isn't based on expensive monitors or other high-tech devices. Managers of these labs wanted researchers to share information and become aware of each others' projects. They now require researchers to summarize their work on large framed posters, which are hung outside the researchers' offices. Other researchers who walk by can quickly learn if aspects of the posted work complement their own, and can knock on the right doors if they want to discuss the details or even possible collaborations.

Connecting the Organizational Dots

This chapter has covered a broad range of topics; in it I've addressed the various ways a firm's organizational environment influences the use of information. This environment includes the business situation itself—strategy, processes, organization and culture, and human resources orientation. It covers the firm's technology investment—the specific technologies employed by the organization to process and manipulate information. And it encompasses the physical factors that affect information, such as the location and design of business units, functions, and offices.

I've already noted that these organizational components have rarely been addressed in the context of information management. As I draw my description of information ecology to a close in the next chapter, I'll take on a topic that's received even less attention: a company's external environment, including its customers, suppliers, competitors, other community stakeholders, even its home country's political turmoil—along with the potential information markets that may open up new sources of revenue.

Assessment Survey for the Organizational Environment

The greater the level of agreement with the statements below, the better an organization manages its business situation, technology investment, and physical arrangement.

Business Situation

✳ My organization has a clear business strategy and has achieved consensus about what makes the business successful.

✳ Information critically increases the value of our products and services.

✳ We collect good information about the operation and performance of cross-functional business processes.

✳ Over the past several years, our information environment has changed in response to changes in our organizational structure and culture.

✳ We understand and value the knowledge and capabilities of our employees.

Technology Investment

✳ My organization uses appropriate technology; specific information and application needs are clearly identified before more IT is purchased.

✳ Our employees are able to connect to each other and to company information easily and in all locations in which they work.

✳ Senior managers have assessed how the technology we have supports or retards their overall information strategy.

✳ My organization has implemented technologies that support text and graphical information—for example, Lotus Notes or internal "Webs."

* All workers have easy access to a wide variety of internal and external information that is in understandable and usable form.

Physical Arrangement

* My organization attempts to locate employees and groups who need to share information in the same physical space.

* When employees who need to share information are scattered in different locations, their ability to share is facilitated through frequent face-to-face meetings or other means.

* My organization's office designs and layouts encourage information sharing.

* Documents, posters, videos, and other physical dispersal mechanisms are used to facilitate information use and sharing.

* We attempt to distribute value-added information to dispersed workers rather than raw data.

Information and the Outside World

Information networks straddle the world.
Nothing remains concealed. But the
sheer volume of information dissolves
the information itself. We are unable to take it all in.

Gunter Grass, *The New Statesman and Society*

All companies have to be informed about the outside world: what customers need, what competitors are trying to accomplish, what regulators insist we must do. Much of a company's internal information, in fact, describes the outside world of business—the third and final environment of an information ecology. But the external environment can also motivate our information actions. A customer demands that our different business units share information about their dealings with them. External suppliers need to know about our business so they can replenish our supply of their products efficiently. As members of an external trade association, we agree to begin collecting and sharing information on aspects of company performance.

It's a business truism that firms must achieve some level of "fit" or congruence with their external environments—a truism that applies to a company's information environment as much as to anything else. When it comes to marketing battles, industry trends, and local governments, no company is powerful enough either to ignore or control its external environment completely. Just as obviously, however, companies can't simply play dead or let external events buffet them. In practical terms, there are at least three ways to interact with the external environment. A firm can

- *adapt* to the outside world;
- *scan* that world for changes to which it must respond;
- *mold* the outside world, through information products or services, to its own competitive advantage.

Some of these relationships may be mediated through the organizational environment. For example, if my competitors engage in lean production activities, I'll be forced to reengineer my business processes, which will also force dramatic change in how I manage inventory information. As with so much of information ecology, the connections form a web of related actions (see Figure 11-1). Later in this chapter, I'll discuss how companies can usefully scan, adapt to, and mold the external environment, along with possible obstacles to any of the three approaches.

The external environment is an ecology in itself—indeed, a very large one. But since a single organization can't manage the outside world, it's more helpful to think of the external environment as a series of markets in which the organization may participate. It may engage in these markets by gathering or providing free information, or by buying and selling information.

For our purposes, then, I break the external environment into three types of markets: general business markets, technology markets, and—last but cer-

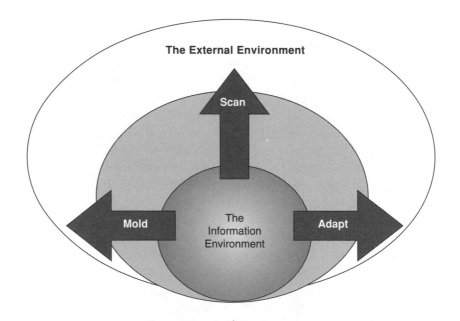

Figure 11-1. How the External and Internal Environments Relate

tainly not least from an ecological standpoint—information markets. Each has fuzzy boundaries, large areas of overlap, and common sources and structures; but different groups within an organization will look at these markets for different reasons. Viewing them separately can help managers focus on the user of the information gained, not on its source or format.

Business Markets

Few managers would disagree with the idea that conditions in a firm's business markets should be understood and reflected by its internal organization. Changes in the worlds of customers, competitors, suppliers, business partners, and regulators constitute critical information for any company. Managers must ask, "What do we need to know about our external environment to be successful? On which customers, competitors, and external stakeholders do we most need information? How will knowledge of these external entities influence our corporate behavior?"

In fact, such questions are at the heart of marketing. Some researchers have called firms that focus their information energies in this way "market-oriented," because of their "organization-wide generation, dissemination, and responsiveness to market intelligence."[1] Yet even firms in the same industry often need different internal information systems for obtaining business-market information. That's because their overall business strategies differ.

Consider two hypothetical firms in the consumer electronics business. One is an innovator, always pushing the envelope in terms of style and new features. The other follows the introduction of any successful product with a more reliable, lower cost product. This "follower" specializes in learning from early sales research and perfecting the technology. Both will gather much of the same information from customers, suppliers, and competitors: preferences on styles and features, cost point preferences, manufacturing techniques, supplier reliability, new product plans. But the manner in which they gather this information will differ significantly. The innovator, for instance, needs an external business market system that's informal and relies little on staff scanning of the environment. The top managers of the organization themselves have to develop their own personal network of industry insiders, trend analysts, conjecture, gossip, and so on. Such a firm won't keep up with the quickly changing industry environment if a staff has to filter the information first for the actual decision-makers.

While there's no one set of information that every organization should know about—or a single approach to acquiring that information and staying current—some types of business information are more popular than others. Let's start with the folks who buy what a company has to sell.

Customers

Customer information can be broken into two groups: potential customers and current customers. Knowledge about potential customers comes from demographic data, market surveys, and other information sources that can be purchased on the open market.

As for finding out about current customers, this broad world of information can be further divided into *customer data* and *customer knowledge*. Customer data typically involves transactions—how many products or services a customer has purchased; how many complaints a customer has registered; how long a customer took to pay an invoice. Customer data may also involve simple, easily structured attributes of the company or individual—for example, the customer's geographic location, organizational structure, and personnel. Of course, these attributes change frequently; maintaining customer data requires eternal vigilance.

So-called "data mining" attempts to extract useful information from the very large transaction databases that include this sort of information. The IT press implies that powerful computers can simply be turned loose on huge databases without human involvement. But in my experience, computers rarely identify information that a human isn't seeking; an intelligent person is necessary to structure the analysis.

That's why customer knowledge—value-added information gained from experience or reflection about data—is both more potentially useful and labor-intensive. Such knowledge typically resides in the heads of customer-service personnel; how managers can extract, formalize, and distribute this knowledge is the real issue. Many firms are adopting technologies that make the capture and distribution of customer knowledge much easier. However, they often fail to motivate customer-service personnel sufficiently to transfer their knowledge to systems. At the end of a long work day, for instance, a tired salesperson needs a good reason to key in the knowledge he learned that morning from a customer into a Lotus Notes system. In this case, it's clear an effective use of information from the external environment is obviously related to the information *and* organizational culture of a firm.

To be sure, there are more formal approaches to gaining customer knowledge. The primary tactic for keeping current with customer needs and attitudes involves asking them questions—through everything from simple customer-satisfaction postcards to unstructured interviews or focus groups. There's no shortage of books about eliciting, and responding to, customer information.[2] They cheerfully describe the best surveys (both mail and telephone) and use of toll-free numbers, comment cards, front line education, focus groups, and face-to-face interviews.

Unfortunately, such books offer little practical advice about how to manage that information once it's received. Because customer knowledge is relatively unstructured, it tends to be stored in filing cabinets if at all, and is seldom leveraged or reused. While customer data is often over-engineered and finessed by computers, customer knowledge remains unmapped, uninterpreted, and ends up in unusable formats.

Both forms of customer information can also suffer from a lack of cognitive authority or engagement. Like any kind of information in an overloaded business, customer feedback must be compelling to force a significant change in the organization's way of doing business. Even if thousands of customers send in postcards scribbled with "I hate this stupid product!" or "Your company belongs in the trash can along with the Whatzit you sold me!", such comments need to be put in a form that's easily communicated to everyone in the organization—not just seen by the marketing assistants who open the mailbags.

One way for managers to overcome corporate inertia is to make personal, planned visits to customer sites just for the purpose of finding out what customers want. As marketing expert Edward McQuarrie points out, "it is one thing to collect information on customers, and another thing entirely to respond to that information.. . .Information that is acquired firsthand is more credible and compelling."[3] Of course, as McQuarrie goes on to explain, the information that's acquired during such visits has to be managed in order to respond effectively to it.

Suppliers

The techniques and sources for gaining information from suppliers are very similar to dealing with a company's own customers—but with one dramatic difference. While suppliers often have a more vested interest in talking with you, they also have more information to hide. They want to build good relationships, but don't wish to give away all their power.

Many firms have found that their customers are also suppliers, and vice-versa. In fact, one firm could be a customer, supplier, venture partner, and competitor. It's difficult enough to maintain consistency on the attributes of external firms in one database, much less several. Therefore, companies like IBM and Hewlett-Packard have developed one "business associate" database that acknowledges the tangled relationships of corporate life. With such a database, structured information about a business associate of multiple types is recorded only once. Still, this sort of database is more useful for supplier data than for supplier knowledge.

Competitors

Every firm wants to know what the competition is doing. Understanding a competitor's intentions and status is valuable information for any manager.

There are almost endless sources available for learning how to manage competitor information.[4] Richard Combs and John Moorhead, two competitive intelligence experts, provide a clearer view of the process of competitive intelligence than other sources. They find that most firms use a four-step process to gather competitor intelligence:

- *Identification* of the information need. Toward that end, Combs and Moorhead emphasize that "the CI [competitive intelligence] researcher must, as much as possible, be an active part of planning for and applying the results of the research."
- *Collection* of information. The basic sources of CI are fairly straightforward: information from inside the company, on-line databases, and people outside your company. But there are also many "creative" sources that take advantage of everything from want ads to counting parking spaces in a competitor's lot.
- *Analysis* of the information. Combs and Moorhead cite a variety of approaches: functional and chronological sorting; market-share analysis; organization charts; benchmarking; product/service comparisons; stock-market performance; value- chain analysis; strength and weakness analysis; vulnerability analysis; and listing distinctive competencies.[5]
- *Reporting* of the information to a decision-maker. As Combs and Moorhead point out, "Unheard, the CI message is meaningless"; they stress the importance of formatting and communicating information in a way that is appropriate to the audience that will be using the competitor intelligence analysis.

In addition to these four steps, Combs and Moorhead also identify issues that are common to all competitor intelligence efforts. They argue that organization of the CI system is necessary for effective and efficient performance of all the steps. The information flow can't be left to chance, but must be actively managed. And ethical rules of thumb should guide the collection of information about competitors. In general, it's best to stick with public information (although that doesn't always mean *published* information.) When in doubt, managers should discuss various practices for gaining competitor intelligence with other professionals, including lawyers.

As with other forms of information, the most effective means of gathering, formatting, and distributing information about competitors will be a hybrid system of human, on-line, and text-based information sources. Certainly, on-line services and computer databases will increasingly play a part in such a system, but they're really only a starting point for creating a full picture of a competitor's strengths and weaknesses. The most valuable and important competitor intelligence will always be carried within the heads of analysts and front-line personnel. As Leonard Fuld, who runs a leading competitive intelligence consulting firm, observes,

> We are all taught as an underlying notion from grade school on up that what you see in print is not only the truth, but is the best way to find information. In the task of gathering intelligence, though, just the opposite axiom is the case, because what you will find in print about your competitor may be old and inaccurate. For up-to-date information, for intelligence that gives a true reading of the market and its competitors, you need to go after the experts through interviews as well as by attending trade shows.[6]

Fuld is somewhat skeptical about relying too much on computer databases for holding competitor intelligence. Computer databases are not efficient at storing data extracted from human sources. As Fuld says, "Resist the temptation to expand the manual file or computer data base immediately...you and your staff will spend more time keying in the data than you spend collecting or communicating it. The result: The information is dated by the time it comes online."[7]

In many respects, handling what a company learns about its competitors is similar to handling other kinds of information in a well-managed information ecology. A hybrid competitor intelligence system should have an easy user interface, allowing access to a wide variety of information sources, of which on-line systems are only one piece of the puzzle. If a database is used, it should point to human sources of additional information. Experts should be encouraged to structure their expertise and make it available electronically to others. Internal Web pages are well-suited to this purpose; both Sequent Computer and Hewlett-Packard have extensive Web pages devoted to competitor intelligence.

Digital Equipment's system for gathering this kind of information is also a hybrid. It includes several on-line databases and different levels of staff support. One staff group deals with requests that take two hours or less to process. Another conducts more extensive research. Still a third group creates original research on Digital's competitors and their products.[8]

Regulators and Public Policy

Managers have begun paying more attention to managing information about the external political arena. In large firms, when this has been done at all it's been handled by specialists—for example, the "regulatory" or "government affairs" department, often with an office in Washington, D.C. Indeed, a local presence where policies are made can be useful, both for receiving and providing information. But as large companies globalize, it's difficult to staff all major world capitals with specialists in government information. Firms will have to rely increasingly on two alternative sources of political and regulatory information: external providers and internal employees on the "front line" in countries where the company does business.

Using external information suppliers for governmental information isn't unusual, but most firms need to add a step to their processing of what these outside sources provide. Information of generic relevance about the country's governmental or regulatory directions should be scanned for relevance to the industry or company in which one is interested, then captured internally along with informed speculation from internal observers about its meaning and implications. A document that synthesizes all of these sources is what a firm's decision-makers should read. While it may be interesting to know that the European Community is reforming its policies for approving new product safety levels, it's even more useful to find out that your company has three products up for approval—and that the last time this happened, six months of hard work went down the drain when you had to re-submit.

The other change in how such governmental information must be managed involves the use of front-line employees to gather and synthesize that information. A marketing department in South America, for example, may have to become a government intelligence department as well. Someone in that group can read the papers, consult with local lobbyists, get on the mailing list for proposed regulations, and attend cocktail parties in the capital—then summarize and share the information with others in the firm. This is particularly important in countries like the United States that are moving away from national services toward the decentralized services provided by states and local governments. Otherwise, you'd need a governmental relations office in every major city.

Technology Markets

Technology markets encompass not only products but also the services available in the outside world of a business. New technology can drive new opportunities. Lower cost fiber-optic communications now enable the transfer of graphic images within organizations and even to customers and suppliers. The pervasiveness of personal computing makes possible widespread information creation, distribution, and storage. The external IT services market includes facilities management, application development, systems integration, and networking services. Firms can use their knowledge of technology markets to choose to outsource particular components or processes of the internal information system. Outsourcing services, for example, frees up cash and time; it can also free up internal information managers to focus on information content.

To leverage information about external technology markets, senior managers must take several crucial steps. They must establish a regular process for assessing technologies. They must let business strategies drive the technologies implemented, as well as allowing important technologies to influence those strategies. Perhaps most difficult of all, they should engage all managers, not just a few specialists, in understanding and assessing potentially useful technologies.[9] There are four basic steps for this process:

- scanning/identification of new external technologies;
- creating the business case for how to apply the new technology;
- technical and market analysis;
- implementation and rollout.

The first step is relatively easy. There's no shortage of technical information in the external environment, and many professionals enjoy staying abreast of emerging technologies. Scanning the technology markets is little different from scanning the rest of the external environment. The only real difference is that the published information about technical advances is quite voluminous and easy to locate. Technology firms have a vested interest in keeping clients and customers informed in such a fast-changing world, so there are plenty of easy-to-acquire, cheap, paper and on-line sources about the latest products and specifications.

Getting information on the latest IT is much easier than learning about competitors or customers. And admittedly, the payoff can be very large: in some accounts, for example, Microsoft began with a 1974 article in *Popular Electronics* called "World's First Minicomputer Kit to Rival Commercial Models." Founder Paul Allen noticed the article and began working with Bill Gates to produce software for this computer.[10]

Even so, it's hard to capture and spread the private learning of individuals throughout the organization. There's also the matter of determining what technologies will be evaluated in depth and tracked with interest. Not all technological advances are equally important to all organizations. Also note that simply identifying information about an emerging technology opportunity didn't automatically determine Microsoft's success. Arguably, the other three steps of the process made the real difference there; and it's these three steps— creating the right business case, market analysis, and implementation—that still trouble most companies.

One way to help carve up the problem of monitoring new technologies is to break them into categories based on their relationship with the organization's work. Along this dimension, we can define IT as either infrastructural, current-use, or innovative.

Infrastructural Technologies

Almost every organization must evaluate and purchase this kind of IT on a regular basis. Such technologies make possible basic infrastructural capabilities like communications, document processing, and transaction processing. For most business organizations, they include phones and voice networks; personal computers; and fax machines. Few companies can get along without these technologies—even consulting professionals who work out of their own homes—or without regularly updating them.

Evaluating infrastructural technologies is usually straightforward for two reasons: (1) since all firms have to evaluate them on a regular basis, there's plenty of published material comparing and monitoring these technologies; and (2) the purchase of infrastructural technologies rarely results in competitive advantage per se. Phones and computers are mass market items, and all have similar features. No competitor is going to outfox you with a slightly better fax machine.

But because these technologies are so common, everyone inside the organization has an opinion about them. Firms can get bogged down in endless conflict over the selection of a new computer platform. Spending a lot of time debating the merits of essentially indistinguishable versions of the same technology is unproductive. What matters most is establishing common, standard technologies so that programs, documents, and messages can be exchanged easily throughout a company. All information managers should try to steer executives away from these debates, so that everyone can focus more time on the process issues of current-use and innovative technologies.

Current-Use Technologies

These are the IT systems already widely used and critical to the daily operations of an organization. They are standard within particular industries, and every member of the industry must monitor them to stay current. Reservations systems have long been current-use technologies for airlines; remotely networked check-in systems have recently become current-use in the rental car industry; and bedside terminals are becoming so in health care.

The operational test for a current-use technology is if it is being adopted to improve efficiency or productivity of a current process. While these technologies don't change the way business is done, they can speed it up, improve its quality, or reduce its expense. But because current-use technologies only increase productivity, they seldom create competitive advantage. Companies that have the very best IT in place may gain such an advantage, but it's often fleeting; the ever declining costs for hardware and software, for instance, mean that the high-tech of today can be easily and more cheaply purchased by competitors tomorrow.

Certainly, firms should spend some time on evaluating and scanning these technologies, especially *before* they become current-use. Once they've been adopted, however, they can usually be evaluated and handled by technical experts who understand the particular technology and its function.

Innovative Technologies

This is the IT that matters most when it comes to scanning technology markets—the systems that promise a new way of doing business, either by creating new products or new services. Implementing the right innovative technologies usually requires organizational, cultural, and strategy changes as well as technical changes. And for innovative technologies to succeed, evaluation and scanning must be part of the firm's overall strategic process.

The value of innovative technologies lies in their ability, as Daniel Burrus puts it in *Technotrends,* to "go beyond the competition," creating new markets where there are no competitors at all and more opportunities for higher profits.[11] But it's not enough just to identify these technologies and then study them for years. Instead, Burrus argues, the whole organization must be prepared to capitalize quickly on new technologies and to make changes to a central part or process within the organization. His process-oriented version involves five general steps: anticipation, communication, flexibility, integration, and orchestration of new technologies. Once again, this is an information-intensive activity. Each of these steps requires an efficient and integrated information system to support it.

Managers often grapple with one particularly difficult issue when deciding on the use of innovative technology: the direction of influence. Should a firm's business direction drive a search for a suitable technology, or should organizations use a technology to enable new business directions? Burrus argues for the latter perspective; the key in technology-driven change, of course, is to perform a careful business analysis of the opportunities made possible by IT. Both types of influence are desirable in specific situations, but establishing a general strategy on this issue is hard, and few firms do it well. Most technology analysts can justify spending on a desired technology, but senior managers shouldn't necessarily rely on such justifications to make the business case for a new technology—especially if implementation will require a big investment. Firms also need to take technology uncertainty into account; options analysis is one such approach.

The third step for assessing external technology, technical and market analysis, is full of pitfalls as well. The IT world changes quite rapidly, and anticipating shifts and responding at almost the same time is one of the greatest challenges in technology management. In addition, innovative technologies often support cross-functional applications and business areas—which is theoretically useful for an information environment. But when myriad business functions are involved, managers will need to determine who sets the dimensions on which the new technology or process should be evaluated. Who makes the decision about actual adoption?

Implementation, the final step, is difficult when any type of organizational change is involved. A new technology—glitzy and thrilling as it may seem to its IT promoters—can wreak havoc if nobody else wants it, or if most workers are inordinately attached to the old way of doing things. Because technologists are usually convinced that the technical innovation sells itself, they don't sufficiently "market" the technology to those who might benefit from it. Research on technology transfer suggests that multiple means of implementing new technologies should be employed, including pilot projects, financial incentives, visits to other sites using the new technology, and any other promotional scheme a company can devise.

One common means of institutionalizing technology scanning and adoption is the development of an advanced-technology lab or group. Such groups may be permanent or temporary; temporary task forces are typically charged with evaluating a particular technology. However, the size of these groups is usually quite small—too small for the task at hand. Exxon's Advanced Technology Group, for example, has seven people in it; Prudential Insurance's group has three. How can such a small group transfer a technology across such a large organization?

A general process for bringing emerging technologies and the appropriate business people closer together on a permanent basis is often more useful than setting up an IT task force. With such a process in place, strategic planning for business would always evaluate relevant emerging technologies, and scanning of technologies would be conducted based on a company's strategic goals. Shell Oil, for example, created "Technology-Driven Business Planning," an all-too-rare approach that evaluated new technologies in the context of specific business unit strategies. Senior managers evaluated a set of "generic applications" for their relevance to business tactics.

Ideally, emerging technologies, and the people who monitor them, should both be included in strategic planning. Not all technological innovations are good for all companies; an interplay between strategy and technology innovations must exist. Only those technologies that potentially support or enable an organization's strategy should be evaluated seriously. This is another variation on the "strategic alignment" issue that has long dogged information systems management.[12]

For instance, Southwest Airlines is a very successful airline but has little in the way of advanced reservation technology. It offers no assigned seating, and tickets can't be reserved through most major reservation systems. (As an interesting aside, Southwest gives its customers plastic number cards for boarding order; when customers have boarded, the cards are counted. As a result, Southwest seems to have better boarding information than more automated carriers). American Airlines, on the other hand, has historically maintained a major business in information technology and travel-related information services. These airlines' differing business strategies (one a commuter airline of short, regular hops, the other a long-range intercontinental airline) has led to different implementation of technology.

Innovative technologies are usually much harder to justify financially in terms of cost savings or increased efficiency. Firms that insist on a quick and sure payoff for all technological implementations, then, will largely be consigned to improving current-use technologies. To adopt innovative technologies takes courage, sound judgment, and tolerance of risk.

Technical managers within the firm should be those most concerned with IT markets. However, as I've already made clear, leaving these concerns in the IT ghetto means technology decisions that truly affect the business can end up out of the hands of senior managers. Techno-utopianism, enhanced by the blandishments of IT vendors and service providers, has led too many managers to believe in an illusory technical fix to their problems. Because information markets are currently smaller than technology markets, and because much of the information needed by managers comes from internal sources, far fewer professionals advocate a focus on external information itself. The next section should indicate why this can be a costly mistake.

Information Markets

Perhaps the most significant external market for an overall information ecology is the one where information is bought and sold. Broadly speaking, information markets include both already-gathered information about external entities (such as customers or competitors) and aspects of the external environment itself (industry data standards, government reporting requirements, or products and services composed of information). External information markets are comprised of a wide range of sources and formats, including on-line databases, published works, opinions of experts and industry leaders, political themes and currents, demographics, and the latest trade show gossip.

Buying External Information

In general, the information market world is large and growing at a rapid pace. There are more than 2,000 on-line databases alone; that doesn't include the many organizations producing and selling information in nonautomated formats, or any of the millions of information sources on the Web. Such external information can be a resource of great value to organizations. At a minimum, information professionals have to know what external information exists to support their firms. Then, when new information needs arise, internal information providers should work with their users to perform "make vs. buy" analyses for specific kinds of information. Internal providers sometimes feel threatened by external sources, but they can add significant value for users and their organizations by connecting internal needs and external sources—or by analyzing, summarizing, and contextualizing external information.

External suppliers can provide not only information, but also information architecture and standards. For example, many large, sophisticated firms, such as Xerox and Digital Equipment, have outsourced the task of identifying and structuring commercial customer information to Dun & Bradstreet Information Services. The company assigns a unique "Duns number" in its Market Identifiers file to over twenty million businesses worldwide; the numbering system allows identification of corporate ownership structure. It would be very difficult for an individual company to track changes in customer structure, name, and location on its own; Dun & Bradstreet provides this tracking service for many firms, some of whom don't even purchase the commercial credit information that was the original basis for creating this company database.

Xerox learned the value of this kind of outsourcing the hard way. When a cross-functional management team at Xerox set out to create an internal standard for customer information, they eventually gave up and adopted the Duns company identifier as its worldwide standard. Several competing identifiers within Xerox contained more information or were more relevant to particular business units; yet the Duns number had worldwide authority, was maintained better than the others, and allowed more integration with business partners that also used the Duns structure.

Needless to say, information markets have become critical to the survival of most firms; they depend on information as much as any other input. Micromarketing, niche manufacturing, consolidation of the value chain, mass customization, rapid response teams, total quality management, reengineering, virtual organizations—all of these trends and a host of others are absolutely dependent on obtaining rapid, accurate information from sources outside the organization. In most cases, the information is purchased, either outright or through business alliances and partnerships, in an exchange that can be characterized as a market transaction.

Not long ago, for instance, demographic information was expensive, difficult to assemble, and used only by large organizations. But now even small businesses can acquire, and depend on, inexpensive information about customers and markets. Large consumer products firms, such as Frito-Lay, have sufficient demographic information to know virtually everything that matters about the people who shop in each retail outlet in which their products are sold. Until recently, these firms stocked retailer shelves on a "national pattern," in which a certain amount of shelf space was devoted to a standard mix of products. Now, however, Frito-Lay can vary product mix not only in its large retailers, but even in convenience stores, based on demographic information. Demographics is only one part of this mosaic; there are literally thousands of sources of inexpensive, on-line information about customers, competitors, suppliers, regulators, and markets.[13]

Selling Your Own Information

While most companies focus on what information to buy from information markets, an increasing number are selling in those markets as well. I've already mentioned Monsanto in this regard. The chemical company has recently begun a new service business called Infielder that sells information about "what works" in agriculture to farmers. For years, Monsanto's agricultural chemicals business has accumulated information on the proper combinations of crops, soil, weather, fertilizer, and pesticides. The company compiled this information into a database that is distributed to growers through the cable television network. Monsanto's Ag managers reasoned that an on-line service would be an expedient way to package this product. More important, in order to allay concerns about proprietary advantage for Monsanto, the company's new information-selling business became a joint-venture with several other firms in the agricultural products industry. The business began in early 1994, and so far is doing quite well.

The software firm Autodesk is planning to sell the engineering and architectural designs its customers create with its AutoCAD software package. Customers can begin their design process by borrowing from existing designs with similar components. Several other firms that produce information systems for their own internal use, such as Fidelity Investments and American Airlines, are also investigating selling customers modules or objects that they have developed. Such potentially salable information is, as Stan Davis notes, a business's "information exhaust." Given that this information is generated anyway, firms that don't participate in these markets may be missing a real opportunity.

Moving into information markets, however, can present some serious challenges. First and foremost, most organizations are not designed either organizationally or culturally to sell information in external markets. Information professionals have not historically viewed themselves as businesspeople with responsibility for producing products and services and then selling them to external customers. Most IS workers have seen themselves as internal support workers, part of a company's general overhead. But as I pointed out in the chapter on information staff, the new-and-improved information professional has to take on more business responsibility, including bottom-line accountability, before a firm can expect him or her to sell information effectively in the open market.

Viewing information as overhead also leads to confusion about how to set prices for information services. When the cost of generating information within organizations is simply assigned to overhead, no direct charge-back or expense system is created for it. While the network, or the PCs, or the office space may all be tracked, the cost of the information itself is rarely accounted for. Thus, pricing for information products or services on the open market becomes problematic, because even internally, there's little understanding of the costs and pricing structure. Fortunately, some research and consulting work on how to price external information has recently become available.[14]

One reason that pricing strategies and business savvy are so critical here is that many information markets lack structure. Information is so malleable that it can be packaged and sold in an almost infinite variety of ways. At least with physical commodities, the size of trucks and the shape of containers lends some uniformity to the lots and transfer technologies. Not so for information; almost everything about it is open to negotiation.

Firms that enter an information market may also run into the larger issue of how to organize or participate in public or quasi-public information networks like the Internet. In this case, most companies, especially those that wish to build cognitive authority through larger distribution, will have to deal with each other as well as with governmental bodies. Information markets need infrastructure just as much as factories need interstate highways. This is particularly true for electronic information that's only of use in real time; if it has to be distributed on paper or CD-ROM through the mail, then it loses most of its value. Again, plenty of research on the economics and infrastructure of external information is available for interested managers.[15]

Adapting to the External Environment

Now that I've detailed the three external markets that influence an organization, let's look at how companies interact with the outside world. No firm is an island; all must pass information to and from the external environment. The three approaches I'll describe here—adapting to, scanning, and molding the outside world—depend on specific business circumstances. But more important, they depend on managers who know how to assess when a company can control outside events—and when it can't.

All organizations, no matter how large or powerful, must adapt to the external environment to some extent. That means the internal information system must be flexible enough to establish the channels, protocols, and content for that information transfer. Below I'll outline several aspects of the external environment to which all firms must adapt.

Government Regulations

Every firm has to report some information to governmental bodies about employees, sales, importing, hazardous materials, safety, and so on. Some of this information is strictly required, with little room for reporting flexibility. Other requirements, however, are more open to interpretation. Firms that actively manage their political environment, for instance, may create a significant competitive advantage.

Citibank and NationsBank have long pushed the frontiers of interstate banking, growing through acquisition and "non-bank banks" when there were ambiguous regulations against them. Health-insurance companies, for better or worse, didn't wait for US health-care reform before beginning to shape public perceptions of the debate. Although there are many reasons for the failure of these reforms, "spin control" by the industry certainly contributed. When the issues are complex and multifaceted, it's a good bet the party with the best-packaged information will win most of the battles.

Customer or Supplier Interfaces

Just as firms must agree with their suppliers and customers about the size of boxes, pallets, and warehouse loading docks, they also must have some common means for communicating information about their interactions. When the information to be exchanged is highly structured and transactional, it's suitable for electronic data interchange. By letting computers communicate directly with computers, firms reduce the number of intermediary hand-offs, and increase the speed and accuracy of ordering and payment information. But for less structured information, few standards exist; information is typically exchanged in document form.

From a technological standpoint, electronic links with customers and suppliers are no longer exceptional. Several Japanese car manufacturers rotate their technical and managerial workers throughout supplier ranks, thus providing continual channels for communication. Information ecologists take note: even with the speed and coordination necessary for just-in-time systems, the human factor is still irreplaceable. In order to remain flexible and to adapt to the external environment, companies can't rely solely on structured data exchange with business partners. All possible channels for exchanging information should be considered, from tying together intranets to regular face-to-face meetings, co-location, and staff rotation programs.

Scanning the External Environment

In day-to-day managerial terms, scanning the external environment, rather than adapting to or molding it, matters most. But getting an organization to look outside itself, and respond effectively to what it sees, is no easy task. An entire mini-industry has grown up around helping organizations scan different aspects of their environments, disseminate that information, and change to fit the environment.

The purpose of this discussion is not to summarize or supplant all that existing work. I'll focus instead on the information flows, both within and outside the organization, that comprise successful scanning. There's a generic process by which any information is identified, located, transferred, and, most important, used to create change within an organization; readers will recognize the basic information management process I presented in Chapter 8. As I emphasized there, organizations that leave any of these steps to chance are unlikely to create or maintain good information environments.

Step 1: Identifying What External Information Is Required

The external information an organization needs should include, at the very least, information about customers, competitors, regulators, suppliers, and technology markets. However, one manager's cup of tea isn't necessarily another's. Frank Aguilar's classic book, *Scanning the Business Environment*, illustrates some of the factors involved in determining what external information is "strategic" or relevant.[16] Scanning for relevance depends on the individual's general predilections toward external information, on his or her knowledge of the domain, on the industry conditions for the organization, and on the type of information being scanned. Aguilar found that the managers he studied were most interested in news of the market, including competitors, customers, pricing, market structure and change; technical news about new and existing products came in second.

Making the identification of information needs an explicit part of the scanning process may cut down on idiosyncratic and repetitive requests for external information. The identification step is also valuable because it casts information managers in a role that's likely to have a productive impact on the strategic direction of the firm. By learning through the strategic planning process what information the company needs, the information managers of the corporation can also generate a set of goals for the creation and acquisition of new information, even if they can't get their hands on it immediately.

Step 2: Deciding Where to Look for Information

Once an organization's information needs are clear, then the search for the right sources can begin. Obviously, firms won't find all the information they want, and some of what they do find will be too expensive or difficult to acquire. Still, any corporate or "special" librarian can direct such inquiries with ease. That's where emphasizing new tasks for information support staff comes in. Effective information managers will continually provide, and push for, diverse information sources that illuminate the widest view possible of the external environment.

Lack of diversity in information sources probably contributes most to blind spots in environmental scanning. If firms get all their information only from "acceptable," "conservative," or "authoritative" sources, they probably won't see fundamental changes taking place in their external environment. A great amount of the important information within an organization comes from face-to-face discussions, rumor, gossip, conjecture, and other soft and tough-to-manage information sources. Yet formalized systems almost ensure that such information is completely expunged from external scanning efforts.

In a recent article, researcher Grandon Gill countered the usual practice of praising automated scanning procedures.[17] One of his prime examples, Mrs. Field's Cookies, is renowned for its use of computerized information systems in business operations. At Mrs. Field's, store managers are guided by computers in many key functions, including when to bake cookies, hand out free samples, order supplies—even when to hire or fire an employee. However, by the early 1990s Mrs. Field's management was caught off guard by major changes in its industries, and the company suffered considerable economic setbacks. The information systems at Mrs. Field's could robotize the process of making cookies, but when bread and sandwiches were added to the menu, neither the systems nor store managers could adjust.

Gill argues that Mrs. Field's executives overlooked major cues from the company's external environment because they were obsessed with computerizing the internal information environment. While he doesn't offer definitive proof for this theory, it makes for fascinating speculation. Does automation "wired" to a particular type of information preclude rapid adaptation to new information environments? Are the most human-oriented information ecologies therefore the most flexible? All the research we'd want for such sweeping conclusions isn't in yet, but I believe a mixture of humanly and technically provided information yields the best trade-off between efficiency and flexibility.

Step 3: Bringing External Information Inside

Once information is located, the information manager faces a new series of hurdles. For example, transferring information across the boundaries of the organization may lead to architectural difficulties. Unless the organization has already adopted standards for the inclusion of external information, the format and structure of such information may fit poorly with the organization's formal information systems. Extensive massaging may be required to fit divergent information within an organization's preexisting categories and channels of communication.

Furthermore, behavior problems often pop up in the transfer process. External information is "not invented here" and may be poorly received by users if it's negative. This is the classic result of many an innovative consulting study. It's all too easy for senior managers or overworked professionals to ignore external information if it doesn't match what they want to hear—even if the organization has paid for it. In short, a process, a person, and a channel must all be developed to pull the information inside the organization and integrate it into a usable form.

For example, at Sematech, a research consortium of semiconductor manufacturers, research information has to flow from Sematech to its member companies. In addition to the usual information distribution channels of documents and databases, each member company has "assignees" who move to Austin, Texas, where Sematech is located, for several years. There are also permanent workers within Sematech who are responsible for ensuring that information flows to each member company, and employees of the member company located within the companies whose job it is to pull the information in. Sematech has a "Technology Transfer" department and a high-level steering committee to address the issue. It's only through such conscious efforts as this that information can penetrate the walls that organizations unconsciously create.

The experience of Microelectronics and Computer Technology Corporation (MCC), another Austin high-tech consortium established to collaborate on developing new technologies, illustrates just how hard it can be to transfer external information.[18] The executives who ran MCC were afraid that confidential information would be stolen by foreign companies or governments, and focused too much time and too many resources on protecting research results. But transferring technology from MCC to the member companies that started and financially supported it became a far bigger problem than maintaining confidentiality. Researchers inside member companies were threatened by MCC's efforts, and adopted protective "not invented here" stances. None of the member companies were based in Austin, and researchers wanted to do research, not travel to other cities to transfer ideas. That meant there was little face-to-face contact between information providers and users. The situation became so grim that MCC could have placed its information on the public street outside its building and no one would have taken it.

Step 4: Using External Information

The final step in managing external information is using and acting on it. Since external information is widely available and for sale, competitive advantage comes from using it more effectively than other firms. Indeed, throughout this book I've described instances in which key information has been ignored by companies—including at both Ford and General Motors, where market research suggested that a minivan would have broad market appeal, but neither company acted fast enough. That left Chrysler to build and market the first minivan in 1983, selling several million of them to American drivers.[19]

Whether or not information gets used in decision-making is a complex issue, one that I can't treat fully here. Information is more likely to be used, of course, if it has cognitive authority, or perceived reliability and accuracy. As McKinnon and Bruns make clear, managers go to great lengths to independently confirm information's reliability through several channels. With external information sources, however, many of the informal means that managers use to cross-check internal information won't be available.

Researcher Patrick Wilson has investigated the murky process by which information acquires cognitive authority.[20] He argues that cognitive authority is a matter of degree. Those seeking to establish the authority of external information sources might follow his general rule of thumb: multiple, well-regarded authorities will be necessary to establish a source's validity. Yet many organizations fail to act on external information because nobody attempts to cross-check external information to establish its authority. Information support staff and providers would do well to remember that it takes more than one well-respected information manager to establish the cognitive authority of an outside source. And information professionals must continually buttress the credibility of their sources.

Molding the External Environment

While adapting to the outside world is necessary for a company's survival—and scanning for industry and market trends is indispensable—active management of the external information environment may represent the greatest opportunity for future business growth. Many possibilities exist for molding the external environment. Companies often can't control their industry or external politics; but managers might consider some of the following ways to put their stamp on the outside world.

Public Relations and Issues Management

One of the most common ways to influence the external environment is through PR that actively crafts the image and perception of a company or its brands. The right kind of public relations can be invaluable, especially for companies whose survival depends on being recognized within mass markets, or on receiving government approval for key actions. A vast industry of public relations firms, of course, are available to nurture this task.

In some companies, PR is little more than "spin control." Managers try to improve the corporate image only after the negative consequences of some action—everything from a merger or business acquistion to poor labor practices in developing countries—have become public. But companies can also adopt a more proactive PR stance, one that's often called "issues management." While the idea is not new, reseachers Betsy Sigman and Sarah-Kathryn McDonald argue that "the systematic identification of emerging issues and their potential impacts clearly is new in the corporate world."[21] They describe five steps for issues management: identification, analysis, preparation of organizational responses, development of detailed implementation plans, and evaluation of organizational responses.

Rogene Bucholz defines issues management as "an organized and systematic effort on the part of a corporation to respond effectively to issues of public concern in its external environment".[22] Based on her work and that of Sigman and McDonald, it's clear that organizations with effective PR operations have an internal information environment capable of not only identifying outside trends, but also of providing information-rich products and services designed to affect the direction of those trends.

Ironically, public relations and issues management are typically handled by professionals who aren't viewed as information providers in an organization. Forging closer working relationships between internally and externally oriented information managers—for example, getting PR people onto information management councils and task forces—makes a lot of sense. Instead of complaining about how PR people "think" or glad-hand the press, why not let them into the information loop?

Market Signaling

Companies can influence behavior and actions within their markets by the selective release of information. Signaling can be a very powerful tool for setting the competitive climate of an industry, and in influencing pricing, promotions, and other marketing approaches. Market signaling is a classic strategy topic, and has been treated in related literature.[23] Market signals are not only important ways to support corporate strategy, but also can achieve strategic ends all by themselves.

The "predatory product announcement" made famous by IBM and Microsoft is a well-known example of market signaling. Just by announcing their intentions to produce a hardware or software product, these firms have discouraged smaller competitors from entering the fray. The information alone creates changes within the market, since the company that signals doesn't necessarily come out with a proposed product on schedule—or ever—a practice disparaged in the computer industry with the term "vaporware."

Information Standards

A final means of using information to influence the external environment is to create standards that the rest of the industry, or even the overall economy, must emulate. Firms do this in one way when they work with the American Institute of Certified Public Accountants or the Securities and Exchange Commission to affect how financial results are reported. In the realm of electronic data interchange, certain companies like General Motors helped mold the Transportation Data Coordination Committee's information standards. GM also shaped the Manufacturing Automation Protocol standard.

On the Internet, early adopters of key functions have set standards simply by doing a good job, but these standards hold for a much shorter time than in other information markets. The "Yahoo" search service quickly set a World Wide Web standard by working diligently to list new and interesting Web pages and by continually updating page categories. However, its categories didn't stick when other search services entered the market. With no other technology can standards be established so quickly—and fade so fast.

Looking Forward, Outward, and Beyond

A company won't survive long if it doesn't know its customers, competitors, and regulators—all aspects of its external environment. A firm won't excel at information technology unless it scans and takes advantage of the relevant technology markets. And it may miss important new business opportunities by ignoring external information markets. Each of these markets contains its respective segments and subsegments, some of which will be more relevant to a specific firm than others. In some cases, companies need to beam information out into the external world; in others, they need to acquire what they don't already know.

Information that could change an industry's competitive dynamic is often there for the taking. But in order for a company to notice that information, bring it to the attention of the right people, and then act on it, all components of a firm's information ecology must function smoothly—no simple task, and one yet to be accomplished consistently by any company I know of.

Still, any organization's need for both external and internal information—*good* information, effectively managed and used—is reason enough to follow the tenets of information ecology. The techno-utopianism that still rules many IT shops is out-dated, naive, and inadequate for today's organizations. The many information problems I've encountered and discussed in this book will only become more complicated as we enter the next century. All companies have a bumpy road ahead; but those with information ecologists at the wheel take with them a new vision, strategy, and set of people-oriented practices to navigate through the constantly changing world of information use.

Assessment Survey for the External Environment

The greater the level of agreement with the statements below, the better an organization manages its business, technology, and information markets.

Business Markets

✳ My organization has identified the external business information that's of particular importance to us.

✳ There is a person or group dedicated to collection and analysis of market information—including information about customers, channel partners, final end users, and market trends.

✳ There is a person or group dedicated to collection and analysis of competitor information—including information about competitor size, market share, strategy, and products and services.

✳ There is a person or group dedicated to collection and analysis of information concerning best practices and/or benchmarks for our key processes and activities, both within and outside our industry.

✱ We have often been able to anticipate changes in our business through the information we've collected.

Technology Markets

✱ My organization has a well-established view of what types of technologies are most likely to bring us competitive advantage.

✱ There is a person or group dedicated to tracking emerging information technology capabilities.

✱ We adopt relevant information technologies at the right time.

✱ My organization has developed technologies or applications that have been seriously considered for sale in the external marketplace.

✱ We participate in associations or consortia that develop new technology solutions or standards.

Information Markets

✱ My organization has evaluated its potential to sell some of our information or knowledge in the external marketplace.

✱ A process is in place to evaluate external information sources for their business relevance, quality, and cognitive authority.

✱ External information is systematically captured, disseminated, and used.

✱ Internal information providers regularly work with users to perform "make vs. buy" analyses of information.

✱ My organization both supplies information to and receives it from industry associations and consortia.

12

Implementing Information Ecology

Metaphor takes us beyond formalism
and rigid measurement . . . and
promotes heightened sensitivity
towards context and cultures.
It . . . deserves a place in every information
manager's professional knapsack.

Blaise Cronin, Information Management

Chances are you haven't ever thought about the subject of information use in quite this fashion. You may be wondering, "What has to happen in order for the ecological approach to thrive?" "What will it feel like if I'm successful?" "What if I fail?" These are all valid—if anxiety-producing—questions. In this concluding chapter, I'll bring the visionary aspects of information ecology down to earth, focusing on the most pragmatic ways to rethink information management. Then I'll wind up with a story about what an ideal information ecology can accomplish—how a fictional company might put into practice many of the specific initiatives I've discussed here.

What Should I Do First?

I've argued all along that information ecologists never do just one thing. Yet it's unlikely that any manager has the support and resources to begin on every aspect of the ecological model at once. To my mind, the best place to start at most organizations is with two components: information management staff and information mapping.

Let's consider the staff component first—particularly who is going to manage all these changes. From what existing information function should the chief information ecologist come? At the very least, a company's IT or information services organization should be consulted on the issue of organizational support for information itself. Of all the information provider groups, it typically has the most resources and clout. However, since most existing IT workers devote their time to the technology, they have few hours or little energy left over to think about information or knowledge.

That leaves two options. One is to outsource the technology—get someone else to do the plumbing, while you focus on slaking information thirst. I've already mentioned that Equifax had a lot more ability to pursue the business opportunities in its credit-reporting databases after it handed over day-to-day management of the technology to IBM. Similarly, the giant oil company BP decided that it would outsource the management of geological data technologies, focusing its own efforts on analyzing and interpreting that data. It's now possible and even common to outsource such traditional IT functions as data-center operations, development and maintenance of commodity applications like payroll and general ledger, and provision and support of end-user computers. Note that not all the people who formerly did such jobs can be transferred to the outsourcer; otherwise, no one will be left in-house to concentrate on information.

The other option for organizational information support might be called "functional mitosis"—taking the existing information services function and splitting it in two. One group could continue the current activities of negotiating with technology vendors, building automated systems, and designing and implementing technology infrastructure. The other group could address information in the manifold ways described in this book. Since the "Chief Information Officer" role has already been taken, perhaps the leader of this function should be called Chief Content Officer.

Actually, a number of firms are already creating such functions, under the banner of knowledge management. Chief Knowledge Officers and Chief Learning Officers have appeared at Coca-Cola, General Electric, Sequent Computer, Young & Rubicam, and many leading consulting firms, including Ernst & Young, Coopers & Lybrand, and Booz-Allen and Hamilton. My consulting and research work with managers in these positions suggests that they don't normally make a firm distinction between information and knowledge, although they try to steer clear of "data" in most cases. Their goals are typically to capture and distribute information with particularly high value, and to motivate increased use of information and knowledge. Therefore, instituting a Chief Knowledge Officer would clearly reinforce ecological information management.

Of course, if senior executives want information or knowledge management to thrive in their organization, they also have to establish other information staff roles. But creating a senior, highly visible position is a good first step. In fact, the advertising and marketing firm Young & Rubicam has recently added a Chief Knowledge Officer to one of its divisions (Wunderman Cato Johnson, an advertising firm). Nicholas Rudd, this CKO, believes that knowledge and information should be managed by all employees, and that his role is to educate and influence them.

The second "first step" toward managing information ecologically is to create a map. Information mapping is not only extremely valuable but also fairly easy to do. Given a specified information domain (which can be identified through a quick, informal information strategy exercise), an initial map can be completed in a couple of months. It's a great way to improve an organization's information access, as well as to help workers become familiar with the concept of information management.

Your first mapping project should cover an information domain that's important to the company, but not overwhelmingly difficult to represent in this way. Since customers matter to just about every organization, mapping customer information is my generic recommendation. Most firms don't have a good sense of how complex their customer information can be, how many different places around an organization it can be found, and how little consensus there is on how it should be managed. It's not the easiest place to start, but a useful customer information map has the most potential for immediately helping a company. For firms with good knowledge of their customers already, or with unusual circumstances that make mapping customer information extraordinarily difficult, information about products, competitors, or a key process may be a better place to begin.

Success Factors for Information Management

Unfortunately, most organizations aren't managing information today the way I would have them do it. Because the ideas and issues presented in this book represent a change from current practice for most firms, implementing information ecology requires some sort of intervention—as with other major efforts like implementing a process management program, a new business strategy, or a new way of managing people. By now, we know something about what makes change programs successful; in this section, I review these factors in connection with information ecology.

Change advocates, for example, almost always report that a high level of *senior management awareness, support,* and *participation* is necessary if a change program is to succeed. This involvement goes beyond mere agreement that information management or information ecology is a good idea; passive involvement isn't enough. Senior executives must also actively persuade dissenters, reward positive behaviors, punish negative ones, and set a good personal example of information management and use. Although you can undertake information ecology initiatives without senior management involvement, you probably won't get very far.

Assuming that you aren't yourself a senior executive, the usual methods for getting the awareness and attention of those at the top apply. It helps to start with an executive who's already an effective information user, who may have an intuitive grasp of information management ideals, and for whom ecological notions won't be a gigantic leap beyond what she already believes or does. You and this hypothetical senior executive can build awareness through internal educational programs, external seminars, circulating articles about other firms' or competitors' information practices, or one-on-one evangelism. Keep in mind that some managers who don't believe in information or who equate it with technology may be beyond persuading, so cut your losses and look elsewhere for support.

Another factor, particularly for the longer term, is *linking information ecology to firm economics.* Successful information management involves competing with other projects for time and resources, as well as spending some money; therefore, the issue of financial return on information ecology has to be addressed at some point. How will better information management help your firm make or save money? If information will help your managers make better decisions, can you begin to identify the economic value of those decisions? Just as companies implementing TQM programs identified the "cost of quality" (actually the cost of poor quality), what's the cost of poor information? What decisions made in the past might have had more successful results if the decision-maker had better information, or had used available information more effectively? Of course, this kind of discussion can be politically sensitive; you might choose to use a manager who no longer works for the company in your "cost of poor information" analysis.

Ardent information ecologists can rightfully point out that we have spent trillions on information technology, often without any good evidence of economic benefit. But information ecology won't profit from the same kind of blind faith that has pushed along many purchases of computers and software. It's easier to find starry-eyed supporters of expert systems or object-oriented databases than to trust advocates of new information staff or information behavior approaches. More to the pragmatic point, we don't want to repeat the same mistakes made by boosters of IT management.

In addition to new staff roles, *some desirable personal characteristics are necessary if managers want information ecology to succeed.* Adopting an egotistical, empire-building approach to information is the surest way to undercut the best of intentions. Information ecology will threaten some people in the organization under any circumstances—especially if others think information ecologists are attempting to expand their own power. For that reason, information providers must view their jobs as primarily facilitative; they support line managers and workers, not the other way around. And they must build coalitions among the various providers in the organization, including IT professionals, librarians, market researchers, and controllers. If "knowledge"—a term that can sound quite intimidating—rather than "information" is the firm's latest buzzword, then its providers and managers must seem even more ego-less.

A related success factor is to *clarify what is being managed.* Information ecology won't seem so threatening if its range is limited, at least at first. While it's possible to apply ecological approaches to data management, the best short-term results will probably be achieved through a focus on value-added information and knowledge. Therefore, information ecologists should make clear to those who work for the IT function, for example, that their efforts won't interfere with data management and transaction-processing applications. Perhaps later on, when ecological approaches have become more familiar and accepted, they can be extended into the realm of data.

A final success factor is *avoidance of excessive structure and misplaced precision.* I've purposely avoided describing a methodology for information ecology, because this should always be an approach that employs careful thought, customization, and selective application. Any of the components of information ecology, from strategy to fiddling with physical arrangement, can be overdone. One firm, for example, decided to "reengineer" its organizational learning and knowledge management processes. With the aid of an overly methodological consultant, it identified and redesigned one process in this area—but also four subprocesses, fifteen sub-subprocesses, twenty-eight sub-sub-subprocesses, and fifty-three sub-sub-sub-subprocesses. Clearly, detail has replaced common sense in this firm. Not surprisingly, very few (five percent, by one manager's estimate) of the redesigned processes have been implemented.

In achieving any major change, it's not enough to focus on avoiding what might go wrong; it's also necessary to have a vision of how the organization might look if everything goes right. For that reason, I'll close the book with an account of what an ideal information ecology could be. If your company is embarking down this road, you may also want to imagine how your own organization will look at its ecological best.

The Ideal: How GoodDrug Manages Information

Fictional GoodDrug Corporation is an international pharmaceutical firm, with its home office in White Plains, New York. Founded in 1897 by Zebedee and Sophronia Winsor, who originally ran a local pharmacy, the company took off when the Winsors began marketing their own "Headache Tamer Tonic." By the 1920s, GoodDrug had become a national corporation with R&D labs in White Plains, Detroit, and Los Angeles. The company weathered the Depression and World War II, introducing new products every year, some of which became top-sellers: a children's aspirin called "Baby Buddy Chewables," GoodDrug's sleeping pill "Terminex." By the 1960s, the firm began moving into foreign markets and has been expanding ever since.

A Model Information Environment

Currently, GoodDrug Corporation has a model research information environment. For one thing, it has a well-defined *information strategy*. Its executives have concluded that achieving worldwide integration and visibility of its drug-research information—as well as increasing the quality of external market information—should be the company's primary goals. To develop this strategy, GoodDrug's managers undertook an analysis of all components of the information environment. This analysis was overseen by the company's Information Management Council, a cross-functional team of GoodDrug's information provider organizations, including Information Systems, Market Research, the Business and Research Libraries, and the Controller's Office for financial information. The analysis identified the key information domains that GoodDrug needed to address, such as specific content areas like competitor intelligence.

Unlike in most companies, GoodDrug managers at all levels are quite aware of the part *information politics* can play—or the havoc they can wreak. The firm's overall political structure is quite democratic and decentralized; if anything, employees may share too much information with each other. So senior managers and the Information Council agreed that centralizing information management made sense, even if that ran counter to their usual practices. In order to integrate drug-development information, top managers appointed a "Research Information Czar," a senior research scientist named Teresa Chiu, who now coordinates current development information; identifies new information requirements; establishes who has what information and where they're located (or on what technical platform it exists); and generally decides which information initiatives to undertake.

Teresa, the Research Information Czar, along with the company's other executives, actively manages the *information behavior* of the firm. Good-Drug's behavioral problems would be envied in some quarters. The strategic analysis made clear that its employees and managers were a bit *too* willing to share information; consequently, many GoodDrug workers have experienced information overload. The Information Council therefore issued a sct of "Recommended Information Practices" that asked employees to stop sending most broadcast and multiple-copy electronic messages. One GoodDrug business unit gives its users an e-mail budget, in which they're only debited for broadcast messages.

GoodDrug, of course, has a terrific (and unusual) *information culture*, one that encourages researchers to share information internally as well as throughout the industry and related scientific community. Top managers believe that participating in conferences, seminars, and academic journals brings in more information than it ultimately loses. GoodDrug scientists present their work frequently and collaborate with university researchers, sometimes even with competitors. Perhaps as a result, GoodDrug has one of the most productive R&D establishments in the industry.

GoodDrug's Research Information Czar and Information Council members constitute high-level *information staff*. The company also has designated experts in key information domains. For example, top managers want to accelerate the drug-approval process in areas where GoodDrug hasn't performed strongly to date, including Latin America, Australia, and Asia; that means the company needs better information on regulatory processes in those countries. To that end, GoodDrug has experts on governmental and regulatory issues in place around the world. In addition, English has become the company's official language so that information on this and other topics can be easily exchanged across borders.

GoodDrug, however, really views all of its employees as members of the information staff. Each person is responsible for their own information needs, managing their personal information environments, and sharing appropriate information with others. GoodDrug's information managers have made clear that twenty-five percent of individual performance evaluation is based on how well employees share, creatively use, and (where appropriate) control information. In fact, one assistant marketer, Selma Rivers, was recently promoted to project director when she persuaded a drug-development team to reformulate the company's most popular allergy medication for twenty-four-hour release. GoodDrug's human resources department had Teresa Chiu write a widely distributed memo that made public why Selma had been promoted.

In addition, GoodDrug managers put great emphasis on defining key *information management processes*. Information managers, for example, have observed how both researchers and developers involved with a new product obtain, use, and share information. In order to speed up new drug applications, managers have documented the process for generating and circulating drug-development information, presenting it to all participants.

They've also eliminated bottlenecks and misdirections of information, such as clinical director Joe Kahlo's previous refusal to sign off on clinical-trials reports unless they were perfectly formatted in twelve-point Palatino type. And information generated early in the process—such as an indication that a drug might cause stomach discomfort—is now communicated to regulatory managers far downstream, so they can begin preparing a regulatory strategy.

Teresa Chiu, the Czar, feels her company has a good drug-development *information architecture*, which largely consists of process-oriented information maps. But she wants to set up a centralized document-management system for drug-development information, and has a small team of analysts surveying available technologies. Teresa also believes that commercial and market information requires a better architecture. Her systems planners are therefore in the midst of completing a map of available financial, competitor, and customer information for GoodDrug.

What About the Larger Organization?

GoodDrug's information environment, of course, is always affected by its current *business situation*. The need for better R&D processes has led to substantial work on drug-development information processes and architecture, under the czar's control. GoodDrug's overall business strategy has rapidly been translated into new information strategies, including its focus on particular geographical markets. And the company's informal but hard-working organizational culture has had a major influence on GoodDrug's open information culture. Winston Winsor, the latest in the founding family's line to sit on the board, originally managed R&D. He's still a legend at GoodDrug, where older employees remember his enthusiam for teams, his drive to meet deadlines without penalizing anyone, and his ability to listen patiently, even when he thoroughly disagreed with someone else.

GoodDrug managers also consciously manipulate its *physical arrangement* to facilitate information goals. When a new product development project at GoodDrug first gets underway, managers bring team members together for a limited time at the company's main R&D site in White Plains. Later, once the team is communicating well and on schedule, individual members can return to their own offices around the country (or the world), communicating through weekly videoconferences and e-mail. Even then, however, a core of researchers on the team share open offices in the same physical space. Support resources for the team, including an information specialist, are also part of this on-sight core. Posters in the cafeteria describe each research team's project status and goals so that others in the company can coordinate their own work with that of the teams.

GoodDrug has made a modest *technology investment* to improve its information ecology in certain areas, though this is not its primary information management focus. For example, the company gives its sales force and researchers laptops so they can access information outside offices; it has implemented groupware like Lotus Notes to help manage less structured information; and established a number of World Wide Web sites. However, based on Teresa Chiu's assessment, GoodDrug halted a planned conversion of mainframe financial systems to client-server hardware, because the heavy investment wouldn't really deliver much better information.

Making the Most of What You Can't Control

Much of GoodDrug's external environment—the ever-shifting mire of the health-care industry—is out of the company's hands. At the moment, the main focus of its *business markets*—customers like HMOs and physicians; manufacturing suppliers—is regulatory affairs. For example, if the US government speeds up its regulatory process for approving new drugs, that will dramatically change the company's R&D operations, its demands on suppliers, and the expectations of customers. In general, US health-care politics are in flux, and no company in a related industry is immune.

Like most companies in its industry, GoodDrug maintains a Government Affairs office in several capitals of its major markets (London, Tokyo, Rome), and a "Regulatory Affairs Information Summary" document is prepared weekly by each office. Yet the Information Council's strategic analysis also uncovered the fact that individual researchers didn't know enough about emerging pharmaceutical customers, largely because the health-care industry was changing so fast. Researchers understood what physicians wanted, but they were less familiar with the views of buying groups, mail-order pharmaceutical distributors, and even employers.

Teresa Chiu jumped in here, assigning market information specialists to each drug-development team. She also approved an internal Web site for market information, including internal and external reports on industry forces, key players, and how GoodDrug products may be affected by industry developments. The Web site has many links, each of which lead users to the firm's expert on a particular topic.

Information managers at GoodDrug continually analyze external *technol-*

ogy markets, evaluating any number of products that may be cost-effective for the company. Lower cost fiber-optic communications, for example, would allow GoodDrug employees to transfer graphic images to R&D sites around the world—even to customers and suppliers. But at the moment, it's still too expensive. Information managers are also considering external technology services for certain functions, since outsourcing of IS services could free them up to focus on information content.

GoodDrug buys considerable information from external sources like the Cambridge, Massachusetts-based firm Pharmaceutical Information Management. But purchasing from external *information markets* is only one way to keep up with changes in the external environment. GoodDrug regularly communicates with its biggest customers about their needs and satisfaction with products. And the company's managers are good at sniffing out information from a variety of sources: job applicants, industry consultants, even their own numbers on trends in product consumption.

GoodDrug has also entered into several early-stage licensing agreements with other pharmaceutical firms. Its licensing partners receive not only access to new drug compounds with the potential for controlling kidney disease, but the more informal information circulated among GoodDrug's researchers in this area. The Japanese company Konichiwa Drugs has access to GoodDrug's IntraNet and drug-development Web sites; in the US, Konichiwa scientists work side-by-side with GoodDrug researchers. These lucrative "information licensing" agreements now earn the company substantially more than drug licensing alone at an early development stage.

Back to the Real World: Messy or Not, Ecology Matters

Even fictional GoodDrug's information ecology is always changing, so managers have to scramble to keep up. Specific information practices may make sense at one point in time, but become less helpful at another. In addition, while I've made sure this company has addressed every component of the information ecology model, many of its initiatives are inextricably intermingled. Putting market information specialists at different sites not only improves external business information but also helps build the company's internal support staff. In turn, making individuals responsible for their own information needs shores up the support staff, while encouraging the right information behavior and culture for GoodDrug.

The real point is that managers can't approach information use as a "fixed" project with a "perfect" end in sight. The nature of the information beast is to evolve and grow—wildly and chaotically at times, in a more controlled fashion at others. GoodDrug's information ecology isn't perfect, but it's as close to information nirvana as we're likely to get.

And why does this nirvana matter? Let me count the ways. No company—including yours—will ever achieve a true competitive advantage through information without adopting more human-oriented approaches to managing it. Many firms have already begun to implement certain aspects of information ecology—to generate new revenues, to find out more about competitors, to get ahead of the innovation curve, to stop bleeding money for inappropriate and confusing technologies. We have tried machine-oriented alternatives for decades now without substantial success. It's time to look to ourselves for the information answers.

Notes

.
.
.
.
.

Chapter 1

1. I have argued this point in two other books: Thomas H. Davenport, *Process Innovation: Reengineering Work through Information Technology* (Boston: Harvard Business School Press, 1993); see also a collection of text and cases on IT-enabled reengineering: Richard Nolan, Donna B. Stoddard, Thomas H. Davenport, and Sirkka Jarvenpaa, *Reengineering the Organization* (Boston: Harvard Business School Press, 1995).

2. Interview with Jeffrey Vinik, manager of the Magellan Fund, the world's largest mutual fund (forty percent of which was invested in information technology companies in 1994), Fidelity Investments, *1994 Magellan Fund Annual Report.*

3. Charles B. Wang, *Techno Vision: The Executive's Survival Guide to Understanding and Managing Information Technology* (New York: McGraw-Hill, 1994).

4. The most recent evaluation I have seen lists IBM as spending a mere 2.3 billion dollars on IT. The company has pared back its spending, and there may have been differences in what was counted in the total. See "The Biggest and the Best," *Information Week* (Sept. 18, 1995): 48.

5. Ida Picker, "IBM's Information Gap," *Institutional Investor* (Feb. 1994): 49–53.

6. The Pearl Harbor story comes from Gordon W. Prange, *Pearl Harbor: The Verdict of History* (New York: Penguin, 1991); this example was brought to my attention by Vince Barabba.

7. Blaise Cronin and Elisabeth Davenport, *Elements of Information Management* (Metuchen, New Jersey: The Scarecrow Press, 1991), 1–2.

8. For example, the distinction between behavioral and architectural/engineering models of information is discussed in Martha S. Feldman and James G. March, "Information in Organizations as Signal and Symbol," *Administrative Science Quarterly* 26 (1981): 46–60.

9. Peter F. Drucker, "The Coming of the New Organization," *Harvard Business Review* 66 (January-February 1988), 45–53.

10. Ikujiro Nonaka and Hirotaka Takeuchi, *The Knowledge-Creating Company* (New York: Oxford University Press, 1995).

11. These types of knowledge-oriented systems are described under the label "sys-

tems of scope" in Andrew C. Boynton, "Achieving Dynamic Stability Through Information Technology," *California Management Review* (Winter 1993): 62–67.

12. See George Lakoff and Mark Johnson's *Metaphors We Live By* (Chicago: University of Chicago Press, 1980).

13. The latter title was used in an article I wrote entitled "Saving IT's Soul: Human-Centered Information Management," *Harvard Business Review* (March-April 1994): 119–131.

14. Charles E. Lindblom, "The Science of 'Muddling Through'," *Public Administration Review* 19 (1959): 79–89; also from Lindblom, "Still Muddling, Not Yet Through," *Public Administration Review* (39:1979), 517–526.

15. One of the earlier statements of emergent management behavior is Henry Mintzberg's, *The Nature of Managerial Work* (New York: Harper and Row, 1973). The most recent refinements of Mintzberg's approach are in his, *The Rise and Fall of Strategic Planning* (New York: Free Press, 1994).

16. Henry Mintzberg, "Crafting Strategy," *Harvard Business Review* (July-August 1987). Also note that the concept of ecology itself has recently been employed to describe the competitive environment for organizations, including evolution, ecosystems, and dominant competitive species. See James F. Moore, "Predators and Prey: A New Ecology of Competition," *Harvard Business Review* (May-June 1993): 75–86.

    Even in economics, a discipline never renowned for its practicality, new approaches that emphasize evolution, behavior, and adaptation are beginning to emerge. The view of economies as complex adaptive systems has become popular over the past few years, with several influential mainstream economists adopting the perspective. While there are as yet few specific useful implications of this line of thought, it more readily explains many aspects of economic reality than does neoclassical economics. See M. Mitchell Waldrop, *Complexity* (New York: Simon & Schuster Touchstone, 1992). A summary volume of work at the Santa Fe Institute, the primary center of this movement, comes from Philip W. Anderson, Kenneth J. Arrow, and David Pines, eds., *The Economy as an Evolving Complex System*. Santa Fe Institute Series in the Sciences of Complexity, Vol. 5 (Redwood City, Ca.: Addison-Wesley, 1988).

    Ecological approaches are also penetrating social policy. The US government, for example, recently unveiled a program for improving life in poor communities that represents "a shift away from a vision of single cause–single effect and toward one admitting complexity and focusing on context." Government organizations have also become highly specialized and focused on narrow aspects of individual and social problems.

17. A few of the companies I discuss wished to remain anonymous and aren't included in the list of firms studied.

Chapter 2

1. James R. Beniger, *The Control Revolution: Technological and Economic Origins of the Information Society* (Cambridge, Ma.: Harvard University Press, 1986).

2. JoAnne Yates, *Control through Communications* (Baltimore: Johns Hopkins University Press, 1989).

3. Andrew Pollack, "Now It's Japan's Turn to Play Catch-Up," *New York Times*, (November 21, 1993): Section 3, 1.

4. For more information on the past and future of corporate libraries and librarians, see Thomas H. Davenport and Lawrence Prusak, "Blow Up the Corporate Library," *International Journal of Information Management* (1993): 405–412.

5. For one attempt at a pragmatic view of knowledge management, see Thomas H. Davenport, "Some Principles of Knowledge Management," *Strategy and Business* 1:2 (1996) 34–40.

6. Ira A. Penn et al, *Records Management Handbook* (Aldershot, U.K.: Gower, 1989), 5.

7. Penn, *Records Management* 4.

8. A detailed discussion of the origins and history of IRM is provided in Eileen M. Trauth, "The Evolution of Information Resource Management," *Information and Management* 16 (1989): 257–268.

9. See, for example, Richard A.V. Diener, "A Tale of Two Paradigms, or Whatever Happened to IRM?" *Bulletin of the American Society for Information Science* (Dec./Jan. 1992): 26–27.

10. John Leslie King and Kenneth L. Kraemer, "Information Resource Management: Is It Sensible and Can It Work?" *Information and Management* 15 (1988): 7–14.

11. King and Kraemer, "Information Resource Management," 10.

12. Karen L. Sampson, *Value-Added Records Management* (New York: Quorum, 1992), vii.

13. IBM Corporation, *Business Systems Planning: Information Systems Planning Guide*, publication GE20-0527-3, 1981.

14. See, for example, James Martin and Clive Finkelstein, *Information Engineering* (London: Savant Institute, 1981); also Clive Finkelstein, *Introduction to Information Engineering* (Reading, Ma.: Addison-Wesley, 1989.)

15. Finkelstein, *Information Engineering,* 94.

16. David De Long, "Growex Corporation Case Study," Mastering the Information Environment Research Program, Ernst & Young Center for Information Technology and Strategy, 1993.

17. Albert L. Lederer and Vijay Sethi, "The Implementation of Strategic Systems Planning Methodologies," *MIS Quarterly* (Sept. 1988): 445–461.

18. Dale L. Goodhue, J.A. Quillard, and J.F. Rockart, "Managing the Data Resource: A Contingency Perspective," *MIS Quarterly* (Sept. 1988): 373–392.

19. If you must learn more about the concept of "enterprise engineering," see James Martin, *The Great Transition: Using the Seven Disciplines of Enterprise Engineering to Align People, Technology, and Strategy* (New York: AMACOM, 1995).

20. Thomas H. Davenport, "Rank Xerox U.K. (A) and (B)," Harvard Business School case studies, case numbers N9-192-071 and N9-192-072, 1992.

21. P.G. Zurkowski, "Integrating America's Infostructure, " *Journal of the American Society for Information Science* 35:3 (1984): 170, and J.F. McLaughlin and A.L.

Antonoff, "Mapping the Information Business," Cambridge, Ma.: Harvard University Program on Information Resources Policy, 1986.
22. James McGee and Laurence Prusak, *Managing Information Strategically* (New York: Wiley, 1993); Thomas J. Buckholtz, *Information Proficiency* (New York: Van Nostrand Reinhold, 1995); Jessica Keyes, *Infotrends: The Competitive Use of Information* (New York: McGraw-Hill, 1993).
23. Ikujiro Nonaka and Hirotaka Takeuchi, *The Knowledge-Creating Company* (New York: Oxford University Press, 1995); Dorothy Leonard-Barton, *Wellsprings of Knowledge: Building and Sustaining the Sources of Innovation* (Boston: Harvard Business School Press, 1995).
24. Fuld and Company and Fujitsu Research Institute, "Information Technology's Role: A Japan/U.S. Competitiveness Gap," April 1995.
25. Roger C. Schank, *Tell Me A Story: A New Look at Real and Artificial Memory* (New York: Scribner's, 1990).
26. Sharon M. McKinnon and William J. Bruns, Jr., *The Information Mosaic* (Boston: Harvard Business School Press, 1992), 162–164.
27. Andrew Tank, "Information for Strategic Decisions," Conference Board Report #1027, 1993, 14.

Chapter 3

1. Garrett Hardin, *Filters Against Folly: How to Survive Despite Economists, Ecologists, and the Merely Eloquent* (New York: Penguin Books, 1985).
2. Mintzberg, *The Rise and Fall of Strategic Planning*.
3. There are at least two academic perspectives on information environments. From an organizational behavior perspective, see G.P. Huber and D.L. Daft, "The Information Environments of Organizations," in Frederic Jablin and Linda L. Putnam, eds., *Handbook of Organizational Communications* (Newbury Park, Ca.:Sage Publications, 1987); from an information science perspective, see Robert Taylor, *Value-Added Processes in Information Systems* (Norwood, N.J.: Ablex, 1986).
4. This would be similar to the concept of strategic intent as discussed by Gary Hamel and C.K. Prahalad, "Strategic Intent," *Harvard Business Review* (May-June 1989): 63–76.
5. The role of principles in IT strategy is discussed in Thomas H. Davenport and Michael Hammer, "How Executives Can Shape Their Company's Information Systems," *Harvard Business Review* (March-April 1989): 130–134.
6. Thomas H. Davenport, Robert Eccles, and Larry Prusak, "Information Politics," *Sloan Management Review* (Fall 1992): 53–66. See also Paul Strassman, *The Politics of Information Management* (New Canaan: Information Economics Press, 1994).
7. Tom Davenport, "Can We Manage Information Behavior?" Mastering the Information Environment Research Note, Ernst & Young Center for Business Innovation, 1993; also David W. DeLong, "Identifying Effective Information Behaviors—An Exploratory Study," Mastering the Information Environment

Research Note, Ernst & Young Center for Business Innovation, August 1993.

8. Paul Osterman, "The Impact of IT on Jobs and Skills," in Michael Scott-Morton, ed., *The Corporation of the 1990s* (New York: Oxford, 1991), 220–243.

9. Thomas H. Davenport, Sirkka Jarvenpaa, and Michael Beers, "Improving Knowledge Work Processes," *Sloan Management Review*, 37:4 (Summer 1996), 53–65.

10. Larry Prusak, "Managing Information Processes," Mastering the Information Environment Working Paper, September 1993.

11. James C. Brancheau and James C. Wetherbe, "Information Architecture: Methods and Practice," *Information Systems Management* 22 (1986): 453–464.

12. See Thomas H. Davenport, "Information Architecture as a Change Process," Mastering the Information Environment Research Note, Ernst & Young Center for Business Innovation, 1993.

13. See, for example, Wanda Orlikowski, "Learning from Notes: Organizational Issues in Groupware Implementation," Center for Information Systems Research Working Paper, No. 241, MIT Sloan School of Management, May 1992.

14. Thomas Allen, *Managing the Flow of Technology* (Cambridge, MA: MIT Press, 1977); also Kim Clark and T. Fujimoto, *Product Development Performance* (Boston: Harvard Business School Press, 1991).

15. Stan Davis and Bill Davidson, *2020 Vision* (New York: Simon & Schuster, 1991).

16. See, for example, Cyrus F. Gibson, Charles J. Singer, Ava A. Schnidman, and Thomas H. Davenport, "Strategies for Making an Information System Fit Your Organization," *Management Review* (Jan. 1984): 8–14.

17. See, for example, Charles Wiseman, *Strategy and Computers* (Homewood, Il.: Dow Jones-Irwin, 1985.)

18. Information on Standard Life was obtained from interviews and from the following documents: article in *Standard Life Magazine* (Feb. 1995): 8–9; Chester Simpson and Michael Vitale, "Standard Life Assurance Company: Making Knowledge Known," Ernst & Young Center for Business Innovation Case Study, June 1994; Jim McGee, "Standard Life Assurance Company: Improving Information Management," Ernst & Young Center for Business Innovation Case Study, December 1993.

Chapter 4

1. As noted above, Mintzberg's perspectives on strategy are best laid out in his *The Rise and Fall of Strategic Planning*. His views on management information, which are also consistent with mine, are described in *Impediments to the Use of Management Information,* New York: National Association of Accountants, 1977.

2. Gary Hamel and C.K. Prahalad, "Strategic Intent," *Harvard Business Review* (May-June 1989): 63–76.

3. Robert Simons, "Strategic Orientation and Top Management Attention to Control Systems," *Strategic Management Journal* 12 (1991): 49–62.

4. Millipore information comes from interviews with Millipore managers and from a case study by Nitin Nohria and S.E. Green, "A Common Language for Common

Systems," Harvard Business School case study #9-494-011, 1994.

5. Mike France, "Reengineer Your Lawyers," *Forbes ASAP* (June 6, 1994): 54–61.

6. The concept of the inquiry center is explained in detail in a book by Vincent P. Barabba and Gerald Zaltman entitled *Hearing the Voice of the Market* (Boston: Harvard Business School Press, 1990).

7. For an overview of this literature, see Anil Menon and P. Ragan Varadarajan, "A Model of Marketing Knowledge Use Within Firms," *Journal of Marketing* 56 (Oct. 1992): 53–71.

8. Information about Ross Operating Valve comes from Steven Goldman, Roger Nagel, and Kenneth Preiss, *Agile Competitors and Virtual Organizations* (New York: Van Nostrand Reinhold,1995), 22 and 67; and conversations with Roger Nagel.

9. For a general discussion of the role of principles in leadership, see Steven Covey, *Principle-Centered Leadership* (New York: Summit, 1991). For a treatment of their role in information technology management, see Thomas Davenport, Michael Hammer, and Tauno Metsisto, "How Executives Can Shape Their Company's Information Systems" *Harvard Business Review* (March-April 1989): 130–134.

10. Robert Simons, "How New Top Managers Use Control Systems as Levers of Strategic Renewal," *Strategic Management Journal* (March 1994).

11. Michael Porter, *Competitive Strategy* (New York: Free Press, 1980).

12. McKinnon and Bruns, *The Information Mosaic*.

13. These questions were developed in consultation with firms that participated in a research project on information management. To use them in a systematic manner, I suggest a Likert scale-type approach, with the respondent being asked whether he or she strongly agrees, agrees, is neutral, disagrees, or strongly disagrees with the given statement. You could conduct such a survey not only to evaluate a particular organization, but also to make comparisons across organizations or different parts of the same organization.

Chapter 5

1. See, for example, Andrew Pettigrew, "Information Control as a Power Resource," *American Sociological Review* 32 (1972): 187–204; also M. Lynne Markus, "Power, Politics, and MIS Implementation," *Communications of the ACM* 26:6 (June 1983): 434-444.

2. Kalle Lyytinen and Rudy Hitschheim, "Information Systems Failures—A Survey and Classification of the Empirical Literature," *Oxford Surveys in Information Technology* (1987): 257–309.

3. Daniel Robey, Larry A. Smith, and Leo R. Vijayasarathy, "Perceptions of Conflict and Success in Information Systems Development Projects," *Journal of Management Information Systems* (Summer 1993): 123–139.

4. This is the conclusion reached by, among others, Richard Walton in *Up and Running* (Boston: Harvard Business School Press, 1989).

5. These were first described in my 1992 article: Thomas H. Davenport, Robert G.

Eccles, and Lawrence Prusak, "Information Politics," *Sloan Management Review* (Fall 1992): 52–65.

6. Robert Simons, "Asea Brown Boveri: The ABACUS System," Harvard Business School Case Study, case # 9-192-140, 1992, 12.

7. Paul Strassman, *The Politics of Information Management* (New Canaan: Information Economics Press, 1995), 43–49. Strassman's book, despite the title, is really more about the politics of information technology management, though it is sprinked with nuggets on information.

8. These principles are described in Chemical Bank's proprietary document, "Corporate Information Management Principles and Standards Guide," 1994. I am grateful to Chemical Bank for the permission to use this information.

9. These criteria for federalism are described in James O'Toole and Warren Bennis," Our Federalist Future: The Leadership Imperative*,"* *California Management Review* (Summer 1992): 73–90.

10. Thomas H. Davenport, Robert G. Eccles, and Lawrence Prusak, "Information Politics," *Sloan Management Review* 34:1 (Fall 1992) 53–65.

11. Information on Hughes comes from discussions with Hughes managers and from Jason I. Frand, H. Alvin Ng, and Jeff Peterman, "Hughes Space and Communications: Scheduling in an Integrated Factory," UCLA Graduate School of Management, Information Systems Working Paper, January 12, 1995.

12. Frand et al., "Hughes Space and Communications," 7.

13. I am grateful to John Henderson for this case study.

14. Michael L. Tushman and Thomas J. Scanlan, "Boundary-Spanning Individuals: Their Role in Information Transfer and Their Antecedents," *Academy of Management Journal* 24:2 (1981): 289–305.

15. James L. Heskett and John P. Kotter, *Corporate Culture and Performance* (New York: Free Press, 1992).

16. Martha S. Feldman and James G. March, "Information in Organizations as Signal and Symbol. *Administrative Science Quarterly* 26 (1981) 171–86.

Chapter 6

1. Michael E.D. Koenig, "The Information and Library Environment and the Productivity of Research," unpublished manuscript, Rosary College, River Forest, Il.

2. Christopher Orpen, "The Effect of Managerial Distribution of Scientific and Technical Information on Company Performance," *R&D Management* 15:4 (1985): 305–308.

3. Work on information behavior in technical and scientific environments has been underway for more than thirty years. For a good overview of this research, see Thomas J. Allen, *Managing the Flow of Technology* (Cambridge, Ma.: MIT Press, 1988).

4. Survey of participants in the "Mastering the Information Environment" research program, Ernst & Young Center for Information Technology and Strategy, December 1992. Participants included such leading firms as American Airlines,

Ameritech, Chemical Bank, General Electric, Hewlett Packard, IBM, Shell Canada, and Xerox.

5. Blaise Cronin, "The Management of Intellectual Capital: from Texts to Markets," in Blaise Cronin, ed., *Information Management: From Strategies to Action* (London: Aslib, 1991).

6. The details of policy deployment are discussed in Yoji Akao, ed., *Hoshin Kanri* (Cambridge, Ma.: Productivity Press, 1991).

7. For a more detailed discussion of the information-process relationship, see Chapter 4, "Processes and Information" in Thomas H. Davenport, *Process Innovation: Reengineering Work Through Information Technology* (Boston: Harvard Business School Press, 1992).

8. See, for example, B. Bowonder and T. Miyake, "Creating and Sustaining Competitiveness: Information Management Strategies of Nippon Steel Corporation," *International Journal of Information Management* 12 (1992): 39–56. For a more theoretical perspective, see Ikujiro Nonaka, "Redundant, Overlapping Organization: A Japanese Approach to Innovation," *California Management Review* 32:3 (Spring 1990): 27–38.

9. For an extended discussion of information sharing, see Stephan Schrader, "Informal Information Trading Between Firms," in Thomas A. Kochan and Michael Useem, eds., *Transforming Organizations* (New York: Oxford University Press, 1992): 320--36.

10. Thomas Davenport, Robert Eccles, and Lawrence Prusak, "Information Politics," *Sloan Management Review* (Fall 1992): 53–66.

11. Wanda Orlikowski, "Learning from Notes: Organizational Issues in Groupware Implementation," MIT Center for Information Systems Research, Working Paper #241, Sloan School of Management, May 1992.

12. J. Kmetz, "An Information Processing Study of a Complex Workflow in Aircraft Electronics Repair," *Administrative Science Quarterly* 19 (1984): 255–280.

13. James G. March, *A Primer on Decision Making* (New York: Free Press, 1994).

14. The first version of this engagement hierarchy was developed by Jane Linder of Polaroid Corporation.

15. Information about Polaroid was obtained from interviews and from a presentation by Jane Linder, "How Polaroid Links Knowledge to Innovation," The Knowledge Advantage Conference, Planning Forum/Ernst & Young, Boston, September 27, 1994. Linder is also a co-developer of many of the ideas in this section on information engagement.

16. Jack Stack, *The Great Game of Business* (New York: Doubleday Currency, 1992).

17. See, for example, Daniel J. Isenberg, "How Senior Managers Think," *Harvard Business Review* (Nov.-Dec. 1984).

18. The classification of disease information is described in Geoffrey Bowker and Susan L. Star, "Knowledge and Infrastructure in International Information Management," Chapter 9 in Lisa Bud-Frierman, ed., *Information Acumen* (New York: Routledge, 1994), 187–213.

19. Asea Brown Boveri has begun to evaluate decisions in this manner.

20. For the original research on the "garbage-can" model, see M.D. Cohen, J.G. March and J.P. Olsen, "A Garbage Can Model of Organizational Choice," *Administrative Science Quarterly* 117 (1972): 1–25.

21. For an overview of this topic, see R.S. Wyer, Jr. and T.K. Srull, eds., *Handbook of Social Cognition,* Vol. 1 and 2 (Hillsdale, N.J.: Erlbaum, 1984).

22. For readings in this area, see Irene Greif, ed., *Computer-Supported Cooperative Work: A Book of Readings* (San Mateo, Ca.: Morgan Kaufmann Publishers, 1988).

23. See, for example, "Workflow: Automating the Business Environment," BIS CAP International, Norwell, Mass., Oct. 1990.

24. Jay Galbraith, *Organizational Design* (Reading, Ma.: Addison-Wesley, 1977).

25. The organizational design of Batterymarch is discussed in N. Venkatraman, "IT-Induced Business Reconfiguration," in M.S. Scott Morton, ed., *The Corporation of the 1990's* (New York: Oxford University Press, 1990): 138–139.

26. For an extended discussion of corporate memory, see James P. Walsh and Gerardo Rivera Ungson, "Organizational Memory," *Academy of Management Review* 16:1: 57–91. For the first major treatment of organizational learning, see Chris Argyris and Donald A. Schon, *Organizational Learning: A Theory of Action Perspective* (Reading, Ma.: Addison-Wesley, 1978).

27. One example of such encouragement—or at least prediction of such behavior—can be found in George P. Huber, "A Theory of the Effects of Advanced Information Technologies on Organizational Design, Intelligence, and Decision Making," *Academy of Management Review* 15:1 (1990): 47–71.

28. For an overview of this approach, see J.J. McCall, ed., *The Economics of Information and Uncertainty* (Chicago: University of Chicago Press, 1982).

29. For a discussion and several case studies of information exchange between consumer goods and retail firms, see James V. McGee, "Implementing Systems Across Boundaries: Dynamics of Information Technology and Integration," unpublished dissertation, Harvard Business School, 1991.

30. For a very useful summary of this research, see Lee Sproull and Sara Kiesler, *Connections* (Cambridge, Ma.: MIT Press, 1991).

31. For a discussion of this phenomenon, see James Matarazzo, *Closing the Corporate Library: Case Studies on the Decisionmaking Process* (New York: Special Libraries Association, 1981)

32. Sproull and Kiesler in *Connections* have described several different types of "information procedures" that are well-suited for encouraging information exchange across electronic networks. See 125–142.

33. This approach has been proposed by Lloyd Baird, Lydia Tuden, and Jon Briscoe, "Implementing Corporate Strategy Through Executive Development," Executive Development Roundtable, Boston University School of Management.

34. Fax poll of 275 readers of *Information Week*, published in July 13, 1992 issue.

Chapter 7

1. James M. Matarazzo and Laurence Prusak, "The Value of Corporate Libraries,"

Special Libraries Association and the Ernst & Young Center for Business Innovation, 1995.

2. See "Information Services: Gateway to Competitive Advantage," Special Libraries Association, Washington, D.C., 1992, see also Thomas H. Davenport and Lawrence Prusak, "Blow Up the Corporate Library," *International Journal of Information Management* (Winter 1993): 405–412.

3. See William J. Reeves, *Librarians as Professionals: The Occupation's Impact on Library Work Arrangement* (Lexington, Ma.: Lexington Books, 1980), see also Linda Wallace, "The Image and What You Can Do About It in the Year of the Librarian," *American Librarian*, (Jan., 1989): 22–25.

4. R. Doidge, "Physical Arrangement and Display, Circulation, and Loan," in L.J. Anthony, ed., *Handbook of Special Librarianship and Information Work* (London: Aslib, 1982), 162.

5. Sharon McKinnon and William Bruns, *The Information Mosaic* (Boston: Harvard Business School Press, 1992)

6. This objective is emphasized in Michael Earl and David Feeny, "Is Your CIO Adding Value?" *Sloan Management Review* (Spring 1994):11–20.

7. Tom Peters also discusses McKinsey's Rapid Response Network. See Tom Peters, *Liberation Management* (New York: Knopf, 1992), 382–399.

8. See, for example, Leslie Willcocks, *Information Management: The Evaluation of Information Systems Investments*, (London: Chapman and Hall, 1994).

9. Richard Saul Wurman, *Information Anxiety* (New York: Bantam Books, 1989), 37.

10. See also Claude E. Shannon and Warren Weaver, *The Mathematical Theory of Communication* (Urbana: Univ of Illinois Press, 1971), 39.

11. McKinnon and Bruns, *The Information Mosaic.*

12. This categorization was suggested by Rodney Lacey, my research assistant.

13. McKinnon and Bruns, *The Information Mosaic*, 197.

14. For more information on information acquires cognitive authority, see the discussion in Chapter 10 on external information environments, or Patrick Wilson's book *Second Hand Knowledge: An Inquiry Into Cognitive Authority* (Westport: Greenwood Press, Contributions in Librarianship and Information Science, Number 44, 1983).

15. See Ray C. Oman and Tyrone B. Ayers, "Improving Data Quality," *Journal of Systems Management* 39:5 (May 1988): 31–36.

16. McKinon and Bruns, *The Information Mosaic*, 212

17. See, for example, Robert W. Zmud, M.R. Lind, and F.W. Young, "An Attribute Space for Organizational Communication Channels," *Information Systems Research*, 1:4 (Dec. 1990); also Rice, R. and Shook, D., "Access to, Usage of, and Outcomes from an Electronic Messaging System," *ACM Transactions on Office Information Systems* 6:3 (1988): 255–276.

18. Cognitive scientists such as Roger Schank argue that stories are also highly accessible to humans. See Roger C. Schank, *Tell Me A Story: A New Look at Real and Artificial Memory* (New York: Scribner's, 1990).

19. *Information Anxiety*, 45. Wurman's book is an excellent source on how to improve this type of accessibility.
20. Henry Mintzberg, "The Manager's Job, Folklore and Fact" *Harvard Business Review* (July-Aug. 1975): 49–61; H. Edward Wrapp, "Good Managers Don't Make Policy Decisions," *Harvard Business Review* (Sept.-Oct. 1967); John P. Kotter, "What Effective Managers Really Do," *Harvard Business Review* (Nov-Dec. 1982): 156–167; James Brian Quinn, "Managing Strategic Change," *Sloan Management Review* (Summer 1980): 3–20.
21. Hugh J. Watson et al, "Soften Up!" *Computerworld* (Oct. 19, 1992): 103–105.
22. Michael Hammer and James A. Champy, *Reengineering the Corporation* (New York: Harper Business School Press, 1993), 122–123.
23. Guje Sevon and James March, "Gossip, Information, and Decision-Making," in *Advances in Information Processing in Organizations*, Vol. 1, (Greenwich: JAI Press, Inc., 1984), 95–107.
24. See Allen S. Lee, "Electronic Mail as a Medium for Rich Communication: An Empirical Investigation Using Hermeneutic Interpretation," *MIS Quarterly* 18:2 (June 1994): 143–157; also M. Lynne Markus, "Electronic Mail as the Medium of Electronic Choice," *Organization Science*, forthcoming.
25. A variation on this TV industry model was first advanced in Thomas H. Davenport and Laurence Prusak, "Blow Up the Corporate Library," *International Journal of Information Management* (Winter 1994).
26. Information about the Coopers & Lybrand Knowledge Network was found in "On Achieving Excellence," The Tom Peters Organization, Nov. 1993; in Carol Hildebrand, "The Greater Good," *CIO* (Nov. 15, 1994): 32–40; and in a presentation at the "Leveraging Knowledge for Performance" conference, Feb. 6-8, 1995, Atlanta, Ga.
27. Janet Novack, "Lender's Best Friend," *Forbes* (December 18, 1996): 198–199.
28. This is actually similar to the original definition of the CIO. When Synnott and Gruber first wrote about the concept of the Chief Information Officer in 1981, they had something different in mind from how most CIOs currently define their jobs. They defined the role as establishing corporate information policy and standards, and maintaining management control over all corporate information resources. Note the absence of the word "technology" in that definition. These researchers presciently noted that what needed to be sold was not the CIO role itself, but a commitment to information as a valuable corporate resource that must be managed as a total entity—whether the information is on computers, in file cabinets, or in an employee's head. See William Synott and William Gruber, *Information Resource Mangement* (New York: Wiley Interscience, 1981).

Chapter 8

1. IBM's process is described further in Maylun Buck-Lew and Thomas H. Davenport, "Informed About Information: Market Information Capture at IBM," Ernst & Young Center for Business Innovation, 1993.

2. John F. Rockart, "Chief Executives Define Their Own Information Needs," *Harvard Business Review* (March-April 1979): 81–93.
3. See the following monographs and articles by Henry Mintzberg: *Impediments to the Use of Management Information* (New York and Hamilton, Ontario: National Association of Accountants and The Society of Management Accountants of Canada, 1975); "The Myths of MIS," *California Management Review* (Fall 1972): 92–97; *The Nature of Managerial Work* (New York: Harper & Row, 1973).
4. See Martha S. Feldman and James G. March, "Information in Organizations as Signal and Symbol," *Administrative Science Quarterly* 26 (1981): 171–186; James G. March and Guje Sevón, "Gossip, Information, and Decision Making," in Lee S. Sproull and J. Patrick Crecine, eds., *Advances in Information Processing in Organizations* (Greenwich: JAI Press, 1984): 95–107; James G. March, "Ambiguity and Accounting: The Elusive Link between Information and Decision-Making," *Accounting, Organizations, and Society* 12 (1987), pp. 153-168.
5. Robert Simons, *Levers of Control* (Boston: Harvard Business School Press, 1994); also "How New Top Managers Use Control Systems as Levers of Strategic Renewal," *Strategic Management Journal* (March 1994) 169–189.
6. Drucker quote cited in "Sensemaking and Group Support Systems" by K. E. Weick & D. K. Meader in *Group Support Systems,* L.M. Jessup & J.S. Valacich, eds. (New York: MacMillan, 1993), 231. Original source: P. Drucker, *Management: Tasks, Responsibilities, and Practices* (New York: Harper & Row, 1974): 466-467.
7. Weick defines five key activities that managers and workers use to make sense of their information environments. They are as follows:
   • Action—taking action to clarify the nature of the problem (e.g., building a prototype system and learning from how it is used);
   • Triangulation—applying several qualitatively different measures or sources about a situation;
   • Affiliation—comparing your views of a situation to that of others;
   • Deliberation—Taking time to reflect on a situation;
   • Contextualization—Comparing the situation to other events or viewing it in broader context.
   For a more detailed discussion of sensemaking and its relationship to computer systems, see Karl E. Weick, "Cosmos vs. Chaos: Sense and Nonsense in Electronic Contexts," *Organizational Dynamics* 14:2 (Autumn 1985): 50–65. For a discussion of sensemaking in relation to information requirements, see David W. DeLong, "Sensemaking: The Missing Link in Determining Information Needs," Ernst & Young Center for Business Innovation Working Paper, Oct. 1994.
8. Henry Mintzberg, *The Rise and Fall of Strategic Planning* (New York: Free Press, 1994), 259–264.
9. The importance of soft information in executive information systems is discussed in Hugh J. Watson et al., "Soften Up!" *Computerworld* (October 19, 1992): 103–105.
10. Information on Toshiba was given to be by Larry Prusak, who with James

Matarazzo published aspects of the example in a 1992 working paper, "Information Management and Japanese Success," (Washington, D.C.: Special Libraries Association).

11. Peter Drucker, "What Executives Need to Learn," *PRISM* (Arthur D. Little), 4th quarter 1990, 76.

12. Quoted in Hugh J. Watson et al, "Soften Up," *ComputerWorld* (October 19, 1992): 104.

13. George Lakoff, *Women, Fire, and Dangerous Things: What Categories Reveal About the Mind* (Chicago: University of Chicago Press, 1987).

14. Clifford Stoll, *Silicon Snake Oil: Second Thoughts on the Information Highway* (New York: Doubleday, 1995), 211.

15. Edward R. Tufte, *The Visual Display of Quantitative Information* (Chesire, Ct.: Graphics Press, 1983), 176.

16. Information on Hewlett Packard was obtained through interviews with Corporate Information Systems managers and from Leigh Buchanan, "The Medium and the Message," *CIO*, (July 1995): 74-76.

17. Mickey Williamson, "Performance Appraisal," *CIO* (March 1, 1995): 45–52.

18. Thomans Davenport and Michel Beers, "Managing Information About Business Processes," *Journal of Management Information Systems*, 12:1 (Summer 1995), 57–80.

19. See Robert G. Eccles and Sarah C. Mavrinac, "Improving the Corporate Disclosure Process," Harvard Business School Working Paper, 1994; also see the report of the Special Committee on Financial Reporting, American Institute of Certified Public Accountants, New York, July 1992.

20. Michael E.D. Koenig, "The Information and Library Environment and the Productivity of Research," unpublished manuscript, Rosary College, River Forest, Il.

21. Marketing Science Institute, "Research Priorities 1990-1991," Cambridge, Ma., 1990.

22. Anil Menon and P. Rajan Varadarajan, "A Model of Marketing Knowledge Use Within Firms," *Journal of Marketing* 56 (Oct. 1992): 53–71.

23. See, for example, the chapters in *Using Social Research in Public Policy Making*, Carol Weiss, ed. (Lexington, Ma.: Lexington Books, 1977). One particularly interesting study of the use of information in federal government is Martha Feldman's *Order Without Design* (Stanford, Ca.: Stanford University Press, 1989).

24. Judith H. Dobrzynski, "Jack and John: Two for the Road at GM," *The New York Times* (July 9, 1995): Section 3, 1.

25. Thomas H. Davenport, Sirkka Jarvenpaa, and Michael C. Beers, "Improving Knowledge Work Processes," *Sloan Management Review* (Summer 1996): 53–65.

Chapter 9

1. "Survey Shows Executives Waste Six Weeks a Year Finding Things," Menlo Park, Ca.: Accountemps, 1992.

2. James V. McGee, "Information Architecture: To the Metaphorical Limits and

Beyond," Mastering the Information Environment Research Note, Ernst & Young Center for Business Innovation, Sept. 1992.

3. Thomas H. Davenport, Michael Hammer, and Tauno Metsisto, "How Executives Can Shape Their Company's Information Systems"; The use of principles at Texaco is described in Gary Richardson, Brad Jackson, and Gary Dickson, "Principles-Based Enterprise Architecture: Lessons from Texaco and Star Enterprise," *MIS Quarterly* (Dec. 1990): 385–403.

4. Chen, P., "The Entity-Relationship Model—Toward a Unified View of Data," *ACM Transactions on Database Systems* 1:1 (March 1976): 9–36.

5. I am grateful to Tia DeWeese, my former colleague at Ernst & Young, for her research on information mapping. Some of the research is described in "Finding the Way: Information Mapping," Mastering the Information Environment Research Note, Ernst & Young Center for Business Innovation, 1993.

   In general, the concept of information mapping is linked to the Information Resource Management movement of the late 1970s and early 1980s. Two consultants, Woody Horton and Neil Burk, developed the idea of mapping as part of an overall program of effective management of the information resource; they argued that managing any resource calls first for an inventory. See Cornelius Burk and Forest W. Horton, *InfoMap: A Complete Guide to Discovering Corporate Information Resources* (Englewood Cliffs, N.J.: Prentice-Hall, 1988).

6. Note that information maps may be the first step in an information audit, in which the budgetary, managerial, and support structures for information are assessed in a systematic manner. Often information audits also assess the IT environment of an organization. See Ellis, D. et al., "Information Audits, Communication Audits and Information Mapping: A Review and Survey," *International Journal of Information Management* (1993): 134–152.

7. Kathleen Lannon, "Managing Information Assets at the U.S. Department of State," *Information Management Review* 4:4 (1989): 47–57.

8. Adapted from Horton and Burk's *InfoMap*.

9. This case study is condensed from Maylun Buck-Lew and Thomas H. Davenport, "Informed about Information: Information Capture at IBM," Mastering the Information Environment Field Profile, Ernst & Young Center for Business Innovation, 1992.

10. Adapted and condensed from Myrna Rae Johnson and Larry Prusak, "Information Mapping at American Express," *Mastering the Information Environment Field Profile*, Ernst & Young Center for Business Innovation, 1993.

11. Johnson and Prusak, "Information Mapping," 3–7.

Chapter 10

1. Richard A. D'Aveni, *Hypercompetition: Managing the Dynamics of Strategic Maneuvering* (New York: Free Press, 1994).

2. Michael Treacy and Fred Wiersema, *The Discipline of Market Leaders* (Boston: Addison-Wesley, 1995).

3. *Business Week*, Gary McWilliams, "At Compaq A Desktop Crystal Ball," March 20, 1995, 96–97.
4. C.K. Prahalad and Gary Hamel, "The Core Competence of the Corporation," *Harvard Business Review* (May-June 1990): 79–91.
5. The Dialogue/Decision Process at GM is explained by its architect, Vince Barabba, in *Meeting of the Minds: Creating the Market-Based Enterprise* (Boston: Harvard Business School Press, 1995).
6. Nitin Nohria and James D. Berkeley, "Lithonia Lighting," Harvard Business School case study, case #9-492-003, 1992.
7. A good business-oriented source on IT architecture is Peter Keen's *Shaping the Future: Business Design Through Information Technology* (Boston: Harvard Business School Press, 1991). Chapter 7, "Positioning the IT Platform," is particularly relevant.
8. Hossam Galal, "Verifone: The Transaction Automation Company," Harvard Business School case study, case #9-195-088, 1995.
9. See, for example, Daft, Richard L. and Robert H. Lengel, "Information Richness: A New Approach to Managerial Behavior and Organizational Design," in B. Staw. and L.L. Cummings, *Research in Organizational Behavior*, vol. 6 (Greenwich: JAI Press, 1984), 191–233.
10. Clark, Kim and T. Fujimoto, *Product Development Performance: Strategy, Organization, and Management in the World Auto Industry* (Boston: Harvard Business School Press, 1991).
11. John Markoff, "Where the Cubicle is Dead," *The New York Times* (April 25, 1993): F7.
12. "Soothing the Panicky Computer User," *The New York Times* (July 19, 1994): D5.
13. Andrew Bartmess and Keith Cerny, "Building Competitive Advantage through a Global Network of Capabilities," *California Management Review*, 35:2 (1993): 2–27.
14. See Craig S. Galbraith, "Transferring Core Manufacturing Technologies in High-Tech Firms," *California Management Review* 32:4 (Summer 1990) 56–71.
15. Robert Eccles and Nitin Nohria, "Face-to-Face: Making Network Organizations Work," in Eccles and Nohria, eds., *Networks and Organizations* (Boston: Harvard Business School Press, 1993).
16. Culnan, Mary J. and M. Lynne Markus, "Information Technologies," in Frederick M. Jablin et al., eds., *Handbook of Organizational Communication* (Beverly Hills, Ca.: Sage, 1987), 420–443.
17. "Verifone: The Transaction Automation Company," Harvard Business School case study, 9.
18. See, for example, M. Saphier, *Office Planning and Design* (New York: McGraw-Hill, 1968); M. Brookes and A. Kaplan, "Office Environments: Space Planning and Affective Behavior," *Human Factors* 14 (1972): 371–391; and Thomas Allen, *Managing the Flow of Technology* (Cambridge, Ma.: MIT Press, 1977).
19. Capers Jones, *Applied Software Measurement: Assuring Productivity and Quality* (New York: McGraw-Hill, 1991).

Chapter 11

1. Ajay Kohli and Bernard J. Jaworski, "Market Orientation: The Construct, Research Propositions, and Managerial Implications", *Journal of Marketing* Vol. 54, (April 1990): 1–18.

2. See, for example, Michael J. Wing, *Talking with Your Customers: What They Will Tell You About Your Business When You Ask the Right Questions* (Dearborn, Mi.: Enterprise, 1993)

3. Edward McQuarrie, *Customer Visits* (Newbury Park, Ca.: Sage Publications, Inc., 1993), 13.

4. Leonard M. Fuld, *Monitoring the Competition*, (New York: John Wiley and Sons, Inc., 1988); *Competitor Intelligence*, (New York: John Wiley and Sons, Inc., 1985). Another good source is by Richard E. Combs and John D. Moorhead, *The Competitive Intelligence Handbook*, (Metuchen, N.J.: Scarecrow Press, 1992).

5. C.R. Mathey, *Competitor Analysis* (New York: American Marketing Association, 1991).

6. Fuld, *Competitor Intelligence*, 23.

7. Fuld, *Monitoring the Competition*, 95.

8. Jane Linder and Margaret King, "Digital Equipment Corporation: Leadership in Corporate Intelligence," Harvard Business School case study, case #9-192-002, 1992.

9. Information on this topic was gathered through analysis of proprietary materials from technology research firms, especially Gartner Group, and from interviews with managers of emerging technology groups. The most helpful were Shana Bertram at Federal Express and Michael Vitale, formerly of Prudential Insurance.

10. "Bill Gates and Paul Allen Talk," *Fortune* (Oct. 2, 1995): 71.

11. Daniel Burrus, *Technotrends* (New York: HarperBusiness, 1993).

12. See John Henderson and N. Venkatraman, "Strategic Alignment: Leveraging Information Technology for Transforming Organizations" *IBM Systems Journal* 32:1. (1993) 4–17.

13. William Dunn, *Selling the Story: The Layman's Guid to Collecting and Communicating Demographic Information* (Ithaca, N.Y.: American Demographic Books, 1992).

14. Anne Woodsworth and James F. Williams, II, *Managing the Economics of Owning, Leasing, and Contracting Out Information Services* (Brookfield, Vt.: Ashgate Publishing, 1993).

15. See Robert M. Mason and John E. Creps, Jr., eds., *Information Services: Economics, Management, and Technology* (Boulder, Co.: Westview Press, 1981) and Margaret E. Guerin-Calvert and Steven S. Wildman, eds., *Electronic Services Networks: A Business and Public Policy Challenge* (New York: Praeger Publishing, 1991).

16. Francis J. Aguilar, *Scanning the Business Environment*, (New York: MacMillan, 1967).

17. T. Grandon Gill, "High-Tech Hidebound: Case Studies of Information Technologies That Inhibited Organizational Learning," *Accounting, Management, and*

Information Techology 5:1 (1995): 41–60.

18. David V. Gibson, Everett M. Rogers, *R&D Collaboration on Trial* (Boston: Harvard Business School Press, 1994).

19. The minivan story is discussed by Vincent P. Barabba in his book, *Meeting of the Minds: Creating the Market-Based Enterprise* (Boston: Harvard Business School Press, 1995).

20. Patrick Wilson, *Second-Hand Knowledge: An Inquiry into Cognitive Authority* (Westport: Greenwood, 1983).

21. Betsy Paige Sigman and Sarah-Kathryn McDonald, "The Issues Manager as Public Opinion and Policy Analyst", in, Alfred A. Marcus et al, eds., *Business Strategy and Public Policy*, (New York: Quorum Books, 1987), 165–194.

22. Her six steps for the issues-management process are: identifying trends and issues; evaluating their impact and setting priorities; research and analysis; strategy development; implementation; and evaluation. See Rogene A. Bucholz, *Essentials of Public Policy Management*, (Englewood Cliffs, N.J.: Prentice-Hall, Inc., 1990) 181–187.

23. Michael Porter, *Competitive Strategy*. (New York: The Free Press, 1980).